Writing Professionally in the Social Sciences

Writing Professionally in the Social Sciences

David Royse

University of Kentucky

Bassim Hamadeh, CEO and Publisher
Amy Smith, Senior Project Editor
Abbey Hastings, Production Editor
Jess Estrella, Senior Graphic Designer
Kylie Bartolome, Licensing Specialist
Natalie Piccotti, Director of Marketing
Kassie Graves, Senior Vice President, Editorial

Copyright © 2024 by Cognella, Inc. All rights reserved. No part of this publication may be reprinted, reproduced, transmitted, or utilized in any form or by any electronic, mechanical, or other means, now known or hereafter invented, including photocopying, microfilming, and recording, or in any information retrieval system without the written permission of Cognella, Inc. For inquiries regarding permissions, translations, foreign rights, audio rights, and any other forms of reproduction, please contact the Cognella Licensing Department at rights@cognella.com.

Trademark Notice: Product or corporate names may be trademarks or registered trademarks and are used only for identification and explanation without intent to infringe.

Cover image: Copyright © 2019 Depositphotos/HayDmitriy.

Printed in the United States of America.

Brief Contents

Preface   xiii

Chapter 1	First Things: What Do I Need to Bring on My Writing Journey?	1
Chapter 2	Where Do I Find Ideas for Writing, and How Do I Evaluate Them?	21
Chapter 3	How Do I Create a Research Question?	39
Chapter 4	Should I Have a Writing Partner?	52
Chapter 5	What Do I Need to Know About the Professional Journals I'm Considering?	75
Chapter 6	What Is the Peer-Review Process?	92
Chapter 7	How Do I Write the *Introduction* and the *Literature Review*?	112
Chapter 8	How Do I Write the *Method* Section for My Manuscript?	132
Chapter 9	How Do I Write the *Results* Section?	150
Chapter 10	How Do I Write the *Discussion* Section?	162
Chapter 11	How Do I Write Abstracts That Hook the Reader?	176
Chapter 12	What Do I Need to Check Before Submitting My Final Draft?	191
Chapter 13	What Is the Process for Submitting My Manuscript?	202
Chapter 14	My Manuscript Was Rejected. What Do I Do Now?	212
Chapter 15	What's Needed to Write a Book Proposal?	229

Index   243

Detailed Contents

Preface   xiii

Chapter 1   First Things: What Do I Need to Bring
on My Writing Journey? 1

Desire to Be Published   1
Time to Write   3
Space (Physical and Emotional)   8
What Other "Equipment" Might I Need?   9
Fear   11
What If I'm Not Interested in Writing a Research
    Piece at This Time? What Else Can I Write to Build
    My Confidence?   13
    First-Person Narratives   13
    Book Reviews for Professional Journals   16
    Writing Articles for Magazines   17
    Writing a Blog   18
Resources   20
References   20

Chapter 2   Where Do I Find Ideas for Writing, and How Do
I Evaluate Them? 21

How Do I Start Developing a Publishable Manuscript?   21
Where Can I Find an Idea for a Publishable Paper?
    Four Ideas   21
    *1. Can Reading Be a Source of Inspiration for
        a Writing Project?   21*
    *2. Can Experiences in Your Life Be a Source
        of Inspiration for Ideas?   23*
    *3. Could Conducting a Literature Search Produce
        Ideas for Writing Projects?   26*
    *4. Can Friends, Colleagues, or Faculty Serve
        as a Source of Ideas?   29*
How Do I Know My Idea Is a Good One?   31
    1. Does the Idea Strike Me as Really, Really Interesting?   31
    2. Is There a Gap in the Literature?   31
    *3. Does My Mentor, Trusted Friend, or Potential
        Writing Partner Like the Idea?   31*
    *4. Is Sponsored Funding Potentially Available for Exploring
        My Topic?   32*
    *5. Feasibility/Practicality: Can I Actually Collect
        the Data?   32*
What Hurdles and Trade-Offs Could Affect the Viability
    of the Writing Project?   33

Should I Proceed When There Are One to Two Issues
That Might Threaten the Project?   35
References   37

Chapter 3   **How Do I Create a Research Question?**............. **39**

Why Is It Important to Start With a Research Question?   39
What Are the Characteristics of a Research Question?   40
    Focus   *41*
    Clarity   *41*
    Relevance   *41*
    Originality   *41*
    Researchable   *42*
How Do I Develop a Research Question?   42
How Are Research Questions Presented
in Journal Articles?   43
Should I Be Worried About Plagiarizing Someone's
Research Question or Material?   46
References   50

Chapter 4   **Should I Have a Writing Partner?**................... **52**

When Must I Offer Coauthorship to Another Person?   52
How Do Journals Judge Authorship?   53
Should I Share Authorship With a Student?   55
What Are the Advantages of Having a Writing Partner?   56
What Are the Disadvantages of Having a Writing Partner?   57
How Do You Choose a Good Writing Partner?   59
Should I Have a Writing Mentor?   60
How Do I Give Feedback to a Writing Partner?   62
How Do I Receive Feedback From a Writing Partner?   64
What Alternative Ways Are There to Improve My Writing
for Publication?   65
    Workshops   *65*
    Writing Boot Camps   *66*
    Other Options   *67*
    Writing Support Groups   *67*
What Can I Do If the Writing Support in My Workplace
or Community Are Lacking?   68
How Do I Figure Out What Kind of Writing Support
Might Benefit Me?   70
Resources   73
References   74

Chapter 5   **What Do I Need to Know About the Professional
Journals I'm Considering?**........................ **75**

Can I Draft a Manuscript and Then Look
for a Journal Later?   75
How Do Journals Differ?   75
    What Are Predatory Journals?   *75*
What Are the Characteristics of Legitimate Journals?   78
    What Are Impact Factors?   *78*

What Are Acceptance/Rejection Rates Like
    in Professional Journals? 80
Why Is It Necessary to Consider the Journal's Audience? 82
How Useful Are a Journal's Author Guidelines? 82
Should I Consider an Open-Access Journal? 84
Given All the Considerations, How Do I Choose
    a Journal? 86
Resources 89
References 90

Chapter 6   What Is the Peer-Review Process? 92

The Editor's Role 93
The Peer-Reviewer's Role 94
The Author's Role 96
What Is an Academic Writing Style? 99
Should I Use Rare and Recondite Words to Impress
    Journal Reviewers? 101
What Is Swampy Writing? 103
    Writing Tips 105
    Explanations to Self-Assessment 107
Resources 111
References 111

Chapter 7   How Do I Write the *Introduction* and the *Literature Review*? 112

What Goes Into an Introduction? 113
How Do I Engage the Reader Early On? 115
    1. Starting the Introduction With a Question
      or a Problem 115
    2. Starting the Introduction With a Controversy 117
What Is Unacceptable Content in the *Introduction*
    Section? 120
How Do I Develop a Literature Review as Part
    of the Introduction? 121
How Do I Write the Literature Review? 122
References 129

Chapter 8   How Do I Write the *Method* Section for My Manuscript? 132

What Basic Information Should the *Method* Section
    Provide? 132
Design 133
Participants 136
Procedures 138
Measures 141
Data Analysis 143
Do I Have to Use the Subheadings Typically Used
    in the *Method* Section? 145
References 148

Chapter 9   **How Do I Write the *Results* Section?** 150

    Should I Be Concise or Lengthy in Drafting
        This Section?   150
    What Is the Problem With Providing Unnecessary
        Information?   151
    Where Do I Start?   152
    How Do You Structure the *Results* Section?   153
    How Many Tables Are Too Many?   155
    References   161

Chapter 10   **How Do I Write the *Discussion* Section?** 162

    What Is the Purpose of the *Discussion* Section?   162
    How Do I Start the *Discussion* Section?   162
    Should I Compare My Study's Findings
        to Previous Studies?   164
    Should I Address Any Issues or Flaws in My Study?   165
    Should I Include Suggestions for Future Research?   167
    Should I Have a "Conclusion" Subheading in My *Discussion*
        Section?   169
    What Questions May Arise When Writing the *Discussion*
        Section?   171
    How Can I Be a Writing Mentor to Myself?   172
    References   174

Chapter 11   **How Do I Write Abstracts That Hook the Reader?** 176

    Why Is Information on Writing the Abstract This
        Far Into the Book?   176
    What Is the Purpose of an Abstract and How
        Important Is It?   176
    How Do I Write a Good Abstract?   177
    What Are the Parts of a Structured Abstract?   178
    What Are Examples of Structured Abstracts?   180
    How Do I Compose an Eye-Catching Title?   184
    References   189

Chapter 12   **What Do I Need to Check Before Submitting
My Final Draft?** 191

    How Do I Proofread for Microstructural Issues
        in the Manuscript?   191
    How Do I Proofread for the Macrostructure
        in the Manuscript?   194
    Read for Organization   195
        Be a Skeptical Reader   196
    How Many Times Should I Revise My Paper?   197
    Resource   201
    References   201

Chapter 13   **What Is the Process for Submitting
My Manuscript?** 202

    How Do I Submit My Manuscript?   202

What Issues Might Journals Be Concerned About
    That Might Escape Me?   203
  Publishing Rights   204
  Protecting the Peer-Review Process   205
  Their Other Informational Needs   206
How Long After Submission Before I Will Hear
    From the Journal?   208
Resources   210
References   211

Chapter 14   **My Manuscript Was Rejected. What Do I Do Now?** ... 212

How Do I Step Away From the Ledge? Understanding
    My Emotions   212
Can There Be a Bad Apple in One's Set of Reviewers?   214
Should I File a Protest With the Editor If I Get
    a Terrible Review?   215
How Do I Deal With Reviewers' Comments That
    Seem "Off"?   216
After the Initial Shock of Rejection, What Do I Do?   217
Does a Revise-and-Resubmit Email Mean That My
    Manuscript Was Accepted?   219
What Are the Reasons Journals Reject Manuscripts?   220
How Do I Go About Revising a Manuscript
    for Resubmission?   222
What Happens to a Revise-and-Resubmit Manuscript
    After It Is Submitted Again?   223
Can I Submit a Rejected Manuscript to Another Journal?   223
What Is the Rule of Three?   224
Resources   227
References   227

Chapter 15   **What's Needed to Write a Book Proposal?** 229

What's Needed for a Book Proposal?   229
  1) Having an Original Idea for the Book   229
What Is Needed Besides Great Ideas?   232
  2) Great Writing Skills   232
  What If You Don't Have an Amazing Writing Ability?   234
What Else Is Needed Besides Originality and Great
    Writing Ability?   235
  3) A Book Proposal!   235
Do I Need a Literary Agent?   237
What About Self-Publishing?   238
Can I Send My Book Proposal to More Than One
    Publisher at a Time?   240
Resources   241
References   241

Index   243

Preface

Dear reader, if you are viewing this preface through a preview feature, I'd like to get right to the point. The purpose of this book is to assist those with an ambition to publish, to become a writer or scholar, to fulfill their dreams. It also serves as a guide for those who have had some minor success but who desire advice for becoming even more successful with publishing in professional journals. My assumption is that you are seeking information about the writing process and that you are motivated—meaning that you are willing to invest the necessary time to take an idea, create a manuscript, and revise it a number of times until it is ready to submit.

You may already have a paper, thesis, or dissertation that you would like to prepare for submission to a particular professional journal. Or, you may not currently have a working idea for a paper. Both situations are addressed. For instance, Chapter 2 will provide a number of strategies for finding a question or material to write about and ways to evaluate these notions as possible foundations for a manuscript. The target audience for the book consists of new PhDs, postdoctoral fellows, full- and part-time faculty, graduate students, and even college students who desire to be published.

This is the truth: I won't pretend to guide you in developing a paper for a humanities type of journal because that is not where my expertise lies. The vast majority of my publications have been empirical with quantifiable data. I can't direct you in drafting philosophical or historical papers or those reviewing music or art.

In this book, I have accessed information from a number of professional journals in the social sciences and the field of nursing. This selection makes the book useful to individuals in a wide variety of disciplines such as social work, psychology, counseling, and nursing. Although most of my publications have been in social work journals, I have also published in other journals such as the *Journal of Child and Adolescent Trauma*; *The Clinical Supervisor*, *Omega—The Journal of Death and Dying*; the *Journal of Burn Care & Research*; *Family & Community Health*; *Journal of Cancer Education*; *American Journal of Drug and Alcohol Abuse*; *The Hospice Journal*; *Adolescence*; *Transfusion*; *Journal of Offender Rehabilitation*; *Rehabilitation Counseling Journal*; and others.

This is also the truth: I view readers as adults who know what they want and are prepared to work for it. Most readers will be working full time with important work responsibilities, and many will have families and need to save time for recreation, shopping for groceries, getting the car repaired, and the thousand other things needing attention in our lives. Realistically, writing a paper for publication for the first time may take you longer than 12 weeks or a semester. Exactly how long it takes is up to you. Some parts of the process may go faster or slower than you expect. However, there is no danger of falling behind because you will read and work at your own pace.

You don't have to read this book in the order in which the chapters are presented. For instance, the chief issue you may be struggling with at this moment is whether you should have a writing partner. If that is the case, you might want to start with Chapter 4 where the pros and cons of such an arrangement are discussed, as well as ways to evaluate potential writing partners and different writing supports if you will be a solo author. I think you will find that this is a flexible book that allows readers to start where they have the most interest, but for many, that will be the first chapter.

It is a fair question to ask about my writing credentials. After all, I have positioned myself as a guide. This is also the truth, as of this writing I have authored or coauthored professional journal articles numbering somewhere in the 90s. I have written 12 books, not counting this one. I have books that are currently in their eighth, seventh, and sixth editions. I've worked with nine or 10 different publishing companies over a span of 30 years. I retired as a full professor from the University of Kentucky, College of Social Work, after more than three decades where I directed the PhD program and was the director of Graduate Studies. Helping students learn how to write well has always been a priority in my teaching and direction of graduate students. I have also been a faculty member at three different institutions of higher education.

As an educator, I believe in the usefulness of posing questions to encourage students to think about the instructional content, and I'll follow that practice with "Your Turn" textboxes in each chapter. They are designed to help you drill down and mine that specific writing portion of the manuscript under discussion—to find the gold, to obtain an assay or appraisal of it, and feedback that will help you to improve and polish before going forward.

It is my sincere hope that this book will be useful to you. I think of manuscripts as tender tree saplings one plants in a choice spot chosen because the sunlight, soil, and moisture content seem exactly right to welcome and nurture the young tree. Although we are not in control of all the conditions affecting the sapling (like the weather and wildlife in the area that might nibble it), there are actions we can take to give the young tree the best chances for survival. The actions *you can take* are where this guide comes in handy. It is as handy as a shovel or trowel, but it alone cannot guarantee success—perhaps only that your planting will have an opportunity for the roots to develop.

Please send me an email if you feel that there are places where the content needs to be expanded or explained better based on your personal experience with writing and the book. I'd like to hear from you and to learn of your stories and your successes. Thank you in advance, and good luck with your writing project!

David Royse, droyse@uky.edu

CHAPTER 1

First Things
What Do I Need to Bring on My Writing Journey?

Life is composed of multiple journeys. We leave the warm, dark, comfortable womb and struggle into a blindingly frightening world of bright lights, unexpected noises, and strange characters. Sometime later, forced out of our now familiar homes, we travel again to daycare, kindergarten, and first grade. Once more, we must learn new rules, and adjust our actions. We repeat this process again and again as we progress through middle school, high school, and beyond. We surmount challenges, pick ourselves up when tripped, and overcome even the sudden gut punch of loneliness as we are left on a college campus and watch the taillights of our parents' car drive away.

Congratulations on beginning another new journey! One where you won't be torn away from home and hearth but coaxed, coached, and tutored—one where you can, sitting in your favorite chair at home or at your work desk, shut the book if the possible decisions and hurdles ahead seem too daunting. Read as little or as much as you wish, as quickly or slowly, reflectively as you want. This is your book, your guide on a journey that *you* have already decided upon. Where it will take you is a mystery. Yes, you may have an immediate goal to publish a paper sitting in your heart or tumbling around in your mind, but what other paths might it open?

Before you lace up your hiking boots, fill your canteen or water bottle, and unfold the map, let's talk about the need for grit and endurance, and the planning and preparation made for your journey. You can skip this section if you wish (of course, you can do that with any chapter), but I believe it might be to your detriment. Why? Attempting to write for a professional journal involves at least three necessities. Let's check to see if you are bringing them along.

Desire to Be Published

You must want this just as much as or more than finishing a graduate or professional degree. A strong desire to see your name in print will sustain you when you are having trouble gathering or analyzing your data, when you must wade through the extensive literature already on the topic and become an expert on it, when a coauthor drops out, and when you receive your first rejection of a finished manuscript. Yes, your journey might be a stroll through Central Park on a Sunday afternoon, but could it also be a climb up Mount Kilimanjaro? You might be lucky and have your first effort accepted within weeks of submitting it, but it is also possible that you could wait months before receiving a letter of rejection that makes you feel like you didn't do anything right. Such a delay (think of it as a detour, but still progress toward your destination) may make you not want to invest any more time into continuing this journey. But could you proceed a little further to reach a signpost suggesting you've made good progress or are close to reaching your destination?

When I think about my own experiences with publishing, a lot of clichés come to mind: it wasn't always "smooth sailing" or "a piece of cake." At times, the process was brutal, and I wished I hadn't worn my "feelings on my sleeve." Yes, you can get your feelings hurt by an indelicate reviewer. At times, you may feel insulted when a critical *peer* reviewer accuses you of taking a sophomoric shortcut or not doing something really fundamental like checking out the statistical assumptions before reporting the findings. You may feel humiliated when you forgot to add something you meant to insert or in your haste left out three references that you cited in the text.

Most people fail, not because of lack of desire, but because of lack of commitment.

Vince Lombardi, celebrated coach of the Green Bay Packers

There are only two options regarding commitment: you're either in or you're out.

Pat Riley, coach of the Miami Heat, New York Nets, and Los Angeles Lakers

You may feel that even a kind reviewer didn't understand what you were trying to do—perhaps they skimmed the manuscript too quickly or missed a key explanation. However, often, maybe even most often, the reviewers just want you to do a little more work, fold in some more detail, expand a section, or explain something (like a variable you created) a little more. You may be exhausted, tired of working on the piece, or too busy to invest any more time in the project, but if you don't, then your manuscript won't get published. Your commitment to the journey is key. Can you make it a little further? Even when the weather is stormy or the path is muddy? Here are a couple of quotes on the topic of perseverance from two famous coaches:

If you have had early success getting something published, that achievement may propel you forward, giving you the courage to go further, to try your hand at other projects. Even then, there can come rude shocks when one of your creations, perhaps one you consider one of your best efforts, is mired in a swamp and difficult to rescue. What happens next is up to you. You can be rational or make a stupid knee-jerk reaction.

As a high school student, I had some success with a regional poetry journal. After several of my poems were published, I was startled to receive a rejection. In those days, the poetry journal always mailed back our paper copies with notations on the printed sheet. My rejected poem contained the words in pencil at the top of the page "No. RAB." The "No" was clear enough and with a little detective work (actually, not much was required), I discovered that "RAB" referred to one of the coeditors. After this occurred another time or two, my estimation of my talent got the best of me. I fired off another poem entitled, "No, RAB. No." Needless to say, it was not the best decision I ever made in my life. Smug in my own cleverness, my high schoolish revenge punished only me.

Years later, I didn't feel quite so secure when, as a new assistant professor at a large state university, it was abundantly clear to me that without publishing in professional journals, I would never achieve promotion and tenure. However, the threat of not having a job if I didn't publish supplied all the motivation I needed to write manuscripts for professional journals. Over the years, I've learned to accommodate reviewers' suggestions that don't seem important or necessary, and when to challenge those I don't agree with.

There is no tidy, compact answer to how much drive you have to have to complete the journey, to be successful at professional writing. The best answer is: You must have *enough* drive to learn how to be successful. Once your journey has conditioned you so that you are no longer the demure, unassured traveler, you will find it easier going. Even a small success will energize and infuse you with a "let's get it done" attitude and long strides. The process won't seem as strewn with boulders, the trail not so steep to climb.

> *Write because you have to, because the process brings great satisfaction. Write because you have a story to tell, not because you think publishing will make you the person you always wanted to be. There is approximately zero chance of that happening.*
>
> Anne Lamott, *Almost Everything: Notes on Hope* (2018, pp. 90–91)

Time to Write

You're a busy person, I get that. Perhaps you are a full-time doctoral student, a new assistant professor working toward tenure, or an individual with dreams but stuck in a lower level job and raising a young family; you want to add some publications to your curriculum vitae (CV) to obtain a better position. On this journey, do you plan to take several short day hikes, or to find a way to take a life-changing journey of many months?

Here's what you need to know: even if you have made wonderful grades in all your courses, you should not assume that a single draft of a manuscript will automatically result in your becoming a published author. You will need time, *dedicated time*, to revise your manuscripts—at least three times if you are a superb writer and possibly five or six times if you are just a good writer. In other words, you need to have ample time for your writing journey—whether you have young children at home or a demanding job sapping most of your energy.

If you don't have a paper, thesis, dissertation, or research report you want to shape into a journal article, then you most likely will need even more time. How much time? In my experience, writing well is not something you can do in 15- to 20-minute leftover crumbs each day. You need substantial writing time—possibly an hour or two a day for as long as it takes for you to complete your draft and polish it. If you ask my advice, I think working in blocks of 2 to 4 hours at a time is much more efficient and productive. Why? A smaller amount of time—say, an hour once a day may turn out to be 40 or 45 minutes. Time is wasted because you may need to reacquaint yourself with where you stopped previously, to refresh your thoughts about how to make the next point or begin the next paragraph, or to remember what resource you wanted to consult.

Maybe you are thinking, "I don't have two to four hours a day!" True, you may not have a great deal of time every day to devote to writing. However, you may be able to schedule a block of writing time 2 or 3 days a week.

Perhaps you can create time for yourself by recapturing time allotted for other purposes. Could it come from declining to be the room mother for your child's first-grade class, taking a sabbatical as a cub scout or Girl Scout leader, or telling your partner that they are going to have to do the grocery shopping or clean the apartment every Saturday for a couple of months while you focus on your writing?

Recaptured time can come from modifying your habits like not watching CNN for 30 minutes every morning or working crossword puzzles as you drink your morning coffee. Put available time to good use; print out a copy of yesterday's draft and edit it as you eat your breakfast. Check references, plan your day, and see if there is any activity you can reduce or cut out to give yourself more time for writing. Take shorter lunches; don't go drinking with your friends after class or work.

One doctoral student I advised began getting up at 3:00 a.m. to give herself a block of time to write before she needed to leave for work at the university hospital. That distraction-free time enabled her to finish her dissertation in two semesters, even while working full-time. Another individual found that he could usually find several hours on Saturday or Sunday by going into his office when no one else was around. He also tried to get to work by 7:00 a.m. on weekdays to have quiet time before the phones started ringing in the office around 8:30 or so. If you are not an early riser, you might find that you do well working after the dog has been walked and the children put to bed. There's nothing wrong with working from 10:00 p.m. to midnight or even 2 a.m.—if you are a "night person."

If you find it difficult to find dedicated time to write, ask yourself, "What are my priorities? What am I willing to give up for a manuscript?" It could be beneficial to make a prioritized list of all your daily activities. Then, look at the last two or three entries at the bottom of your priorities. What can you reduce from five or more times a week to only twice or three times a week to give yourself some time to write or edit yesterday's effort? Would it be possible to cut out a few activities completely for a month or longer?

Kallestinova (2011) from the Graduate Writing Center at the Yale Graduate School of Arts and Sciences has discussed seven rules that "allow the writer to prepare a well-structured and comprehensive manuscript for a publication submission" (p. 181). Her first rule? "Create regular time blocks for writing as appointments in your calendar and keep these appointments" (p. 182).

Choose hours of the day when you feel most productive—whether it is 10 p.m. or 3 a.m. Do your boring chores when you expect to be interrupted by the telephone or individuals stopping by your office. Protect your writing time from meetings, social gatherings, grocery shopping, or other distractors. A note here: a well-published colleague of mine once told me that he likes to clear out all other major projects before writing. I do it the other way—I like to resolve all of the minor things that might take my attention away from writing (e.g., scheduling my dental appointment, getting the car's oil changed, and so forth). With no nagging details to address, I can let other major projects sit for a day or so because I won't forget about them. Find what works for you. Maybe it will be only 15 minutes a day initially, but put your project in gear!

You cannot wait for the "right" time to begin writing. Years ago, our college hired a new faculty member who not only loved to teach, but students loved her teaching. She had some experience with theater, I believe, and her classes were lively and well-attended although she was no pushover for an easy grade. She devoted herself thoroughly to her courses and received delightful evaluations from students, but she made no time for her writing. At the end of each academic year, she would tell herself that she would focus on writing projects all summer and "knock out one or two articles." Only that didn't happen. She was so exhausted by the month of May that she needed time to recharge her Energizer bunny within, and she and her husband would take nice vacations to make up for the impoverished times of no relaxation or recreation when classes were underway. Later, she did not get promoted or tenure due to a lack of academic publications in her portfolio.

It is a valuable lesson for academics who think they can throw themselves totally into writing for a couple of summer months—ignoring the fact that what looks like a huge block of days for writing doesn't include time for the messy things in all our lives—the wonky computer motherboard on its way to going out, the unplanned visit from friends or relatives passing through town, tornadic winds knocking out the electric lines in your neighborhood, a family member's illness or accident, children needing transportation to play sports in summer leagues—need I go on?

I don't think the scenario I just shared is all that unusual. I was reminded of my colleague's inability to set aside time to work on writing while recently reading a book by Deetjen (2020) who wrote about the issue of finding time:

> And even when I gather the right motivations, daily distractions keep me from completing the work. ... How often have I let meetings, email, and extracurricular commitments steal time away from my research projects?
>
> I tell myself it's okay because summer will come around. Summer will give me months of uninterrupted time to catch up. Except in summer I can't quite focus. My fast-paced semesters have trained my brain for sporadic activity instead of undistracted depth. My lack of focus yields unsteady progress, and I eventually realize that I'm not gaining ground as quickly as I had hoped. I take holidays here and there to deal with the resulting stress. But, by the end of the summer, I'm anxious, exhausted, hitting dead ends, and anticipating another fast-paced semester where catching up on research will only become more challenging. (p. 9)

If it helps, personalize your writing project. Give it a name like Burt or Bob, Nancy, Judy, or Linda. Just like a lover or family member, Burt or Linda need time with you. Schedule reoccurring afternoons or evenings when you can spend "quality time" together or have "date nights." That might sound a little weird, but Nancy or Bob will feel neglected if you have a cup of tea together on March 1 and then nothing until the 28th when you can put a lunch on the schedule. Protect whatever time you can afford on a regular basis to be with this project you profess to love.

While I am, obviously, of the strong opinion that a writer needs writing time each week, typically in 2- to 4-hour blocks, I also realize that the scheme may not work for all people. (I can't legislate that amount of time anyway—so no worries.) Some individuals may be able to work a whole day two or three times a month and that is about as "regular" as it gets. I understand, and I don't mean to depreciate those who find that extended or binge-writing episodes are what works best for them—or is all that they can do. I'm a pragmatist and know what works best for me. Everyone else has to figure out what approach advances their writing and is most effective for them. If you don't make progress, then try a different approach.

The possibility exists that even if you set a regular time for writing, you may not be productive during the time set aside. That can stem from a host of different causes such as an emotional upheaval in your life (e.g., loss of a loved one or the breakup of a close relationship) or health and medication issues. In some situations, you may need patience and time for healing. In others, you may need to be proactive and contact a medical professional. In some situations, you might consider going into counseling to get the emotional support you need. I'm sorry, but I am unable to provide solutions to all the unique and different problems that could be creating difficult obstacles in your life. However, Wendy Belcher has done a fine job of discussing possible solutions to many of the obstacles that writers encounter on her website (https://wendybelcher.com/writing-advice/).

Your Turn 1.1

What can you do right now to plan for or set aside time for your writing project?

_____

_____

_____

_____

Could you ask your partner, spouse, or other persons to relieve you of some responsibilities to free up time for your writing?

_____

_____

_____

_____

(continued)

What days and times have you identified or are planning to be scheduled for your writing?

_____

_____

_____

Space (Physical and Emotional)

Sometimes on journeys, you have to share rooms. Roommates can be compatible and easy to live with—they may seldom be a problem. However, six or seven people sharing the same bathroom or shower could be. In my opinion, writing is a private activity, best done alone and without conversation, TV, or other noise in the vicinity to distract. If you agree, you should find a private space where you can leave folders or notebooks and have a place for your laptop and any papers or books you need. It doesn't have to be a large room—it could be the laundry room once the house is quiet, or a corner in the basement or bedroom. Some individuals can work in a Starbucks, but others cannot (count me among them!). If your writing time is in the evening but you can't escape a noisy television, there are white noise machines, ear plugs, and ear protectors. Listening to classical music to cover up other background noise might work for you. However, you may need the tranquility found in libraries.

I use a table where I can position my laptop in the center and have room to the left and right—providing space if I want to read a printed draft or article there. I have neat piles where I keep things that must be attended to immediately (e.g., bills to be paid), and a pile of books and articles I want to read or take a quotation from. Small desks where there is only enough room for my laptop don't work well for me. At times, it is important to spread out pages or notes or other material so I can see them and maybe even organize them.

This is what Annie Dillard, author of *The Writing Life* (1989) has written about the need for physical space:

> The materiality of the writer's life cannot be exaggerated. If you like metaphysics, throw pots. How fondly I recall thinking, in the old days, that to write you needed paper, pen, and a lap. How appalled

> I was to discover that, in order to write so much as a sonnet, you need a warehouse. You can easily get so confused writing a thirty-page chapter that in order to make an outline for the second draft, you have to rent a hall. I have often "written" with the mechanical aid of a twenty-foot conference table. You lay your pages along the table's edge and pace out the work. You walk along the rows; you weed bits, move bits, and dig out bits, bent over the rows with full hands like a gardener. (p. 46)

I'm not sure every writer will need as much desktop space as Annie Dillard, but having some space of your own is surely better than no space at all.

Space also applies to emotional or psychological space. You need the support and cooperation from your spouse, partner, or significant other to occasionally free your time and help out with the numerous but necessary tasks associated with running a household: putting the kids to bed, doing the dishes, and cleaning or running the vacuum on occasion. You must have time to write; don't feel guilty about it. Look for responsibilities or things that you can put on hold or temporarily say "no" to. You are the best judge of "time-eaters," which are unessential tasks that can get by without your involvement for a while. You may have to negotiate shared duties like shopping, doing the laundry, or cooking, but the point is to plan! Find time to write. If you can't write every day at the same time, then make a schedule. With dedicated time (another way of saying *commitment* to a schedule!), you will be able to finish your writing project much sooner than if the time allotted to writing is haphazard. And who wants to begin a journey that is off again, on again, off again? Plans may need the support of family, friends, or significant others. Are they willing to support you on your journey? Can they help carry the tent or a backpack? Clean up the campsite?

What Other "Equipment" Might I Need?

In addressing the necessities you need on your publications journey, you might have noticed that I never once said you have to have an astonishing clever idea to be published. If the major hurdle you feel before you is the lack of a good idea to build a publication around and not, desire, time, space, or support from others, then take a breath. Breathe. We'll discuss finding and evaluating good ideas in the next chapter. Before we get to that place, let's think about some other equipment you may need.

You probably already have a laptop or computer you can use when you want to write. If not, shared computers can work if schedules don't conflict. But there are advantages to having your own computer; the main one is privacy and protecting your fragile project in development. I don't show my early drafts to anyone. Later on, I might, but certainly not when they are in the early, formative stages. Sometimes writers are advised to "just get it down," and "clean it up later." That is good advice. I don't want others weighing in with their opinions prematurely if they review my early drafts.

Peternelj-Taylor, the editor in chief of the *Journal of Forensic Nursing*, has commented on her own difficulties with writing. "At times, I become so caught up in trying to craft the perfect paragraph that I am unable to move forward, although many learned colleagues have suggested that it is important to write first and edit later" (2018, p. 1). An elegant phrase or a crackerjack introduction may slip out of our heads when we don't incorporate these ideas right when they pop into our heads. We can fold such nuggets into a manuscript without the necessary introduction or transition. I know when a piece I have written is choppy, and I don't want to share it with others in its unrefined state—especially anyone who might feel it is necessary to point out that the piece is not finished. Your own computer allows you to have more privacy than you might otherwise have—a good piece of equipment for the journey.

If your computer is old and not working as it should, you might want to consider getting one that is more dependable, has more memory, and will allow you to work more efficiently or with fewer headaches. At a minimum, make sure all the key apps have been updated, and remember to make backup copies of all your drafts.

Your Turn 1.2

As you reflect back over what you have read, what one thing do you need to do (besides finding time) to get fully into writing a manuscript?

_____

_____

_____

_____

What is another thing you can do to address the desire or space needed to develop a manuscript?

_____

_____

_____

_____

Fear

I hope you are able to be honest with yourself. That is, you may have all that you need in the way of desire, time, or space (physical and emotional/psychological), but what holds you back from taking your writing journey is your fear. This is what I know: there are many things to fear in life. There are things that may keep us tossing and turning at night because of a situation (like potential job loss or a child not doing well in school) that can leave us with a feeling of hopelessness. However, many of the things we may fear (like a shark attacking us during a summer vacation at the beach) are rare statistical occurrences—sort of like winning a multi-million-dollar lottery ticket in reverse. Yes, they can happen, but not often, and probably not to you on this day or on the handful of days when you are at the beach. Many bad things do occur in life, but many good things do, too. In the words of fabulous hockey player and coach, Wayne Gretzky, "You miss 100% of the shots you don't take." You can't succeed if you don't try.

Yes, it is true that our best efforts at publication may be rejected. However, if you experience such an event, *what will you learn along the way* about writing for *that* particular professional journal? Could it possibly prepare you, make you more skilled, so that your next effort, your next submission of the same or slightly revised manuscript would be successful? Instead of fearing rejection, craft a backup plan for yourself. Select another journal to send the revised manuscript to or consider another topic that could be developed for publication if your first submission gets rejected.

In all of our conscious actions, each of us must weigh whether the risks are worth the potential payoff, the effort worth the opportunities presented, and how our lives might be enriched, changed, or disadvantaged. Let's be realistic. Put your fear on the scale. What does it weigh? It weighs as much as you allow it to weigh. Visualize it as weighing nothing. How might a rejection of your manuscript be the end of the world? What would it cost you? (Compute that cost in any way you want.) Would the cost be greater than the payoff or the sense of accomplishment you would feel if the piece were published? (Compute the payoff in any way you want.)

Rather than fearing some editor or reviewer will write horrible comments that will slice like razor blades, your fear may not be so much that your piece will smell like week-old garbage as much as that you might disappoint those who love you or have worked with you on the project. This fear of not being good enough can attack even those who know that they are smart, get good grades, and even compliments on their writing. I know this from a doctoral student of mine, a graduate of an Ivy League university who had an amazing mind and analytic ability. She completed all of her graduate courses without any difficulty at all but stalled repeatedly at putting together a plan for a dissertation. She never finished her degree, although I'm reasonably sure her GRE scores were higher than mine. She, not a critical doctoral program director, mentor, editor, or anyone else, was responsible for producing this fear. She could not, in my opinion, risk being potentially embarrassed because of negative feedback. She was, actually, literally, her own worst enemy.

We can't completely dismiss the fear of failure that may exist in the back of our minds. Everyone who writes likely has at least a little fear. To cite the editor once again of the *Journal of Forensic Nursing*, Peternelj-Taylor (2018) confessed, "I still cringe when I read reviewers' feedback and even now turn to my mentors for sage counseling." Critical feedback on our writing efforts should be expected; however, it rarely will make you want to jump from a 40-story building.

For the time being, let's suspend any thoughts of failure. Instead of focusing on the negative, let's get on with planning and ignore any big-footed fear that could stomp our writing progress. It may help you to know that we're going to spend a whole chapter toward the end of the book dealing with the topic of rejection of a manuscript and what you can do at that time *if* it occurs. For this writing journey, you are about to take, you will be prepared—even if there are unexpected rockfalls, detours, or annoying insects buzzing about—and clouds of beautiful butterflies, too.

Your Turn 1.3

What is one thing you fear most about developing a manuscript for publication? Be precise, detailed—write it down completely. No need to show this writing to anyone.

_____

_____

Write several paragraphs about how this fear affects you.

Lastly, what can you do about your fears and how they affect you? Can you block them, ignore them? Can you feel the fear and start your writing anyway? Make a list of things you can do as you prepare for your writing journey.

What If I'm Not Interested in Writing a Research Piece at This Time? What Else Can I Write to Build My Confidence?

First-Person Narratives

Congratulations on being in a pleasant place with the time and space to accompany your desire to write something meaningful. I understand that not everyone is ready to begin drafting a research paper. If I were an advice columnist, I might note that you didn't mention that you could be feeling a little fear about plunging into what might feel like the icy waters of authoring a research paper—no worries though. Writing just about anything can build your confidence. You can write letters to the editor of the local newspaper, write your life story for your grandchildren, begin a blog, or compose a poem. (Heck, in college I once wrote a small poem on a piece of sycamore bark. The young woman who received it was appreciative.) There are many options that may not feel as high stakes as submitting a research paper to a professional journal. There are places to go where there is no pressure, and while you would be glad to see it in print, you wouldn't be destroyed if that piece never made it into print.

You may not realize it, but you could have an avenue into a realm where you know more than most people.

What I'm suggesting is that you might want to consider writing a personal account of something you have experienced. Researchers and practitioners might call it a case study, but interesting enough, many journals will publish personal accounts or narratives. If you have had a unique experience or incredible insight related to work, culture, or travel, you might want to consider writing a first-person account.

I firmly believe we often think that others have more interesting stories to tell than we do, when, in fact, it may be that what made the other person's story so fascinating was just the skill with which the writer had us hanging on to every sentence before leaping to the next. A wonderful writer can make the every day, the mundane, fresh, and wiggly. If you doubt that sentence, just watch a few back episodes of *Seinfeld* to see how much of the storyline revolves around something trite—like getting a piece of spinach stuck in a front tooth. If you write well, or at least are eager to improve your writing skills, drafting a personal account might be a way to gently test a venue that might not be so competitive. Examples are provided below to help you see how reflections and personal accounts are put together. Read several of the examples to see if this is something that you could get excited about writing.

First-Person Accounts and Narratives in Professional Publications

Amari, N. (2021). On becoming a counselling psychologist: Making sense of presence. *Journal of Humanistic Psychology, 0*(0). https://doi-org.ezproxy.uky.edu/10.1177/0022167821995371

Baldwin, D. (2020). A personal account of reducing and stopping antidepressant treatment. *International Clinical Psychopharmacology, 35*(4), 194–200. https://doi.org/10.1097/YIC.0000000000000315

Del, C. (2021). Training pains: A personal account. *Psychodynamic Practice, 27,* 83–89. https://doi.org/10.1080/14753634.2020.1759960

Edwards, S. L. (2016). The personal narrative of a nurse: A journey through practice. *Journal of Holistic Nursing: Official Journal of the American Holistic Nurses' Association, 34*(2), 154–161. https://doi.org/10.1177/0898010115587582

Ergas, R. (2020). Bearing witness in asylum work: A personal account. *Journal of Humanistic Psychology, 60*(6), 761–766. https://doi.org/10.1177/0022167820945957

Faulkner, S. L. (2021). Buttered nostalgia: Feeding my parents during #COVID19. *Journal of Social and Personal Relationships.* https://doi.org/10.1177/02654075211012478

Gray, B. (2019) The power of psychiatry: A service user's first-person account and perspective, *Psychosis, 11*(2), 178–183. https://doi.org/10.1080/17522439.2018.1542022

Hannam-Swain, S. (2018) The additional labour of a disabled PhD student. *Disability & Society, 33*(1), 138–142. https://doi.org/10.1080/09687599.2017.1375698

Idowu, B. D. (2023). A personal reflection upon navigating into a senior academic role. *Frontiers in Sociology, 8,* 979691-979691. https://doi.org/10.3389/fsoc.2023.979691

Larsen, P. (2019). Family caregiving: A personal story. *Rehabilitation Nursing, 44*(6), 301. https://doi.org/10.1097/RNJ.0000000000000242

Müller, M., Broadhead, J., Simpson, T., & Abas, M. A. (2022). Effect of acute depression associated with COVID-19 infection on health-seeking behaviour: A psychiatrist's personal account and case report. *BJPsych Open, 8*(4), e119. https://doi.org/10.1192/bjo.2022.521

Newhill, C. E. (2019). Personal account: One out of a hundred. *Schizophrenia Bulletin, 45*(3), 498–499. https://doi.org/10.1093/schbul/sby043

Rhee, S. (2017). A caterpillar morphs into a butterfly. *Reflections: Narratives of Professional Helping, 22*(3), 18–21.

Seinen, J. (2021). "Room for failure was abundant": A personal account of SummerWorks. *Canadian Theatre Review, 187,* 42–46.

Singh, S. P. (2022). Stairway to heaven: A first-person account of noesis. *Journal of Nervous and Mental Disease, 210*(11), 850–854. https://doi.org/10.1097/NMD.0000000000001550

Smith, D. E. (2022). The potential of psychedelic medicine—a personal account. *Journal of the Neurological Sciences, 434,* 120128. https://doi.org/10.1016/j.jns.2021.120128

Smith, H., & Parkinson, C. (2022). Experiences of a service user advisor to a post-qualifying social work course: A personal account. *Journal of Social Work Practice, 36*(4), 473–479.

Super, J. T. (2018). A personal narrative on responding to the Pulse tragedy in Orlando: An interdisciplinary supervisory perspective. *The Clinical Supervisor, 37*(1), 142–157. https://doi.org/10.1080/07325223.2017.1413471

Whittaker, T. T. (2019), "Get off my property": A personal narrative addressing violence against African Americans by law enforcement post–Hurricane Katrina. *Journal of Multicultural Counseling and Development, 47,* 161–171. https://doi.org/10.1002/jmcd.12139

The main thing to remember is to find a receptive, friendly journal. Not every journal will accept a personal account. Look into their archives or back issues to see if they have ever published a *first-person account, personal narrative,* or *personal account* or *anecdote*. If there are no guidelines to follow for submission, then try to keep your final word length within those that the journal has published before. Do a draft, cut the dry stuff out, and leave in the details that help others experience what you saw, felt, heard, ran toward, or away from. Give it to someone you trust to give you honest feedback. Revise and send it off.

Book Reviews for Professional Journals

You might want to consider writing a book review as another way to build confidence. After all, you read books, don't you? And discuss them? (If you don't read books, you really should; they are a fine way to learn more about the craft of writing.) If you read books, which most of you do already, it is not so much of a hop, skip, or jump to summarize the content of one and recognize the parts that you liked and the parts you didn't.

This is what editor Felber said about book reviews in 2002: "It is a dirty secret of the journal publishing business, perhaps known only to editors, that professors may be reluctant to write book reviews" (p. 166). She went on to say, "The editor's job is often discouraging. It can take five or more contacts to arrange the review of a single book, and the dropout rate for those who consent is about twenty percent" (p. 167). In the journal, she edited at that time, "30 reviews and review essays" were published in a prior year, which makes it seem as if there are an adequate number of opportunities for getting a review published—assuming other journals have a similar interest in new books being reviewed. Not every journal publishes reviews, and those that used to years ago, may not anymore. Once again, you will need to do some sleuthing to determine where an editor might be interested in your offering.

Here is a brief list of journals that regularly carry book reviews:

Frontiers in Psychology

Innovation in Language Learning and Teaching

Journal of Baccalaureate Social Work

Journal of Evidence-Based Social Work

Journal of Gerontological Social Work

Journal of Scholarly Publishing

Journal of Social Work

> *Publishing Research Quarterly*
>
> *Research on Social Work Practice*
>
> *Social Work*
>
> *TESOL Quarterly* (concerned with English language teaching and learning and standard English as a second dialect.)
>
>   Additionally, one can find sites on the internet that list literary magazines that will publish book reviews. See, for instance,
>
> - https://trishhopkinson.com/2020/06/11/where-to-submit-book-reviews-60-lit-mags-journals/
> - https://www.alinastefanescuwriter.com/blog/2020/4/20/a-list-of-places-that-like-book-reviews

Still thinking about it? Lewis (2022) provides specific examples of ways to express your opinions and states, that "There is not one perfect format for a book review as reviewers have their own styles, perspectives and priorities and it is important that these come through in a book review as it will allow the readers to 'connect' with the ideas and perspectives" (p. 255). Here's another resource from Wiley giving suggestions about how to review books:

https://authorservices.wiley.com/Reviewers/book-reviewers/reviewing-published-books.html.

Writing Articles for Magazines

Writing for an online or print magazine in your field is a third way to begin writing in a low-stakes way. It may give you helpful feedback, but even if that is minimal, at least you may be able to try out your writing skills without a great deal of stress. A couple of suggestions of social work magazines that may be receptive to your ideas for developing short articles are provided below. Contact the editors before developing an article. If your idea and article are accepted, this could be a publication to add to your CV, however, these publications may

> **Examples of Social Work Magazines**
>
> *The New Social Worker.* Guidelines for writers: https://www.socialworker.com/Guidelines_for_Writers/
>
> *Social Work Today.* Writers' guidelines: https://www.socialworktoday.com/writers_guidelines.shtml#:~:text=Do%20not%20list%20references%20that,%2C%20and%20e%2Dmail%20address.&text=Submission%3A%20Send%20all%20queries%20and,mail%20as%20Microsoft%20Word%20attachments.

not count for faculty or aspiring faculty in research or tenure-track academic positions. Unlike commercial magazines, you will not receive any remuneration.

Writing a Blog

Developing a blog or submitting blogs for an established site is still a fourth way to write and exercise your writing muscles and test the flowing waters of publication possibility. Be mindful, though, that first-person narratives, book reviews, blogs, and poems penned on tree bark are not likely to impress your colleagues or dean if you are in a tenure-track position or want to see your efforts receive academic recognition. This does *not* mean that writing for these venues can't be enjoyable or fulfilling. These forms of writing can also be ways to make sense of the world, to relax. It could become an activity you do after you have finished with your day's or week's work. In fact, writing blogs can open the door for book publishing—giving you writing practice and an opportunity to be noticed. It is something I'll talk a bit more about in Chapter 15.

> **Your Turn 1.4**
>
> Do you have an interesting, life-changing experience that you could share? Were you ever tempted to be a whistle-blower on a colleague or supervisor? Lost in Mexico City without a knowledge of Spanish? Found a good way to teach or relate to others very different from you?
>
> _____
>
> _____
>
> _____
>
> Have you found an outlet that could be receptive to your story? If not, have you asked your friends where they would go? Have you thought about asking your university's research librarian? (Even if you are not a student, most are glad to help the public.)
>
> _____
>
> _____

Your Turn 1.5

If you were forced to decide in the next hour, would you rather write a first-person account, a book review, an article for a magazine, or a blog?

_____

_____

_____

_____

On a scale from 1 to 100, how interested are you in pursuing one of the ideas above?

_____

_____

_____

_____

What is the first step you need to take?

_____

_____

_____

_____

Resources

Bagri, G., & Jones, G. V. (2018). The role of first-person perspective and vivid imagery in memory for written narratives. *Educational Psychology in Practice, 34*(3), 229–244. https://doi.org10.1080/02667363.2018.1431522

Collado, J. (2019). *Make a living with blog writing: How to write blog posts that clients pay for and where to find clients—a beginner's guide.*

Flanagan, K. (2018). *Writer's Digest guide to magazine article writing: A practical guide to selling your pitches, crafting strong articles & earning more bylines.* Writer's Digest Books.

Gornick, V. (2002). *The situation and the story: The art of personal narrative.* Farrar, Straus and Giroux.

Journal of Scholarly Publishing. Information on reviewing a book for JSP. https://www.utpjournals.press/journals/jsp/book-reviews

Nash, R. J. (2019). *Liberating scholarly writing: The power of personal narrative.* Information Age Publishing.

Nash, R., & Viray, S. (2013). The who, what, and why of scholarly personal narrative writing. *Counterpoints, 446,* 1–9.

Reflections: Narratives of Professional Helping. (https://reflectionsnarrativesofprofessionalhelping.org/index.php/Reflections)

Sprott, Z. E. & Zuckerman, C. (2022). Annual bibliography of works about life writing, 2021. *Biography: An Interdisciplinary Quarterly, 45,* 163–248. https://doi.org/10.1353/bio.2022.0030

Zinsser, W. (2005). *Writing about your life: A journey into the past.* Da Capo Press.

References

Deetjen, T. (2020). *Published.* Productive Academic.

Dillard, A. (1989). *The writing life.* Harper Perennial.

Felber, L. (2002). The book review: Scholarly and editorial responsibility. *Journal of Scholarly Publishing, 33*(3), 166–172.

Kallestinova, E. D. (2011). How to write your first research paper. *Yale Journal of Biology and Medicine, 84*(3), 181–190.

Lamott, A. (2018). *Almost everything. Notes on hope.* Riverhead Books.

Lewis, M. N. (2022). Here's a good book: Hints on writing a book review for academic journals. *RELC Journal, 53*(1), 253–260. https://doi.org/10.1177/0033688220916239

Peternelj-Taylor, C. (2018). Do you have a writing mentor? *Journal of Forensic Nursing, 14,* 1–2.

CHAPTER 2

Where Do I Find Ideas for Writing, and How Do I Evaluate Them?

How Do I Start Developing a Publishable Manuscript?

The first thing needed to start a draft of a manuscript is to have a topic, a problem, or a research question in mind. If you don't have one, don't worry—this chapter will discuss sources where ideas may be found. However, if you are already in possession of an idea for a possible paper or have research from an academic paper, thesis, or dissertation that you want to polish and shape into a format suitable for submission to a professional journal, then you may want to skip ahead and go to the latter part of the chapter. (This would also include those of you who have submitted a previous manuscript that you believe can be better prepared.) The later section will discuss ways of assessing whether your idea for a manuscript may have qualities likely worth investing time and energy in. This chapter is mostly for readers who have a dream of publishing an article and being an author but haven't yet settled upon an interesting idea they want to develop, and those who have the bud of an idea but don't know whether it is a good one.

Let's look first at several strategies or sources, idea ponds if you want to call them that, where you can go fishing. There are many sources of ideas. In the next section, we will consider tried and true sources where publishable ideas might be found.

Where Can I Find an Idea for a Publishable Paper? Four Ideas

1. Can Reading Be a Source of Inspiration for a Writing Project?

Sometimes in reading for pleasure or even reading material assigned as part of a university or graduate education, you can be cruising along minding your own business when unexpectedly you are momentarily struck by a statement or question raised by the author. "Huh," you think, "that would be really interesting to check out." Or perhaps, your reaction is more skeptical, and you say to yourself, "That doesn't make sense. I wonder if someone explored it with a different approach if the findings would be the same?" At times, we read something that leaves us hanging. We want to know more, go deeper. Is more known about the problem than the author has described? Was the study so exploratory it overlooked several relevant questions? Closely scrutinizing what we are reading can give rise to researchable questions.

Indeed, essays we read, news stories, or even professional journal articles may, because of space limitations, not fully review all that is known about a problem or topic. Information is developed and disseminated so rapidly these days, that even professional journal articles written 2 to 3 years ago may not reveal the most recent information. However, a little investigation on our part may reveal a surprising lack of research or literature on the topic. This can especially happen when a new development or problem in one field is slow in coming to the attention of others in an allied field or discipline. Even if more is known than presented in the original article, there may be no studies taking the approach you had in mind or examining the question exactly the way you might go about it, and that is okay. Science moves forward in small increments, usually. Sir Isaac Newton, credited for his theory of universal gravitation and the inventor of calculus, acknowledged the contributions to knowledge of those who came before him. He is attributed with saying, "If I have seen further, it is by standing on the shoulders of giants" (Elshaikh, n.d.).

If you look closely, you may find flaws or weaknesses in published studies. What might these be? Perhaps unwarranted generalizations from a convenience sampling design, small sample size, or use of a questionnaire with unknown reliability or validity. If a small set of articles on your proposed topic exist and they are all qualitative studies, you may want to explore further with a more objective or quantitative approach. Similarly, if you have skimmed the literature and found only quantitative studies, you might want to consider a mixed method or qualitative study.

Where should you start reading? Begin with the journals that are most germane to your area of interest or where you are most likely to find articles related to your budding research question. Let's assume you find two or three professional journals along this line; you don't have to read every article in each issue of the journals. Work smart. Do key word searches, title searches, skim abstracts, and read only the articles that are of most interest to you. If you find an article that is right on target or close to it, look at the references cited at the end of the article. These can expand your knowledge of the topic and also introduce you to other professional journals and articles that you may not have known about.

After finding professional journal articles that are a good match for your topic, go to their *Discussion* sections. Frequently in the concluding paragraphs of articles, one can find a call for future research. This is where the author or authors make suggestions about the use of new instruments or samples with different characteristics. With an eye toward moving the research forward, their recommendations can be highly specific. The value of finding these future research discussions is that they can be used to confirm that an idea you have may well be worth pursuing because other researchers or authors on the topic have concluded the same thing.

You might also want to look in the *Discussion* section for the place where the authors are discussing the study's limitations. By identifying the areas in their own study where there are weaknesses, you might be able to use some or much of that study's methodology but can improve upon it. Simply put, overcome the flaws of an already published paper, and you may have a publication.

Read fiction, too, for ideas. One of my favorite books is Pat Conroy's *Prince of Tides*. In that book, he vividly describes a fictional character's experiences growing up in a highly dysfunctional family—which may have been partly autobiographical. The abuse and chaos in this family give rise later to a fictional sister attempting suicide. Hmm. One might wonder about a possible relationship between growing up in an abusive, tumultuous home and later suicide attempts. Whenever in your reading you find yourself wondering, wanting to know more, you may be on a journey of discovery that has the potential for a publishable paper.

2. Can Experiences in Your Life Be a Source of Inspiration for Ideas?

If you have an inquisitive mind and want to better understand the people and the events in the world, potential topics to write about will be dropped into your lap (figuratively speaking) with some regularity. You don't have to be a lab scientist or have an IQ that runs into the genius range, just notice what is going on around you and ask yourself, "Why?" To illustrate this point, I will share a story, although it will surely date me.

Decades ago, when acquired immunodeficiency syndrome (AIDS) was a new term in the popular press, there was a serious lack of information. As we have discovered with the COVID epidemic, some individuals took it upon themselves to try to explain how the disease was transmitted and ways to keep ourselves safe, but often speculations had no basis in science but originated in fears. For example, early on, individuals wondered that if a mosquito bit a person with AIDS and then drew blood from a second or third person, might these individuals develop AIDS? People questioned whether they could acquire AIDS from toilet seats or if a server in a restaurant with AIDS might pass the illness on to those being served in the restaurant or bar by handling plates or glasses. During that time, I was visiting a social work intern placed in a large urban hospital being supervised by a licensed social worker whose caseload dealt mainly with patients hospitalized with AIDS. We met in an office inside the hospital, and in concluding the meeting, we had to sign some paperwork. Since none of us could find a working pen, the social worker went to the outer office and borrowed a ballpoint from the assistant. When that was concluded, we went out into the hall and were in the process of saying goodbye and shaking hands when I noticed out of the corner of my eye that the assistant had come out of the office. She had the ballpoint in her hand that we had used and was washing it in the water fountain. I was stunned that she might have thought that the social work supervisor who traveled into the hospital rooms of patients with AIDS might be a carrier of AIDS that could be transmitted to her via the pen that the three of us had just used.

As a result of that experience, several colleagues and I published a small article based on surveying social work students and looking at their knowledge, fear of AIDS, and empathy toward persons with AIDS. A short time later, another colleague and I published a study on homophobia and attitudes toward AIDS among medical, nursing, and paramedical students. Neither one of these two articles was earthshaking nor in the most prestigious journals, but that didn't matter to us. If we informed even a few people, that was satisfaction enough.

On another occasion, I had a graduate student working as a coordinator of volunteers for a hospice organization tell me that several of her volunteers had been asked by their hospice patients if the volunteers would help them to commit suicide to end their suffering. This was an intriguing question because the medical community's position was basically that no one needs to suffer from pain—and yet for a proportion of the hospice patients, it sounded like life was too painful or that their quality of life was minimal. Were most hospice volunteers receiving these requests? Wanting more information, we prepared a brief survey, and that study was published too.

More recently, a doctoral student who was a foster parent decided to focus his dissertation and publish on topics related to foster parenting. If you are working in a field of practice, social work, counseling, clinical psychology, nursing, and others, I promise you there are tens, if not hundreds, of questions worthy of investigation if you are paying attention. Of course, you may not be interested in all of them. A portion of them will require too much time, funding, or staffing to fully investigate. But on the other hand, there will be a few that can be explored on a small scale whether you have access to funding or not. In fact, the way to think about this is that the findings from a small pilot study may provide data that would secure funding for a more comprehensive investigation.

Here are eight possible strategies that can result in a research question:

1. Evaluate a novel or innovative intervention or practice.
2. Replicate a study with a variation of the dependent variable, completely different dependent variable, or with a different methodology, or data analysis. Examine the "host" study and conduct a similar study but without all of the limitations listed in the original article.
3. Test a theory or practice theory.
4. Conduct a systematic review of the literature examining an understudied practice, intervention, or application.
5. Regarding an emerging problem, summarize current knowledge for the practitioner and specify the research gaps.
6. Step outside the quantitative literature and seek insiders' perspectives about a problem, culture, or current issue.
7. Test folk wisdom applications. Do they work better than current treatment methods?
8. Examine a pattern of incidents. Has something been overlooked that could explain the phenomenon?

(These ideas were modified from Stamler (2002) who cited Gillis and Jackson (2002) with 12 possible sources for research questions.)

Probably the best part about being a faculty member is reading a student's end-of-term paper and finding superb writing or creativity. Yes, sometimes the question or the methodology has to be shaped or adjusted, but students are a constant source of ideas for exploring. Students often are aware of new developments and topics being discussed on social media. They may introduce you to new slang or terminology that suggests movements or directions within segments of society that are unknown to you. They may inform you or write about these in assigned papers about current problems or issues. One advantage of writing about these new topics is that there won't be a basketball arena of literature to have to wade through in professional journals. That can be a plus—or a minus in the sense that you might have to hunt in related disciplines to find literature that is "in the ballpark" and has some commonalities with your topic, even if not being an exact fit. Being a faculty member can be a source of potential questions to explore if one is open to working with students.

Please don't misinterpret what I am saying about ideas you hear from students. I'm not saying that if you are a faculty member, you ought to exploit students or steal their ideas. I am saying that they *may* bring ideas for papers in the normal course of an educational experience. Depending on the extent of their involvement with the topic and their ability to make a significant contribution as a writing partner, you may want to partner with them and explore the potential for a possible journal publication. Stealing students' ideas would always be wrong and could result in severe repercussions for the instructor. I'll talk more about coauthoring with students in Chapter 4. Looking back over my years of teaching, I could have written a lot more about students' life experiences that they shared during advising or freely contributed to class.

Questions can also come to you from experiences other than teaching. I was visiting my 87-year-old aunt in the hospital; she had unfortunately fallen and broken her hip. During her hospitalization, one day a volunteer visitor arrived with a therapy cat. My aunt, even though she was having some issues with dementia, loved cats, and particularly enjoyed petting and stroking the therapy cat that was placed on her bed. From that experience, one might wonder if there were some objective ways of measuring the visit of the therapy animal. For instance, do patients request less pain medicine or eat more of their meals afterward? Do family members or hospital staff notice that patients receiving visits from therapy cats smiled more or were more pleasant? Pushed the call button fewer times during the night? Did the cat's visit allow them to reminisce and share happy moments with family members during visits? One might also investigate what the hospital staff thought about bringing therapy animals in. What special concerns might they have? Did they prefer certain animals (e.g., cats or rabbits, over dogs)?

Life brings us all kinds of experiences; you may have had a friend, neighbor, or family member who committed suicide and wonder why they hid their depression from you. Is that always the case among those considering suicide? Perhaps you have a friend who disclosed being adopted, who found and called her biological mother and was told by the mother to never call back again. What is it like having a member of the family who is mentally ill move in with you and whose fragile state forces every family decision to be considered in light of its effect on her? What is it like to be a minority in society trying to always place your best foot forward when it feels like circumstances are always making you take two steps back, to have so little support for the person you want to be?

Look around and be intrigued by the questions that make you wonder, "Why?" or "What the heck?" Ask questions about things you don't understand. Albert Einstein once noted, "I have no special talents. I am only passionately curious."

3. Could Conducting a Literature Search Produce Ideas for Writing Projects?

Maybe you don't think of searching for literature as a source for inspiration, but sometimes a search will turn up zip, zero, nada, and you know then that anything you write on the topic may be a giant step closer to being published than you were before you began the search because there has been almost nothing published on your topic.

As I indicated in the previous section, I believe every one of us has had conversations and life experiences that could be the source of an idea for a published paper. Let's say that a close friend confided in you that they had been abused or seriously neglected as a child. Even if they don't share details of the terror or trauma in their lives, you might go away from the friend's disclosure and wonder about how those early childhood experiences might have affected your friend's functioning as an adult.

The topic of child abuse itself is too broad for a research question and literature search. Research questions must be focused—which is another way of saying that they must be very narrow. If our literature search is too broad, we will suffocate trying to wade through hundreds, if not thousands, of articles or "hits" that our search engine will discover. Using the topic of child abuse as an illustration, we can develop a narrower focus (and corresponding research questions) by examining various aspects of the problem of child abuse. See how a slightly different lens each time can lead to different studies:

> Effects of child abuse (or neglect) on preschool children, elementary, and middle school children, teenagers, and adults—(just select one of these population groups)
> Best ways for diagnosing child abuse and neglect
> Types of child abuse (e.g., physical, emotional, and sexual abuse, neglect)
> Treatment for children who have been abused or neglected
> Treatment for adult survivors of childhood abuse (or neglect)
> Characteristics of perpetrators of child abuse
> Causes or factors contributing to child abuse
> Treatment of perpetrators
> Efforts to prevent the occurrence of child abuse and neglect
> Macro/organizational issues: societal responses to the problem of child abuse (e.g., foster care, adoption, training of child protection professionals, stress, secondary trauma, and job turnover among child protection professionals), diversity and differences in reported statistics in the United States and other countries)

These narrower facets of child abuse can then be examined even more specifically by the characteristics of the children (e.g., age, sex/gender, race/ethnicity, type and severity of abuse) or by the parent's or care provider's characteristics (e.g., age, sex/gender race/ethnicity, education, mental status, substance use, survivor of abuse or neglect as a child) and by even other variables that may interest you (e.g., within homeless families, military families, foster care families).

Don't think you are on a search for the magical "right" set of foci from literature. That might be the case, but even more valuable might be how the elements of a story or experience interact with each other and create a new question or topic. For instance, suppose your close friend later discloses that she grew up in a rural area of the state and was traumatically mistreated by an elementary school teacher. Despite the fact that the adult perpetrator could have caused your friend to have negative associations with school, your friend is planning on being an elementary school teacher herself. "Hmm," you wonder, "is that a typical response? It seems more logical to expect that she wouldn't want that career." This seems like it could be the start of a legitimate research question regarding how child abuse could possibly affect career choice, doesn't it? A literature search might confirm the lack of research on career choices by adult survivors of abuse.

One set of authors has discussed the "pruning function" of delimiting questions to narrow down the literature. These are questions such as, "In which people?" "Under what conditions?" "At what time?" "In what location?" "By observing which events?" "By manipulating which variables?" (Locke et al., 2000, p. 51).

If you begin a literature search and don't feel overwhelmed by the vast number of seemingly relevant articles, the next step would be to begin reading them or grouping them by specific content or relevance so you can see what might be missing. At this point you are probing the literature, doing a simple reconnaissance of it. What elements or factors haven't been written about yet? Have others done anything like what you are considering? If so, experiment with a variation or modification of the original premise.

For instance, let's assume you are reading about veterans and come across the story of a vet who, having served in Iraq and Afghanistan, described the grief of losing friends in combat; he was tormented that he survived—feeling he should have died too. What if you take the concept of survivor's guilt and apply it to individuals who experienced childhood abuse?

Let me tell you a little more. I once interviewed a young woman student in graduate school, the survivor of horrific sexual abuse from her father, who described something akin to survivor's guilt stemming from her inability to prevent the abuse occurring to her young sisters—especially after she left the home. Her survivor's guilt was as powerful as the veteran's. Is there a possible research question there about the similarity of the two concepts? Or about the negative effects of sexual abuse on survivors when they can't protect their siblings? Consult the literature; test the waters. If you are not flooded with hits, if there is only a trickle, maybe you've found a topic that would be worth developing into a manuscript. In quantitative research articles, the absence of studies on a topic is called a gap in the literature. Finding a disclosed gap in the literature when reading a published article nearly always justifies further investment in the topic. And here's the thing: authors of articles routinely tell readers about gaps in the literature they've found.

We'll spend more time on conducting a literature search in Chapter 7, How Do I Write the Introduction and the Literature Review? For now, just recognize that seeing the extent and focal areas of what has been published on a topic is a useful way of discovering and refining ideas for writing projects.

Finding a gap in the literature is passing the baton of a good idea on to you. Here's what you might experience in the words of Stanley Kubrick:

> You sit at the board and suddenly your heart leaps. Your hand trembles to pick up the piece and move it. But what chess teaches you is that you must sit there calmly and think about whether it is really a good idea and whether there are other, better ideas.

4. Can Friends, Colleagues, or Faculty Serve as a Source of Ideas?

My first published article in a peer-reviewed journal came about when a friend and coworker returned from a conference where he had presented a description of a novel federally funded project that employed us. The editor of the journal appreciated the innovativeness of the project; he invited my friend to write a description of it to send to him at the journal. Which we did, with successful results. (Except our boss was angry that we didn't put her name on the manuscript. Longer story there). While that publication might have been explained away by just great luck, I don't think so. Years later, I was attending a conference and met another attendee who wanted to join me in writing a book. Had I not been at the conference, we would not have decided to team up, and I probably wouldn't ever have written that book on my own.

Presenting at conferences, joining roundtable discussions, and talking to those who may have similar interests to you can, like dandelions in a lawn popping up in the spring, give you a new vista, new challenges, and writing topics to consider. My fourth, seventh, eighth, and ninth publications came about with people I met at meetings of statewide associations.

As a young assistant professor, I had two mentors who both worked on manuscripts with me—with success. One of them suggested that I should present at professional conferences and then take those presentations and turn them into publications. I took his advice, and it was a good strategy, although I admit to being fonder of writing than presenting. The other colleague I wrote several articles with also and will discuss him a bit later in the chapter.

Within university settings, there are often opportunities to work with colleagues from different disciplines and located in colleges or departments different from your own. Opportunities sometimes pop up unexpectedly. I worked a couple of summers with a researcher in a different college. We didn't know each other at first but learned that we worked well together as a team.

He brought interesting ideas from his funded projects, and we wrote about them. We had four publications together.

Your university may have a database listing faculty with special expertise, publications, or recipients of sponsored funding projects. If there is no one in your immediate circle of contacts who seems like a promising partner, don't be hesitant about reaching out to others, exploring common interests, and writing ideas.

To make your mark on the world, go for coffee or lunch with colleagues or potential ones. Talk to them about what they are working on; ask what projects they are planning or have gotten underway. Speak up and express an interest when they hit upon a subject you would like to explore, too. If they seem compatible, tell them what you are considering writing about. Whether you are a teaching assistant or faculty member, keep an open mind. Consider even ideas a little removed from your silo of knowledge— especially if the colleague has an expertise but needs help writing. If the research question captures your interest, if there appears to be a gap in the literature, if you could see yourself working with the topic and developing it into a publication, then don't reject an opportunity that may come from an unexpected direction.

As a college student, I met the celebrated composer, author, folksinger, and folklorist John Jacob Niles (best known for "I Wonder as I Wander," "Black Is the Color of My True Love's Hair," "The Frog Went a Courtin'"), and after his concert, we had a brief but enjoyable discussion about song lyrics as poetry. He told his personal assistant to remember my name when I called to set up a meeting time for us to continue talking about poetry. However, I was too shy to call. Now I wonder what direction my life might have taken if I had followed up. When opportunities knock, open the door. Shyness won't get you a cup of Starbucks or anything else!

If you are open to drawing upon "people resources," Heppner and Heppner (2004) identified four more sources of people who could be willing to discuss your ideas about potential research projects. They suggest you could (a) directly contact the *author* of a captivating article written recently. The author may be willing to discuss your "seed" of an idea and suggest ways to distill it or shape it better; (b) if you will be attending a conference where scholars in your area are meeting, you can consider approaching a *presenter* there and inviting that person to have coffee or lunch to discuss a common interest, perhaps a project you would like to explore further; (c) if you have found a recent *dissertation* where the author's work was similar to the topic and methodology you have in mind. Reaching out to that person could be beneficial to learn of problems experienced and suggestions for improving the next exploration; (d) lastly, you may find a *group of interested persons* on the internet who discuss the methodology or the topic. They may be aware of resources or literature that you did not find. To this list, we should also add research librarians in your university. They may be able to take an idea or concept and help with locating synonyms for searching, databases, or connect you with a resource like the American Psychological Association's Thesaurus of Psychological Index Terms. Hepper and Heppner (2004) write, "The librarian is your friend! If not, the librarian should fast become your friend!" (p. 60).

Inspiration comes from everywhere. From life, observing people, etc. From movies and books you love. From research.

Holly Black, author of over 30 fantasy novels for teens

How Do I Know My Idea Is a Good One?

In this section, we will consider ways to assess the viability of an idea for a potential writing project. They are not presented in a preferred order, as you may have more confidence in one approach than in others. This is what seems to have worked for me:

1. Does the Idea Strike Me as Really, Really Interesting?

Does the idea or research hook my interest? Even simple writing projects can take 1 to 3 months to complete and sometimes even a year when data collection is difficult or complex. I ask myself, Am I willing to spend 1 to 3 months of my life on this project? Would I enjoy exploring the idea? Writing about it? Do I have a better idea? A therapist friend once told me that he discovered his clients reported their romantic involvement with others occurred when that person intrigued them. Am I intrigued by a topic and want to learn more about it?

2. Is There a Gap in the Literature?

Does a preliminary search through one or more research databases (e.g., Web of Science, PsycInfo, Medline) or one or more recent peer-reviewed articles that I have read confirm that my idea would, in fact, respond to a gap in the literature that needs assessing? Can I find the gap stated in a recent article?

3. Does My Mentor, Trusted Friend, or Potential Writing Partner Like the Idea?

Within my circle of closest friends or support systems, do they evaluate the idea as positively as I do? Do they see pragmatic difficulties or problems that I haven't considered? (For instance, might it take too long to create the data collection instrument and gather the data?) Is it too large of a project for me at this point in my career? Is the idea too inconsequential or so underdeveloped that the project can't be evaluated yet for its potential to be published?

Weigh the enthusiasm differentially. For instance, if you are a faculty member and the writing partner is a student, then the student could be excited and flattered to work with you but not as able to judge as well as, say, a faculty member with publications in your area. Also, you may need to evaluate the responses of others well positioned to evaluate your ideas who are overly negative and sometimes don't have adequate explanations for their positions. (I could tell a couple of stories here—about two different faculty who torpedoed ideas for journal articles that were later published.) You can encounter something like professional jealousy stemming from their failure to think of the writing project or unhappiness that they wouldn't have a role in writing it. (This happens all the time in academia, unfortunately.) If you get some unexpected negative feedback and you feel your idea is a good one, consider increasing the sample size of those giving you their opinions. For instance, if only one of two faculty think the idea is a good one, you might want to consult a third person you trust. When two of the three people consulted enthusiastically support the idea, that should weigh more than a single negative opinion—all opinions being equal in your consideration. Consult only people you know well enough to trust.

4. Is Sponsored Funding Potentially Available for Exploring My Topic?

While sponsored or financial support is not always necessary to begin a writing project, favorable opinions that your idea could potentially attract funding is a plus for the sustainability of the project. Ask: Has my chair or dean given me enough financial support (e.g., summer funding or a course release) so that I could complete a study based on my idea? Has the chair/dean identified a potential source of funding for my project and encouraged me to apply for financial support? Have I or a coauthor sent a brief letter to a foundation and received a positive response to our idea?

5. Feasibility/Practicality: Can I Actually Collect the Data?

Ask yourself: Do I have access to the data? Can I find enough participants to interview? Will the findings advance our knowledge? Be useful to others? With these criteria, you might want to consult with practitioners instead of academics to get confirmation regarding the possible practicality or usefulness of the proposed study.

Your answers to these five questions should inform whether you should proceed with your idea or perhaps revise it in some way or consider a completely different idea. You may be reluctant to abandon an idea too early, and that's okay. Let's go a little further in evaluating the feasibility of a potential project.

The questions asked at the end of the next section will give you another opportunity to think about the ease or complications that could affect the research.

What Hurdles and Trade-Offs Could Affect the Viability of the Writing Project?

While in my doctoral program, I attended a colleague's class where a vice squad officer, prostitute, and owner of a brothel each spoke as part of a panel presentation. The audience, consisting mostly of students, asked questions. I left the university that afternoon convinced that I wanted to write my dissertation on the lives of prostitutes. The panel had shattered misconceptions and introduced me to new ways of thinking about the "oldest profession in the world." For several weeks I turned the idea over in my mind before finally having to let it go.

Why? As a brand-new father of an infant son, I knew interviewing prostitutes would require me to be away from home many evenings. I wasn't sure whether the brothel owner would allow me to interview his staff when they weren't working or whether he would or could introduce me to other operators. I wasn't interested in standing around in the shadows of a dark street waiting to talk to women who were attempting to solicit business or hanging out with them after the customers had all gone home at who knows at what hours of the morning. Ethically, I felt that since these women would be giving of their time to be interviewed, I might need to pay them some sort of honoraria. However, I had no funding. Most importantly, I was concerned that pimps of prostitutes not affiliated with brothels might see me as jeopardizing their sources of income and might not want me to learn too much about the money they received or the drugs that might keep their women going. I was worried, too, about whether there might be criminal interests involved in the operation of the brothels who might want to know what the prostitutes working for them might have learned or might say. What if one or more of them wanted out of the life and asked me to provide them safe passage? While I'm a pretty altruistic guy, I certainly didn't want a couple of shady characters to show up at my home and threaten my wife and son. If I had friends on the police force or in the social service system who assisted trafficked women, it could have been different. I didn't have any connections that would have given me the ability to gather data with reasonable security. Not having these key resources, I thought it was best to choose another topic.

What hurdles might prevent you from completing the project you are considering writing? Here are possible hurdles to consider presented as a checklist for issues revolving around time, effort, funding, and things beyond your control associated with the data collection.

> **Checklist 2.1 Possible Hurdles to Overcome**
>
> ☐ Issues raised by the Institutional Review Board (IBR) requiring complicated procedures, informed consent, or resulting in lengthy delays in getting approval.
> ☐ Inability to collect the needed data within an acceptable amount of time. This can occur when staff or agencies have few clients who are screened eligible for inclusion or few persons of interest can actually be identified for data collection.
> ☐ The agency and/or staff are not excited about your project and don't really facilitate it. Staff claim they don't have the time to assist; you don't have funding to reimburse them. Funding is also an issue if expensive equipment (e.g., biometric devices) or travel (e.g., to Kazakhstan for data collection) is required.
> ☐ People you want to interview or survey don't want to talk about their organ transplants, their traumas, their combat experiences, or the shameful things done to them by bullies or abusers.
> ☐ Too much effort is required. That is, you personally have to sit in a hallway close to the emergency room waiting to talk to family members who may not be willing to discuss their feelings or reactions after the almost catastrophic loss of a family member.
> ☐ Your colleagues or intuition tell you that the department or tenure-voting faculty might not view this line of research or writing as important or making much of a contribution. An example of this might be topics where spirituality/religion overlap with other topics (the near-death experience), and you are *not* a member of a philosophy or religious studies department.
> ☐ Personal, family, or participant safety issues.

On occasion, some hurdles might be easily overcome or offset by other strengths supporting the approach. Yet, every decision will not be a Heck-Yes! or a Heck-No! in terms of proceeding with the writing project. There may well be a mixture of positives with a few lamprey-like potential problems to be overcome.

These 11 considerations should give you a metric (although one without demonstrated psychometrics) for evaluating the strengths or assets you could have with a good idea for a writing project. Obviously, the more checkmarks you accrue, the better, the more viable the idea, and the fewer difficulties you might expect to encounter.

> **Checklist 2.2 Final Checklist for Evaluating the Viability of a Good Idea**
>
> ☐ I personally believe the idea is a good one.
> ☐ There appears to be a gap in the literature.
> ☐ I've been encouraged to publish a portion or all of my research. Also, my mentor, potential writing partner, or colleagues believe the idea is worth pursuing.
> ☐ Financial funding for the project appears available.
> ☐ Submitting IRB protocol and receiving approval is not anticipated to be a problem.
> ☐ Time required for data collection is reasonable, not excessive.
> ☐ Agency partners/staff are excited about gathering data or evaluating this intervention.
> ☐ A pilot test has shown exciting data; alternatively, participants have shown they want to tell their stories.
> ☐ The amount of effort to collect data is reasonable.
> ☐ My department/tenure-voting faculty have been thoroughly supportive of other similar research on this topic or actively support this project.
> ☐ Threats to safety are not an issue.
>
> ___Total Checkmarks

Should I Proceed When There Are One to Two Issues That Might Threaten the Project?

Damn the torpedoes! Full speed ahead! Apologies to Admiral Farragut, but he actually said more than those six words. They do, however, convey the message that we may decide to trust our inner intuitions and proceed anyway—despite whatever well-intended advice we have received. Why might you decide to pursue a writing project even though you expect several problems discussed in the previous section? Here are some reasons:

- This writing project is your life's work (part of a research trajectory), and you are not troubled if data collection takes a long time or if the IRB crimps and slows down your plans. This may be a project you feel called to investigate or write about. It may stem from one of those experiences that a family member or friend had, and you want to honor them by writing about this situation or set of circumstances.

- You may have financial resources, for instance, to personally purchase computers or tablets used for data collection. You were planning to travel to Ireland anyway, even if your request for funding isn't approved. Maybe you can even find a cheaper way to conduct the study by locating a set of secondary data. Maybe you can't reimburse agency staff, but you can appeal to management to give participants an hour or so as time off in lieu of pay. In return, you might provide free consultation to the agency or assist with another research project as a volunteer. Also, you know of places where you can apply for funding.

- You believe that the problem of participant reluctance can be overcome. A different approach may assist in securing a larger sample. Sometimes people are reluctant to participate in research projects because they don't know what questions will be asked. Potential participants may not be highly educated and more comfortable with telling their stories than writing in computer boxes. Perhaps a family member can be asked to assist the person of interest in completing their forms. Also, you may want to give them time, perhaps a week or two, and try explaining the project again over the phone or via email. If funding can be found, a monetary incentive to participants could make an enormous difference.

- The effort required may be solved by training students, giving them credit for a research project or independent study, or possibly finding volunteers from support groups of individuals interested in the topic you want to write about. Or, instead of interviewing individuals in person, you modify your data collection and do it by Zoom, electronic survey, or focus group.

- Perhaps the strongest reason for doing this project is the faith that you currently have in it, your belief that it is a good idea and one worth your expenditure of time and effort. In second place would be the affirmation you receive from a faculty mentor, trusted friend, or department chair. Those who know your writing abilities and intellect the best may point out that your idea is one that has *buildability*. That is, from the proposed study, you may be able to build out from it and create a research trajectory of studies or articles that examine various aspects of the problem or phenomenon you are interested in writing about. You may be the one who fills the research gap, who becomes the expert on this problem.

A good idea will keep you awake during the morning, but a great idea will keep you awake during the night.

Marilyn vos Savant, American magazine columnist

Your Turn 2.1

As you have read this chapter, did you produce an idea, topic, or problem that you think you would like to develop into a manuscript? If so, when you evaluated the idea in terms of the criteria in Checklist 2.2, did you find sufficient support (in your opinion) for the idea? If not, do you have another idea or need to talk to someone about ways to modify your original plan?

_____

_____

_____

_____

Your Turn 2.2

When you looked at the possible hurdles to overcome in Checklist 2.1, are they minor issues or large problems? Did you think of other complications that may thwart your data collection or writing? Can they all be managed without too much difficulty, in your opinion? What will you tackle first?

_____

_____

_____

_____

References

Elshaikh, E. M. (n.d.). *Standing on the shoulders of invisible giants.* Khan Academy. www.khanacademy.org/humanities/big-history-project/big-bang/how-did-big-bang-change/a/standing-on-the-shoulders-of-invisible-giants

Gillis, A., & Jackson, W. (2002). *Research for nurses*. F. A. Davis Co.

Heppner, P. P., & Heppner, M. J. (2004). *Writing and publishing your thesis, dissertation & research*. Thomson.

Locke, L. F., Spirduso, W. W., & Silverman, S. J. (2000). *Proposals that work: A guide for planning dissertations and grant proposals* (4th ed.). SAGE Publications.

Stamler, L. L. (2002). Developing and refining the research question: Step 1 in the research process. *The Diabetes Educator, 28*, 959–962.

CHAPTER 3

How Do I Create a Research Question?

The previous chapter discussed ways to find ideas, topics, or problems to be the seed of a developed writing project. Depending on your discipline, you might be surprised that our discussion has now moved to developing or framing good *research questions*. Although you might be more comfortable with language that would address developing or framing a good *argument*, you'll need to mentally make that conversion, as the task is the same. And according to one source, "A precisely formulated research question is becoming increasingly important within the humanities" (Wisse & Roeland, 2021, p. 22).

In some fields, a hypothesis is favored over a research question to start the process of exploring data. Hypotheses are declarative statements that can be tested; they often predict what researchers expect to find in the planned observations. Null hypotheses state that there will be no difference between two samples or among different groups. Hypotheses are commonly derived from theories, but they and research questions don't have to be. A hypothesis is the "formal version of a hunch or speculations about what the data may reveal. … Hypotheses and research questions are both legitimate starting points for the research process, as long as they are not frivolous or unethical. One's hypothesis can be converted into a research question and vice versa" (Royse, 2020, p. 25).

Research questions allow you to capture the readers' interest by presenting a bit of a mystery, conundrum, puzzle, or question that will reward their skimming of abstracts by giving them something they want to think or read more about. Yes, you can also make an argument; however, in the social sciences, it would likely take the form of a research question or a hypothesis. I'm going to use "research question" most often in this book, but you can mentally replace it with hypothesis if that is your preference.

Why Is It Important to Start With a Research Question?

Here's the easy answer: because the research question or problem you want to investigate is the *organizing principle*, the *raison d'être* upon which the other components of the manuscript are secured. This means that the question or problem must be strong. What do I mean by that? It has to be engaging, interesting to read, and have the capability of capturing readers' interest because they want to know more about this problem and to discover what you have learned about understanding or addressing the problem. Think about trying to slow readers going down the road at 75 miles per hour. Capture their interest because your question is unique, different, or brings a perspective that has a sense of freshness to it. Make your question or problem as worthy of considering as a rest stop during a long drive. Will you potentially uncover something no one else has found? That would be grand, wouldn't it? Perhaps you won't get a request for a TV or radio interview right away, but how wonderful it is to give readers a different way of thinking about time-worn theories, ways of practice, or lack of information on a problem. How great it is to give humanity new information that can make the world a better place!

Your research question or problem has to be important, too. There is no point in wasting your time and that of others if what you are going to write about is trivial or inconsequential. If the research truly contributes, then readers will be excited and want to learn more—particularly if it has definite implications for practice, teaching, or the profession. Strong questions in the social and medical sciences must be answerable. Philosophers may love the questions that can be debated to eternity and back, but not so most researchers and practitioners.

> Research is to see what everybody else has seen, and to think what nobody else has thought.
>
> Albert Szent-Gyorgyi, Noble Prize winner for first isolating vitamin C

What Are the Characteristics of a Research Question?

Particularly with quantitative articles, and perhaps less so with other types of articles, one of the most important steps is deciding upon a central question around which all of your activities related to developing a manuscript will be connected like the trusses supporting a bridge. The road across this bridge begins with the question and ends when you have arrived with findings to discuss.

Although we talked generally in the previous chapter about four sources for ideas, in this segment, we want to move more specifically into refining ideas so that they become researchable questions. This involves taking the germ of an idea and refining it into a research question. The characteristics of a research question are that it is focused, clear, relevant, original, answerable/researchable, and makes for a question that is interesting to ponder.

Focus
The research question is seated within a segment of literature, but don't choose a topic as large as a glacier. Especially if you have little or no experience with publishing professional journal articles, do not take on a topic that already has a mountain of material written on it.

Don't let that news be discouraging. Even within a topic that would take a lifetime to read everything written about it, there will be gaps or facets of the problem that have been under-researched, overlooked, or investigated with less than the best methodologies. Find a niche for yourself where little is known. There will always be both avenues and backstreets for you to explore.

Clarity
Locke et al. (2000) have written this:

> The clarity of a research question hinges on adequate specificity and the correct degree of inclusiveness. The major elements of the investigation must be identified in a way that permits no confusion with other elements. At the same time, the statement {question} must maintain simplicity by including nothing beyond what is essential to identify the main variables and any relationship that may be proposed among them. (p. 12)

Don't make your research question too long or complicated. In a few words, explain what you want to know or do so that an average person can understand the thrust of it. (Of course, sometimes authors of technical papers will have to ignore that last sentence.)

Relevance
The research question should address an issue or problem that has practice, professional, or societal implications—certainly, it should be of interest to those whom you consider to be your colleagues or students. Mattick et al. (2018) suggest this test: "Ask yourself what will happen if this research is not done—does it really matter? Who will benefit from it?" (p. 105). How might it improve outcomes for a particular population or a special problem?

Originality
This characteristic asks that your research question provides new insights into a problem or understanding of a phenomenon. Don't serve up leftovers to your company of readers or look at the issue in the same way that 35 others have looked at it with the same tired, old, expected results. What is fresh, different, or unique about your study?

Researchable
The methodology used to conduct your study must be feasible enough to provide a reasonable chance of answering the research question. The question cannot be answered with a "yes" or "no" finding and must not be so simplified that it can be answered with a 3-minute Google search. Unless you are a philosopher, avoid philosophical questions with no easily obtainable answers.

How Do I Develop a Research Question?
What might be useful to you in developing a research question is the use of a structural framework. Students in the health professions and social sciences often learn the mnemonic PICO which stands for

Patient problem

Intervention

Comparison (or control)

Outcome.

A recent paper has argued that the PICO scheme need not be limited to settings of clinical practice and experimental manipulation but instead has much greater generalizability when the P (problem) is conceptualized as a research object or population being observed, when the I (intervention) is conceptualized as the application of a method or theory (e.g., pedagogical approaches), when C (comparison) is conceptualized as an alternative theory or previous method, and O (outcome) is considered the aim of the study or knowledge generation—an explanation for some problem. The author notes that despite the use of this mnemonic, "It does not, for instance, offer minimal criteria of what makes a study aim worthwhile, significant, interesting, or examinable" (Nishikawa-Pacher, 2022, p. 7). Obviously, the shaping, perfecting, and elegant phrasing of a research question are still left up to the fertile mind of the manuscript developer or researcher.

Gibbs (2007) has discussed a slightly different approach. He identified four parts to the well-built question:

1. **Client type and problem** (describing a group of clients of similar type)
2. **Possible course of action** (applying a new treatment, preventing a problem, surveying or interviewing clients, assessing or screening to assess risk)
3. **Alternative course of action** (comparing to current treatment or previous client perceptions or satisfaction)
4. **Desired result** (wanted or preferred outcome or accurate description of clients assessed; Gibbs, 2007, 148–149)

Here are two examples of well-built questions contained in his paper:

> If disoriented persons who reside in a nursing home (1) are given reality orientation therapy (2) or validation therapy (3), which will result in better orientation to time, place, and person (4)?

> If sexually active high school students at high risk for pregnancy (1) are exposed to the Baby Think It Over program (2) or to lecture material on the proper use of birth control (3), will the former have fewer pregnancies during an academic year (4)? (Gibbs, 2007, p. 149)

If neither of these two approaches to developing a research question works for you, there is still good news—that is, other frameworks are available. For instance, Cooke et al. (2012) have described the SPIDER tool for qualitative studies.

It is reasonably easy to convert a research question into a hypothesis and vice versa.

How Are Research Questions Presented in Journal Articles?

The last part of this chapter has taken excerpts from several recent articles to show how different authors have presented their research questions or hypotheses.

Kloda et al. (2020) used the PICO framework to explore four different research questions involving students in occupational therapy (OT) and physical therapy (PT).

1. Do students in OT and PT who are taught information literacy skills using the alternative clinical question framework conduct literature searches with similar search results as those taught the PICO framework?
2. Do students in OT and PT who are taught the alternative clinical question framework demonstrate similar search skills as those taught the PICO framework?
3. Do students in OT and PT who are taught the alternative clinical question framework show a difference in information literacy self-efficacy when compared to those taught the PICO framework?
4. What are the perceptions and experiences of students with regard to clinical question frameworks (pp. 186–187)?

Here are the research questions from an article that I shamelessly helped to write:

> The purpose of this study was to enhance our understanding of child welfare workforce turnover as a means of promoting improved strategies to increase retention and reduce turnover. As noted previously, extant research on child welfare workforce retention and turnover focuses on those who intend to leave and/or those who intend to stay. However, decisions around remaining employed may not always be dichotomous, but may rather occur on a continuum, including those who have decided to leave, those who are undecided, and those who have decided to stay. The current study adds to our understanding of retention and turnover within the child welfare field by answering the following research questions:
>
> 1. How satisfied are frontline child welfare workers with respect to key factors known to influence retention and turnover, including workload, salary, recognition, professional development, accomplishment, peer support, and supervision?
> 2. Does satisfaction with workload, salary, recognition, professional development, accomplishment, peer support, and supervision differ among child welfare workers who intend to stay, those who intend to leave, and those who are undecided?
> 3. What factors predict intent to leave and indecision about continued employment in child welfare (Griffiths et al., 2017, p. 112)?

Here's an excerpt showing hypotheses used in a different study about the language used in TED Talks authored by MacKrill et al. (2021, pp. 1030–1031). You'll see a brief explanation regarding the first three and then the second set of three hypotheses.

> The literature shows that language can be differentiated based on the bidimensional factor of analytic/authentic. TED talks are a highly narrative "storytelling" style of presentation, designed to convey emotion and spoken with authenticity (Ludewig, 2017; Romanelli et al., 2014). As such, we hypothesized that:
>
> **Hypothesis H1.** *TED speakers who have a more analytic linguistic style would have less popular talks.*
>
> **Hypothesis H2.** *TED speakers who have a more authentic linguistic style and use more positive words would have more popular talks.*

Hypothesis H3. *Greater use of the word "I" would be associated with greater talk popularity.*

Due to the increase in science communication by experts, our final hypotheses concerned the differences between talks by academics and non-academics ... Academia also has a strong hierarchical organization (Martin, 1998). As such we predicted that:

Hypothesis H4. TED talks by academics would have a greater use of analytic words as well as clout.

Hypothesis H5. TED talks by nonacademics would use more authentic words, characterized by a higher use of "I" and more positive emotion words than academics.

Hypothesis H6. Due to academic talks having a greater analytic linguistic style, they would be rated more negatively by viewers than nonacademic talks and on average would attract less views overall.

The journal where you want to submit your manuscript may allow you to state clear objectives instead of research questions or hypotheses. Here is one example that was positioned in the last paragraph of the paper's introduction:

> There is a significant gap in research focusing on the high-risk practice of identifying sex partners through social media among women in general, and women in socially isolated areas like rural Appalachia in particular. This paper has two primary objectives: (1) Profile substance use, sexual risk behaviors, and social media use in this sample of rural, Appalachian, justice-involved women; and (2) Explore risky drug use and sexual behaviors among women who self-report using social media to connect with sexual partners. (Staton et al., 2022, p. 2549)

In the next example, the authors received the Emerging Scholar Best Article Award for 2020 from the *Journal of Youth and Adolescence*. After listing their two objectives, they go further with elaboration on them. However, because of fair use standards, only the explanation of the first hypothesis has been reproduced here.

> The primary objectives of the current longitudinal study, therefore, are to: (1) identify subgroups of early adolescents based on their time spent using a variety of social media platforms; and (2) examine whether social media subgroup membership predicts psychosocial

functioning six months later in a diverse community sample of early adolescents (11- to 14-years). Based on uses and gratifications theories (Katz et al. 1973; Sundar and Limperos 2013) and initial studies in emerging adults (Hargittai and Hsieh 2010; Scott et al. 2017; Yang and Lee 2018), it was hypothesized that at least three social media use subgroups would be identified using latent profile analysis. It was expected that the subgroups would distinguished by: (1) infrequent social media use across most platforms (e.g., "dabblers", "samplers"); (2) frequent, daily use of solely Instagram and Snapchat in light of research demonstrating the popularity of these platforms among adolescents (e.g., "devotees", platform-differentiated users) (Pew Research Center 2018a); and (3) frequent, daily-to-hourly social media use across most platforms (e.g., "omnivores"). (Vannucci & McCauley Ohannessian, 2019, 1474–1475)

The next paragraph went on to explain the second study objective about psychosocial outcomes of membership in high social media use subgroups. They hypothesized that membership in the high social media use subgroup would predict widespread psychosocial adjustment problems relative to the other social media subgroups.

Should I Be Worried About Plagiarizing Someone's Research Question or Material?

These are the occasions when you should be most worried:

(1) You have copied and pasted *any* material authored by another person or group and presented it as your own without proper acknowledgment. This means that you did not provide a footnote or attribution to the original source—you did not inform the reader that the material was not original to you but from another study, website, article, or book. (2) You've used a fragment of a sentence or an idea that you think came from something you've read, but you can't find it. You use it anyway.

This is an occasion when you should not be worried:

You read about a study investigating whether health disparities in HIV may be perpetuated by differences in relative attention to HIV-prevention communications across racial groups. Earl et al. (2016) investigated that question by having research assistants unobtrusively observe individuals in an adult sexual health clinic to see whether they spent more time watching a video on flu prevention or one on HIV and sexually transmitted illness prevention while in the clinic's waiting room. Since you are teaching a large lecture class with a nice mixture of racial groups, you are considering exploring the same question with a different methodology—one where students would, for extra credit, watch two brief videos on the topics and use a rating sheet to assess how much they learned, how interesting the videos were, and the videos' overall value for public health. There is no problem with using different approaches or methods to explore interesting research questions. No one owns research questions, and they can't be copyrighted. Indeed, science advances as different studies continue to explore the same question with improved methods of measurement and new materials. All that said, yes, you probably would want to acknowledge those who framed the question originally.

Because human recall is imperfect, it can sometimes let us retrieve something from memory, a nice eloquent phrase we've read or heard perhaps, and allow us to believe that we put those words together on our own when the phrasing came from someone else. I used to tell undergraduate students that they couldn't get up some morning and see a beautiful sunrise and then talk about the rosy fingers of dawn—because "rosy-fingered Dawn" is a passage from Homer's *Odyssey*. They would be plagiarizing the Greek poet. I stopped doing that when I realized they didn't know who Homer was anyway.

Plagiarism is confusing to a large segment of the academic population. There is, for example, no rule that says only if you borrow a certain number of words that you are guilty of plagiarism. Yet, I once had a friend who got his PhD from a well-known university who said his major professor claimed borrowing more than eight words was plagiarism. Five, six, or seven words wasn't. Not so. I had another friend who at one time was considering doing some research on the women in postwar Germany who had to become prostitutes to earn money to live and support their children. In a conversation, my friend described the opposite of sex for hire as "domesticated sexuality." Those two words put together that way is so creative and distinctive that anyone using them should double-check their materials to see who among the authors read might have applied them in their writing so that they could be cited.

Wendy Belcher (2019) does a superb job of presenting the topic of plagiarism. Some of the points she makes follow (the comments are mine).

- Plagiarism is serious: "It's now an absolute that a plagiarized article will be caught" (p. 162). How serious is it? Here's a true story: Some years ago, a PhD student from my university (but not one of mine) was applying for a faculty position at a distant university, and in trying to finish his coursework and teaching assistant responsibilities, he copied his dissertation proposal from someone at another university. His committee chair was devastated but reported it to the Graduate School, and it was determined the student not only would not be unable to finish his PhD, but he could never apply any of his doctoral work to any new degree at the university. In other words, he had committed an academic felony. It is that serious. (Belcher also reported a similar occurrence of someone losing the opportunity "to ever obtain an academic job, all because of the kind of plagiarism many don't know they're doing" (p. 163).

- "Representing others' work as your own is morally wrong" (p. 163).
- "Many journals now run all submissions through plagiarism-detection software" (p. 162). Note that if you are creating a journal article from your dissertation, you are likely thinking that you could cut and paste passages from the longer document into the smaller one, saving you a great deal of time. Realize, however, that this is referred to as self-plagiarism and could be caught by the journal's software. While you may be able to use a few paragraphs from the dissertation, it would be better to paraphrase them. Or, if you feel the need to use whole paragraphs verbatim, clearly attribute them to your dissertation. And between you and me, I wouldn't do that a whole bunch of times. An editor could then remark, "We'll just read the dissertation!"
- "Some types of paraphrasing are plagiarism as well—slightly or even heavily varying sentences or paragraphs even when the source is cited. If your wording is too close to the author's, it may be problematic despite the citation" (p. 164). Most authors, particularly those who draw upon many sources, worry about plagiarism—especially those who frequently bring in the thoughts of others into their own writing. If you are not worried about it, you either have an eidetic memory, or you are mimicking the ostrich with its head in the sand.
- "The best way to ensure that you cite sources accurately, completely, and fairly is to maintain good research and writing habits" (p. 165).
- "Review others' work briefly rather than at length" (p. 166).
- "Paraphrase without looking at the source." "Check your co-authors' work." "Check that you correctly copied your quotations" (p. 167).

To these many fine points made by Belcher (2019), I would also suggest that you have a good understanding of how and when to correctly attribute text back to the original or secondary source. Many times in grading undergraduate and graduate students' papers, I have found a single citation at the end of a paragraph or even a whole page. The students thought they had done all that was required when they should have double indented, used quotation marks, or cited the work multiple times.

Many universities have information on their websites or writing centers about plagiarism. Faculty sometimes include helpful tips to avoid it in their syllabi.

There are free plagiarism detection sites available on the internet, and if you are a student, you may have access to one that is licensed to your university, like Turnitin. If you don't want to try one of the free ones, you can try highlighting a portion of any text where you worried that your paraphrase was too close to the original and do a Google search with that paragraph or section.

> **Your Turn 3.1**
>
> Do you have a problem, idea, or topic in mind that you can turn into a research question or hypothesis using the PICO or a well-built framework? If so, write it down.
>
> _____
>
> _____
>
> _____
>
> _____
>
> Does it have all of the characteristics described in this chapter?
>
> _____
>
> _____
>
> _____
>
> If not, how can you revise to improve it?
>
> _____
>
> _____
>
> _____
>
> _____

> **Your Turn 3.2**
>
> If you are reasonably happy with your research question, do you feel comfortable showing it to a classmate, faculty member, or friend to get some feedback?
>
> _____
>
> _____
>
> _____
>
> _____
>
> What does their feedback suggest you need to do?
>
> _____
>
> _____
>
> _____
>
> _____

References

Belcher, W. L. (2019). *Writing your journal article in twelve weeks: A guide to academic publishing success.* University of Chicago Press.

Cooke, A., Smith, D., & Booth, A. (2012). Beyond PICO: The SPIDER Tool for qualitative evidence synthesis. *Qualitative Health Research, 22*, 1435–1443. https://doi.org/10.1177/1049732312452938

Earl, E. A., Crause, C., Vaid, A., & Albarracin, D. (2016). Disparities in attention to HIV-prevention information. *AIDS Care, 28*(1), 79–86. https://doi.org/10.1080/09540121.2015.1066747

Gibbs, L. (2007). Applying research to making life-affecting judgments and decisions. *Research on Social Work Practice, 17*(1), 143–150.

Griffiths, A., Royse, D., Culver, K., Piescher, K., & Zhang, Y. (2017). Who stays, who goes, who knows? A state-wide survey of child welfare workers. *Children and Youth Services Review, 77*, 110–117. https://doi.org/10.1016/j.childyouth.2017.04.012

Kloda, L. A., Boruff, J. T., & Cavalcante, A. S. (2020). A comparison of patient, intervention, comparison, outcome (PICO) to a new, alternative clinical question framework for search skills, search results, and self-efficacy: A randomized controlled trial. *Journal of the Medical Library Association: JMLA, 108*(2), 185–194. https://doi.org/10.5195/jmla.2020.739

MacKrill, K., Silvester, C., Pennebaker, J. W., & Petrie, K. J. (2021). What makes an idea worth spreading? Language markers of popularity in TED Talks by academics and other speakers. *Journal of the Association of Information and Technology, 72,* 1028–1038. https://doi.org/10.1002/asi.24471

Mattick, K., Johnston, J., & de la Croix, a. (2018). How to … write a good research question. *The Clinical Teacher, 15,* 104–108. https://doi.org/10.1111/tct.12776

Nishikawa-Pacher, A. (2022). Research questions with PICO: A universal mnemonic. *Publications, 10,* 21. https://doi.org/10.3390/publications10030021

Royse, D. (2020). *Research methods in social work*. Cognella.

Staton, M., Dickson, M. F., Pike, E., Surratt, H., & Young, S. (2022). An exploratory examination of social media use and risky sexual practices: A profile of women in rural Appalachia who use drugs. *AIDS and Behavior, 26,* 2548–2558.

Vannucci, A., & McCauley Ohannessian, C. (2019). Social media use subgroups differentially predict psychosocial well-being during early adolescence. *Journal of Youth and Adolescence, 48*(8), 1469–1493. https://doi.org/10.1007/s10964-019-01060-9

Wisse, M., & Roeland, J. (2021). Building blocks for developing a research question: The ABC-model. *Teaching Theology & Religion, 25,* 22–34. https://doi.org/10.1111/teth.12603

CHAPTER 4

Should I Have a Writing Partner?

This question arises early for those who have worked favorably and productively with a classmate, lab partner, or colleague on a project—and also may affect the thinking of those whose experience may have been negative and unproductive with a partner or group member who disappointed and "hitchhiked" on the efforts of others. In the first instance, the inclination might be to consider working with a writing partner or even to consider having several coauthors. However, individuals still remembering one or more unfavorable experiences with those not carrying their fair share of a team or group project may have the inclination to go solo, to develop a manuscript on one's own, but would it be better to invite others to join you? What are the advantages and disadvantages of working with one or more writing partners? Let's first examine your obligation to others involved in the creative process and then the pros and cons of jointly writing with others.

When Must I Offer Coauthorship to Another Person?

The American Psychological Association's Publication Manual (APA, 2020), referring to the APA's Ethics Code Standard 8.12a, states, "Authorship is reserved for persons who make a substantial contribution to and who accept responsibility for a published work" (p. 24). Substantial contribution is not defined in the standard, but let's consider what it might suggest.

All writing projects begin with a germ of an idea; without a central premise, argument, or question, there would be no manuscript. Therefore, if the idea for the project originated with someone else, they should be given credit or acknowledged, possibly recognized as a coauthor. This could also be true if you took the idea and revised, tweaked, or reconstructed a research question or topic that is still based on the original. Even if you don't want to involve the individual in writing the manuscript, it is better to figure out some way to give them recognition than to be charged with stealing the idea later on. Let's look at a couple of situations.

In Scenario #1, imagine you are sitting in a classroom, and during a lecture, the professor asks rhetorical questions to provoke class discussion. If you are taking notes, write down some of the questions, and later decide to develop a paper around one of the questions, you might argue the professor's rhetorical question wasn't a substantial contribution since it was merely designed to provoke deliberation, conversation, or even debate. If, on the other hand, you are meeting with a faculty member and an idea emerges during a one-on-one mentorship, conference, or consultation, and the two of you talk about it for a while—that seems like a substantial contribution—whether or not various methodologies are discussed for advancing the idea. I would hope that a faculty member tossing out rhetorical questions in a classroom would not expect to be a coauthor of a paper unless invited to participate in a more active and meaningful way during the paper's construction.

In Scenario #2, you are a faculty member and for the required term paper, Emilia, one of the better students, develops a paper with a new perspective that arose from readings assigned to all the students. Although her paper didn't review all of the key literature, and her paper wasn't polished as you would have liked, you see promise in the fresh slant and think the paper could be expanded, edited better, and then would be suitable for publication. Should you make Emilia a coauthor? I say so. Your status as a faculty member is not diminished in any way by elevating the work of a student.

In group projects and with lab partners where the writing project is solely concerned with meeting course requirements, a paper that is later developed from that exercise and improved upon probably may need to involve as coauthors any persons who were co-participants or cocreators. However, not every student in a group project, in my experience, might deserve an invitation to be a coauthor. Sometimes students in groups don't make substantial contributions to the group project. They may also not want to do the work that would prepare it for publication—pragmatically deciding the project would take too much of their time. If one of the group members volunteers to proofread the final draft or to put the references in correct format, these would not be substantial contributions in my opinion. However, editing a manuscript that is a complete mess and requires "heavy editing" could be a substantial contribution.

How Do Journals Judge Authorship?

Fortunately, you do not have to guess as to what constitutes a substantial contribution. The National Information Standards Organization announced in February of 2022 that the Contributor Roles Taxonomy (CRediT) has become a standard for academics and publishers representing "thousands of journals." The following are the 14 roles that authors typically play in scientific scholarly work (also available at http://credit.niso.org/). As you will see, coauthors can make many different contributions. Should one of your students, colleagues, lab partners, or other involved persons perform one of these roles, they have earned the right to be a coauthor.

14 Roles Authors Typically Have in Scientific Scholarly Work

Conceptualization	Ideas; formulation or evolution of overarching research goals and aims
Data curation	Management activities to annotate (produce metadata), scrub data and maintain research data (including software code, where it is necessary for interpreting the data itself) for initial use and later reuse
Formal analysis	Application of statistical, mathematical, computational, or other formal techniques to analyze or synthesize study data
Funding acquisition	Acquisition of the financial support for the project leading to this publication
Investigation	Conducting a research and investigation process, specifically performing the experiments, or data/evidence collection
Methodology	Development or design of methodology; creation of models
Project administration	Management and coordination responsibility for the research activity planning and execution
Resources	Provision of study materials, reagents, materials, patients, laboratory samples, animals, instrumentation, computing resources, or other analysis tools
Software	Programming, software development; designing computer programs; implementation of the computer code and supporting algorithms; testing of existing code components
Supervision	Oversight and leadership responsibility for the research activity planning and execution, including mentorship external to the core team
Validation	Verification, whether as a part of the activity or separate, of the overall replication/reproducibility of results/experiments and other research outputs
Visualization	Preparation, creation, and presentation of the published work, specifically visualization/data presentation

Writing—original draft	Preparation, creation, and presentation of the published work, specifically writing the initial draft (including substantive translation)
Writing—review and editing	Preparation, creation, and presentation of the published work by those from the original research group, specifically critical review, commentary, or revision—including pre- or postpublication stages

It might be surprising to learn some roles aren't specifically identified—such as surveying the literature and preparing the literature review, listing the references used and or putting them in the proper format for the journal, double-checking the data shown in graphs or tables, and proofreading. The role of writing the important *Discussion* section isn't mentioned either. It makes sense, however, that writing key sections such as the *Introduction, Literature Review,* or *Discussion* sections of a manuscript constitutes a substantial contribution and should be credited with authorship.

The International Committee of Medical Journal Editors (ICMJE) lists four conditions needed for authorship, and all four must be met:

1. Substantial contributions to conception and design, acquisition of data, or analysis and interpretation of data;
2. Drafting the article or revising it critically for important intellectual content;
3. Final approval of the version to be published; and
4. Agreement to be accountable for all aspects of the work in ensuring that questions related to the accuracy or integrity of any part of the work are appropriately investigated and resolved.

Additionally, the ICMJE also has stated, "Contributors who meet fewer than all four of the criteria for authorship ... should be acknowledged." Examples could include the acquisition of funding, supervision of a research group, writing assistance, and technical editing (https://www.icmje.org/recommendations/browse/).

Should I Share Authorship With a Student?

Occasionally, it is possible to hear on a college campus a story about a faculty member taking a student's idea and then publishing a paper without giving any credit to the student. Clearly, that is wrong. Even if you have to completely overhaul a student's paper, expand its breadth or research, give the student who produced the idea on their own and authored the original paper credit—even if you have to throw out almost everything they wrote.

Over my career, I have been happy to give students ideas for writing and research projects and don't really expect many of the projects to come to fruition. However, sometimes they have followed through with my suggestions, and we both have been coauthors. Approximately 25 or more students have successfully published with me as a coauthor. Some of these became faculty members; other students were content just to have one publication. I can't speak to how many of these enjoyed the process of learning how to write professionally, but all were pleased to see their names in print.

In the journal articles I have written with students, they can appear as first or second author. First-author determination is usually based on the metric of who does the most work. Drafts of sections written by students go through multiple revisions until we have addressed all problems and polished until it feels silky smooth. That might take five or six drafts. Students sometimes drop out and lose interest after the second draft, but if they hang in there and originated the idea, I give them first-author status. This is especially true when the individual has completed a dissertation and put together a well-written draft for a journal. Even though I may have supplied the research question, suggested the methodology, or helped with data analysis, I know that taking a dissertation of 150 or 200 pages or more and editing it down to about 20 pages for a journal submission is a lot of work. The student becomes the first author.

What Are the Advantages of Having a Writing Partner?

Let's start with the ideal. A well-chosen writing partner is one who is as enthusiastic as you about getting published, who has good written communication skills, who is open to feedback, and able to complete tasks at a reasonable pace is a joy, a blessing, a gift, an extender of your time and effort. Such a writing partner may be the "winning ticket" you need for helping to produce articles needed for tenure.

Even after I got tenure, I continued writing with a congenial colleague. We published about a dozen journal articles together. What made him so special was that we were well matched in interests, personalities, and skills. Sometimes he took the lead on a manuscript, and sometimes I did. When I took an idea to him, we would negotiate which parts we each wanted to write. On one occasion, I told him the idea would be viable both as a conference presentation and as a journal article. I wanted to go to the conference in a city I had never been to before, so I was the first author on the conference abstract, and he was first author on the publication. We had our names on both. We never argued or had any serious disagreements. (My main peeve was that he didn't paragraph often enough. He thought there was an intrinsic beauty in a 250-word paragraph. I broke each of his overly long paragraphs into smaller ones by the final draft each time, although he never acquired my love of shorter paragraphs.)

Over the years, I've had many successful writing partners. I purposely involved others when a particular project would benefit from another individual's special expertise. The supposed African proverb "If you want to go fast, go alone. If you want to go far, go together" seems to apply. I certainly got more accomplished with writing partners than I would have on my own. However, I didn't grab just anyone to be my writing partner but considered their talents and personalities before they became a "well-chosen writing partner." I'll discuss the important qualities of this type of partner after the next section.

As you discuss the proposed writing project with someone who will likely become a coauthor, try to resolve any potential major problems (like order of authorship) before the writing begins. While agreements may never need to be revisited, it may also be helpful to record important aspects of the partnership, project design, specific responsibilities, and so forth in your notes that you can email to your coauthor. This allows all parties to be "on the same page" so to speak and to have a record of what they have agreed to. In the resources at the end of the chapter, there are three sources of additional information for authorship disputes.

What Are the Disadvantages of Having a Writing Partner?

When you are one of the newest members on a faculty or in a graduate program, you may not know the personalities of those you might consider for a writing partner. Why would personality have an influence? I am so task-oriented that sometimes I can't sleep well at night thinking about the projects I want to finish. I don't match up well with someone more laid back—someone who feels they have all the time in the world to finish something. It may not be just personality either. A young parent with an infant at home, teaching a full load of classes and trying to conduct research and write about it might slip important deadlines. Sometimes care-taking responsibilities of adult family members, demanding jobs, illness, and other complications (relationship break-ups) have a way of slowing down potential coauthors. All of this is a way of suggesting that depending on others for key parts of a manuscript can, at times, put the whole project on hold. That's a major disadvantage if you are in a hurry to improve your CV or tenure portfolio or when you have a job interview coming up soon and want to say that the research paper has been submitted.

Not knowing well those you invite to be a writing partner can also lead to disappointment when they cut corners or don't pull their own weight. You can be disappointed when your expectation is that they would have done more with their section—perhaps cutting out repetitious segments, enhancing sections needing more or better analysis, infusing with more literature or relevant comparisons, or expanding the implications. I recall trying to help out a young assistant professor and offering a coauthorship. His contribution wasn't initially thoughtful at all and seemed like something hastily thrown together. I didn't bounce him off the article, but gave it back to him and asked for some greater effort—which he agreed to do.

It is common when working with students who have not had any mentoring or experience with writing professionally to have to ask them to revise, add to, clarify, or in some way continue working on their piece of the manuscript. In many, if not most, classrooms across the country, students submit papers without any real instruction in how to write professionally. Term papers are, for the most part, tepid and mediocre, and they don't receive much more than a few passing comments from the faculty member. There are, of course, faculty members who take the time to show the student how their arguments could be made sharper and their conclusions more salient, but there are other faculty who merely assign numerical or letter grades with no internal comments. It is easy to understand why many undergraduate and even graduate students don't write well. I fully expect that it will require more of my time when I coauthor with a student. However, I don't begrudge that investment, as it is a wonderful gift back to me when these students become talented writers and researchers.

The most egregious problem I ever had with a writing partner wasn't because the individual was lazy or overcommitted, or anything like that. This person was brilliant, a prolific author, but somewhat narcissistic. The brief version of the story is that this individual wanted to upset the order in which the authors were listed, assessing her relatively small part of the project as being more important than the second-place coauthor who had contributed quite a bit more than she. It is one thing to make a request, but this was a major brawl. The upshot was that she left the project. One might consider this episode just an instance of my own personal bad luck, but I had a friend pulling together an edited book, and one of the coauthors (there were three) not only wanted to move from third place to second place as coauthor, but she also wanted to replace the originator and facilitator of the project and move into first place! This was even after the first author had to ask her three or four times to provide the chapters that she had agreed to write.

A less serious problem on another project was that the coauthor didn't write the agreed-upon section the way I wanted and was unreceptive to my suggestions about how I thought it should be altered or amended. This issue didn't affect the viability of the project, and to keep the peace, I decided not to get angry over it. I have had other coauthors who had to "write their way" or edit a team-produced document so that it read "their way." Each of us may bring certain styles or mental templates into writing projects. Let me just say, however, when one partner is incapable of compromising and keeping agreed-upon deadlines, it takes a lot of fun out of ever wanting to have another writing partner again.

You and your writing partner should be positive and supportive of each other. If it is a minor strain for one or both of you, just try to finish the project and then look for a different partner. I'm a big believer in going to lunch with people and giving them a draft of something to read and then waiting a couple of days before I ask, "What did you think of that?" If it takes someone more than a week to get back to you, don't choose them for a writing partner. If they hand you back your manuscript within 48 to 72 hours all edited, you might want to invite them in.

How Do You Choose a Good Writing Partner?

Here's Dave's time-tested Six Rules for Choosing Writing Partners:

Rule 1. Choose a known entity, someone with a solid *record of publications*—the more publications they have, the better. Look at their CV or use a search engine to confirm that they have recent publications—that they haven't, for some explained reason, quit writing or conducting research (as happens with some tenured faculty).

Rule 2. Choose an individual who has *knowledge* or *skills* that you don't have (e.g., statistical analysis, or expertise that you haven't acquired yet). However, this person could also be someone with similar skills or talents as you who enjoys literature searches, or editing manuscripts. They don't have to tower over you in ability, just be able to contribute in a meaningful way that you both recognize.

Rule 3. Choose someone who is dependable, who keeps promises made, who is time conscious, *respectful of deadlines*, someone who is not already juggling too many projects and has time to assist as a writing partner. It is a joy to have a partner who is quick to respond to drafts.

Rule 4. Choose someone whose *personality allows negotiation*, who has a sense of humor, and who is self-deprecating. If at all possible, find someone who is optimistic and who can say kind and supportive things if you hit a low spot. They should be able to take criticism in stride in order to improve the manuscript. Avoid anyone who takes feedback intended to improve the project as personal criticism. If after a session with constructive feedback, they pout or don't answer emails, text messages, or phone calls, consider dissolving the partnership or at least never working with that person again.

Rule 5. Choose someone who is as *enthusiastic* as you are about the project—or at least almost as enthusiastic.

> *Writing for me is a pretty scary thing, so it was a huge comfort to have someone in the room working with me. It became less like work and more like play.*
>
> Kate DiCamillo, children's fiction author of over 25 novels

Rule 6. They must be detail oriented. Beware of the writing partner who doesn't bother to run spell-check and is sloppy with commas and capitalization. What you see in any example of their writing may well be what you get from that person on your writing project. Sometimes the most loveable of potential writing partners have great ideas but are sloppy in the execution of the product. Can you live with that?

Should I Have a Writing Mentor?

Here's the short answer: if you don't know where to start, if you don't know whether your idea or research interest is potentially publishable, if you need a sounding board for your ideas, if you are very insecure about your ability to write for a professional or academic audience, if you don't know the first thing about submitting a manuscript to a professional journal, then Yes! A "yes" to any of the questions posed in the first sentence suggests that securing a writing mentor could be of great assistance. Writing mentors can be invaluable to the novice author in these ways:

> Writing mentors provide direction with topic selection, intent of the manuscript, and clarification of the message. They offer guidance on narrowing the content, navigating the publication requirements, formatting, and editing advice. Most importantly, mentors can offer the support and encouragement to make the writing process a rewarding and satisfying experience. (Demeyer & Demeyer, 2018, p. 340)

These authors go on to bullet list the specific benefits that mentors provide:

- Accountability (especially when they are content experts)
- Feedback and teaching how to grasp and assimilate it as constructive criticism
- Faster problem solving

> - Focus on goals
> - Instruction on how to write clearly and editorial advice
> - Increases in self-confidence (especially when the project becomes published!)
> - Avenues for building a professional network
>
> (Demeyer & Demeyer, 2018, p. 340)

Sometimes senior faculty will be assigned to junior faculty for mentoring. If that is not the culture in your department, then consider looking for a senior faculty member who is willing to be a mentor. You should realize they may agree to mentor you because they want to become a coauthor on your manuscript. If you want a mentor, the chair of your department may be able to recommend a faculty member to you or able to assign you a mentor. You might also consider asking one or two colleagues you trust to suggest someone who might be able to be a mentor for you.

You want to secure a mentor who is willing to read your work and give you an honest assessment of your manuscript—complete with detailed identification of its strengths and weaknesses. If there are several faculty to choose from, check out their publication records and choose the one who is most published. (There will always be faculty who can give you their impressions of your manuscript, but if you are trying to get published in a professional journal, the mentor needs to be someone with "firsthand" experience and who will be particularly valuable if they have recent knowledge of that journal's style and approach.)

A word of caution: Choosing a writing mentor when you are a junior faculty member, or doctoral or graduate student, can have political implications. That is, you may feel that the best person to help you develop your writing is another junior faculty member and not the senior one assigned to you as a mentor. Advisors take pride in the number of graduate students they have in their lab or for whom they have chaired theses or dissertations. Even if senior faculty don't have as many recent publications as more junior faculty, senior faculty may feel treated disrespectfully if you pair up with someone perceived to be inferior to the contribution they would make.

You shouldn't feel obligated to work with someone who can't advance your writing or if on a personal level you just feel as if you would rather work with someone else. If your "assigned" mentor is perceived to be one of those, then have a discussion with the department chair or other faculty member. Think before acting spontaneously. As a junior faculty member, for instance, might you need the support of the senior person when you go up for promotion?

As a graduate or doctoral student, could your decision affect your fellowship or stipend? Your qualifying exam?

As an assistant professor, I had no assigned mentor, but I worked with several senior faculty on different projects. One of my favorite colleagues joined me on a couple of papers that were successful. He wasn't exceptionally well published, but he always found time to read a draft manuscript if I asked. I'm not sure how many he read, as I reserved him for those that I felt had some problem. Almost without exception, this individual found something positive to say that generally ended up with "I think you should submit it." He was an invaluable support to my writing, never picky-picky, or overly critical. If you can, find yourself a positive, supportive mentor like that. Other faculty were helpful, but more businesslike in tone. Not much on the personal level.

After the submission of your drafts, mentors can "help to dissect the criticisms received and underscore lessons for their mentees. ... Mentors can place these experiences in perspective and encourage mentees to stay the course" (Northridge et al., 2015, p. S15).

As a final note, you may not need a writing partner if you have a supportive mentor. Mentors can also become writing partners; they may or may not want that much involvement in your project. If they end up having real roles as we've discussed earlier and not just reviewing and making comments, you probably should invite them to join you as a coauthor.

Checklist of Positive Characteristics Needed in Writing Partners and Mentors

- ☐ They have professional journal publications (a track record).
- ☐ They have skills and talents; ability to contribute to the paper.
- ☐ They are respectful of deadlines, are dependable, and have the time to assist.
- ☐ They have a pleasant personality and sense of humor, and are able to compromise.
- ☐ They are enthusiastic about the project.
- ☐ They pay attention to details.
- ☐ They are supportive.
- ☐ They are trustworthy.

How Do I Give Feedback to a Writing Partner?

The answer to the question is one word: *cautiously*. No one I know of (and you can weigh in too) likes to be criticized, told that what they have written stinks like a harbor seal after a fish-feeding frenzy. Sometimes writing partners just don't invest the amount of time in revising or perfecting their portions of a manuscript, but they are capable of producing a better quality of writing. How can you communicate that their section is unsatisfactory?

First of all, don't use any terms that communicate failure like "unsatisfactory" used in the previous sentence. Similar terms to avoid are deficient, disappointing, unacceptable, atrocious, awful, crummy, dreadful—you get the point. This is your writing partner, someone who has goodwill and cooperation you need. After all, even if you will be first author, you are not *the chancellor of writing.*

Even if you are distressed about your writing partner's effort (or lack thereof), start by saying something positive your partner will hear as a compliment. It may involve noting a clever opening sentence, a nice turn of a phrase, or two or three directly applicable references that have been added. Then move to the area of your concern by saying, "I had a question about this sentence (or this paragraph). I'm wondering if there was something else you were intending (or perhaps something you left out) when you wrote this?" Simply pose a question that has no barbs (similar to "Have you seen my cell phone around?"). This question should allow your writing partner to begin explaining or perhaps rereading the paragraph to realize that it wasn't all that well developed. If your partner doesn't see anything wrong with the passage, then you can pose another question where you say, "I'm wondering if a reader might grasp this easier if we insert a short paragraph immediately before it that brings in ..."

Other approaches you can try: "I like the paragraphs in this section, but think they build interest better if we move the third paragraph to first place. What do you think?" If your partner immediately responds, "I think they are fine just the way they are," then you have to decide how important the suggested revision is. You have three choices: (a) you could argue your point a bit more (which works sometimes), (b) you could make the revisions yourself in the next revision, or (c) you could simply let the matter drop.

Depending on how long you've known your writing partner and the quality of your relationship, issues might be addressed in a more straightforward manner: "You have strong references here, but it feels like we're a little light on the more current studies. Could you take a look at that?"

In short, you don't want to get red in the face, curse, threaten, or be a bully. Approach your partner as a team player and ask if there is something you could do to help. Maybe it was a simple miscommunication or the partner had something to come up which was urgent (like a sick family member) that took priority over writing a section of the manuscript. Always give the partner benefit of the doubt, if at all possible.

Feedback is, of course, a two-way street. You have feelings, and your writing partner might not have the most diplomatic way of expressing their opinion that your writing needs something else. I remember how angry I felt when a writing partner handed me back a manuscript that we were both working on and said, "So what?" I immediately became defensive, and fired back "What do you mean so what?" He then explained that the *Discussion* section didn't make a point, didn't lead the reader to see the implications of the findings—which he thought should be expanded beyond what I had drafted. I didn't completely agree with my partner, but because we were partners and respected each other's work, I went back and revised that *Discussion* section to draw out the implications more clearly. In retrospect, I'm sure he was correct—but hearing that from him and possibly believing I was the better writer, made his criticism difficult to hear. However, that's what writing partners have a responsibility to do—to point out where a manuscript can be improved.

I don't recommend using "So what?" with a writing partner. Even if you say nicely, "I believe the conclusion could be made stronger here," or suggest "This section could have a real punch if you. ... ," you should expect your partner may be unprepared for the comment, go on the defensive, and may argue with you. Don't cut off discussion because you are convinced that you are right. Instead, listen fully and closely to truly hear your partner's objections to revising a section. If you have a number of major and minor points, you might want to prioritize them with the idea if things get too heated, you might be able to let go of some of the minor suggestions you might otherwise make.

A friend and I once swapped some short stories we had written, each eager for some constructive feedback. I remember pointing out several things in his story that I found didn't make any significant contribution. In a smoky tavern scene, he had country music by George Jones being played over a jukebox. I assumed he had made up the name and wrote, "Use a country singer readers might know." He wrote back, "George Jones received the Country Music Hall of Fame in 1992 and in 2008 received the Kennedy Center Honors for lifetime achievement." I learned not to make comments in areas where I had no expertise. It is better to be positive than to be fussy. Nobody likes picky, sticky, or icky.

How Do I Receive Feedback From a Writing Partner?

When a friend, a mentor, or a writing partner has some suggestions about a piece you have drafted, the first thing you need to do is to *listen* and *hear* what is being said.

> - *Don't* jump to the conclusion that it is a catastrophe and the whole piece might have to be thrown away.
> - *Don't* hear in the recommendations that you are an idiot and should have known better and realized that the sentences were not organized in the best way.
> - *Don't* say to yourself, "I have no time to make these changes. I've just wasted 3 months of my life."

When your adversary (otherwise known as your friend, mentor, or writing partner) has relaxed back into their chair and the room is quiet again (but your thoughts are racing), take deep breaths before speaking. Smile. Then pleasantly begin to ask for clarification on each point that was brought to your attention. Make sure you understand whether these are minor issues that can be quickly fixed (potato spelled with an "e") or whether a substantial revision is being requested. You may find it helpful to take notes or to write comments on the margins of the manuscript. Doing so will give you time to think as you write, and you may want to refer to your notes if you both agree to think on the issue overnight and then continue your discussion. If you don't understand something, ask again. It is better to ask a second time than to spend time revising only to find out later that you misunderstood.

Be completely honest. If the revisions being asked of you come at a bad time due to scheduled travel out of town, other work obligations, children out of school, and so forth, don't be shy about stating your needs in terms of the amount of time you require to complete the new draft. If there is something your writing partner could help with, then ask. Maybe the two of you can rebalance the workload. End your meeting with a smile, possibly a handshake, and a "Thanks!"

What Alternative Ways Are There to Improve My Writing for Publication?

If you don't want a writing partner (or at least are not ready for one yet) and don't have or don't want to work with a mentor, a tutor, or hire a consultant, there are still ways to improve your writing skills. Besides trying to find a university-level course that might be of interest, you might want to consider methods such as workshops, boot camps, and writing support groups. These will be described next.

Workshops

These normally involve active instruction with a knowledgeable author. They may have, however, different formats from meeting several days with an instructor, followed by participants actively writing, and then meeting as a group once a week or every other week for a period of time. Participants may share parts or all of their writing. Workshops may not always be available or easy to find. You might be able to locate one by searching at your university, or other local colleges known to have writing programs. Most universities have writing centers and you may want to start there. Those folks may know of upcoming workshops or those being sponsored by others in the community.

Orman et al. (2018) have described a 6-month workshop series for clinical nurses in a Colorado hospital that taught them about the writing process, mentored the nurses through various phases of their writing, and prepared them to submit a manuscript for publication. Meeting once a month, two to three participants would work together after the first 2-hour overview, submitting a draft for each of these sections of a manuscript: the introduction, methods, results, discussion, and implications for practice. The workshop leaders and other participants offered constructive feedback with suggestions for improvement.

Orman and colleagues (2018) have reported that in three 6-month workshops where 21 mostly two-person teams were formed, nine teams published articles, and two teams submitted manuscripts that were rejected. In an evaluation "query" of 15 workshop respondents, lack of time was the most frequently reported barrier to the writing process, and interestingly, 53% reported in the future they would seek individual mentorship.

Workshops have the strength of providing personalized critiques from instructors with significant publication experience in a format less demanding than a typical university course. However, the format of the workshop might mean that you receive feedback from the other participants instead of the instructor. Also, workshops in which participants work in teams might mean your specialized interest or research problem might not be the one chosen by the group. In that instance, there still could be valuable learning occurring, but the feedback or consultation may not directly advance your own manuscript.

Noone and Young (2019) have described a multiday retreat held in a large communal room on a university campus where lunch and snacks were provided. Persons interested in the retreat were asked to send a draft of a document, outline, or concept paragraph ahead of time. Most of the retreat involved giving participants dedicated time to write; however, discussions at lunch involved issues about writing of interest to the group and learning about participants' progress. There was an expectation that time spent at the retreat would be used to complete an article, grant proposal, abstract, presentation, outline for an article, and/or to review material for their manuscript.

Writing Boot Camps

These are somewhat similar concepts that also involve meeting over a period of time of several days or weeks with a guide. In an article by von Isenburg et al. (2017), the guide was a librarian who supplied support for literature searches, gathered tips on writing for publication, and made resources available from the medical library website when needed by participants. Specific writing tasks (10 of them) were done over a 12-week period. Participants were again formed into groups and read each other's completed manuscripts. Sixty percent of participants submitted a manuscript by the program's end.

In a later refinement, participants were not assigned to a group but could choose to work with a partner or in a small group. Weekly "Shut Up and Write Sessions" were provided in quiet spaces around the medical center to give participants a 2-hour block of time. No emails, phone calls, or pagers were allowed. However, most participants found their schedules not flexible enough to allow them to attend these sessions. Upon manuscript completion, participants could request editorial services free of charge. In the revised program, 35.5% of participants submitted a manuscript.

Other Options

In a brief Australian communication, Johnston et al. (2014) have reported a "writing buddy" approach where pairs of participants made pledges to each other to write regularly 30 to 60 minutes daily. Writing buddies would call or text before or after each scheduled writing session to help establish routines, provide motivation, and accountability. All the writing buddies would meet together every 2 weeks for support, networking, and public setting of their writing goals.

A research/writing group (RWG) for nontenure track faculty in a School of Pharmacy has been described in an article by Fleming et al. (2017). The RWG set monthly, 1-hour lunchtime meetings to discuss members' current scholarly activities. Participants would share their progress since the last meeting. Group meetings were intended to motivate, offer accountability, and provide deadlines to keep projects on track. They didn't involve instruction in teaching faculty how to compose manuscripts or conduct research. Group members served as a sounding board for ideas on improvement, resources, and possible platforms for presentation/publication. Members also provided encouragement, mentorship, regularly reviewed manuscripts for one another, assisted in choosing target journals for publication, discussed feasibility of projects, and helped each other brainstorm and develop future research/writing projects.

Writing Support Groups

At universities, sometimes new faculty, as well as doctoral students, may recruit several friends or colleagues to meet together as a small informal social group to troubleshoot issues they may be having in writing, finding the right approach to investigate a research topic they want to explore, and so on. These

Successful publication is an endurance event.

Northridge et al. (2015), *American Journal of Public Health* support groups can meet sporadically, but meetings might be called by a member who wants to circulate a manuscript or to read a piece of it to others for feedback.

In some writing groups, a more regular meeting schedule is chosen to "encourage" the completion of projects. The scheduled meeting dates are functional deadlines for finishing segments of a paper and encourage group members' writing so that they can report progress on their projects. Generally, there is no guide or instruction associated with support groups. However, members may share information about resources, upcoming conferences, journals wanting manuscripts for a special issue, and so forth.

What Can I Do If the Writing Support in My Workplace or Community Are Lacking?

Here are four ideas:

Idea #1. If you are a doctoral or graduate student or recently affiliated with a university, you are in the best possible position to find a tutor, a consultant, or a faculty member to mentor you. If you are a graduate or new faculty member from a small academic unit, don't limit yourself to considering only the faculty in your department. Think more broadly. Ask a reference librarian if there is a website listing university faculty's expertise, publications, or recently funded research. Are there any on that website who have written extensively in your area of interest—even if they are in a different department? Check out who is publishing in the professional journals that you follow, the ones where you might be likely to submit a manuscript. Look at the literature searches you have conducted recently to see if any articles involved faculty from your university. If you find a name of someone who publishes frequently, even if you don't know them, send an email and ask for a brief meeting. Prolific researchers often have data sets that they haven't had the time to analyze and write about. You could make their day! Even if you don't want to work with their data, it may be that your topic could be interesting enough and/or be a complementary area of interest to them. Don't be shy. The worst-case scenario is that they may say no to your request for mentorship. However, they might be able to refer you to a colleague who could possibly help.

Idea #2. Writing partners are usually drawn from your own circle of friends and acquaintances. But again, you don't need to limit yourself to only people you know. Go to professors or the chair of the department and ask them for any names of students they have been impressed with—who are thought to have the potential for publication. Then, contact these individuals to see if they want to collaborate with you. The same advice applies even if you want a "writing buddy" as described earlier whose role is primarily to help you set a routine for writing regularly.

Idea #3. You can organize a writing workshop or boot camp or one of the other approaches we've talked about. Perhaps the chair of your department or the dean would be willing to host such an event—providing funding to provide lunch for participants or honoraria if you want to bring in a particular well-known individual who might be the instructor or reviewer supplying feedback on draft manuscripts. If you desire a resource that is not currently available to you, what can you do to bring it about?

Ideal #4. It is easy to find online supports; they are as numerous as the cell phones in a college classroom—more than you care to count. Be advised that you need to pay for most of the services advertised; however, vanity presses may make promises to review your work for free. Of course, you should realize their main interest is in getting thousands of dollars from you to publish a few dozen copies of your book.

There are, also, legitimate sites that may be of assistance. For instance, the Association of Writers and Writing Programs (https://www.awpwriter.org/store/overview) has a directory of writing programs across the country and one of community writing programs and conferences (free to access). For some of their services, you have to become a member to access them. (Volunteer mentors were available for those interested in writing poetry.) Other websites provide writing coaches from $45 to $65 an hour (as of March 2023). The Educational Testing Services provides an app (https://mentormywriting.org/) that gives writing prompts and computerized feedback on practice writing paragraphs. It will also provide feedback (under the Extended Writing tab) on up to 5,000 words. Writing coaches on internet sites are often authors of fiction, so you may want to look closely at their credentials if you are wanting help with academic writing. If you are looking for writers' groups in your community and another source of conferences, you might want to subscribe to *Poets & Writers* (https://www.pw.org/groups) or *Writers Digest* (https://www.writersdigest.com/), which also has informative "how to" articles and houses 350 tutorials available for a monthly fee.

Lastly, practically any book on writing will advise you to read, read, and read. The more you read, the more you will learn about the styles and techniques that other writers use. Take notes for yourself. Study the examples that you might want to emulate. While this approach may not be as intense as taking a workshop, or university course, or working with a mentor, it should not be overlooked as a "self-improvement" strategy.

> **Your Turn 4.1**
>
> What do you need to assist you with your goal of writing professionally?
> - Someone to periodically ask about your progress, to set due dates?
> - Social or emotional support?
> - Writing instruction or professional guidance?
> - Would you prefer to "learn the ropes" by being on a team or group project?
> - Someone to critique your writing?
>
> _____
>
> _____
>
> _____
>
> How will you acquire what you need?
>
> _____
>
> _____
>
> _____

How Do I Figure Out What Kind of Writing Support Might Benefit Me?

Haas (2014) has created a wonderful scheme for considering the various ways writers' groups can vary—particularly if you need to create the kind of support that would be ideal for you personally. Here's a summary of his typology:

Purpose of Group: What is the overall intent of the writing group? The choices he suggests are these: Emotional Support, Academic Socialization, Increased Understanding of Writing, Increased Writing Skill, and Productivity

Desired Membership: Group Size, Characteristics of Members, Discipline, Expertise

Leadership Preference: Formal Leader, Peer Leader, No Leader

Duration of Group: Defined Length of Time, Ongoing

Meeting Characteristics: Set Time of Day, Length of Meeting, Frequency of Meetings, Format, Location

Meeting Activities: Goal Setting, Reading, Writing, Feedback, Discussion, Other Research Activity, Social, Ground Rules (e.g., confidentiality, mutual respect)

Between Meeting Activities: Working on Goals, Preparing Peer Feedback, Self-Directed Writing, Submitting Work for Publication, Keeping Reflective Journal

As you can see, there are multiple facets of the group meeting pattern, activities, and structure to consider. The unavailability of the specific type of group you want may necessitate creating or advocating for the kind that will meet your needs.

An immediate issue will be recruiting the membership and how best to go about that. Personally, I would caution against "casting your net" for membership everywhere. Start small, and then if you need individuals who can give more thoughtful feedback or have other good qualities, then add one or two at a time. I was in a support group several years ago composed of four very compatible individuals. On the recommendation of one of the participants, we added a fifth person who didn't have quite the same qualities as the others. The group soon disbanded. Certainly, groups larger than four can function simply fine—particularly if you know each other well and all share a similar preparation and motivation.

Your Turn 4.2

Choosing Group Writing Supports

Characteristic	What I Want Or Need: (Describe)
Group Purpose	
Desired Membership	

(continued)

Characteristic	What I Want Or Need: (Describe)
Leadership Preference	
Duration of Group	
Meeting Frequency	
Meeting Activities	
Between-Meeting Activities	

Your Turn 4.3

You know yourself better than anyone else. Reflect on the approaches mentioned in the later part of this chapter that have been used to support and develop writers and improve their productivity, which approach would you be most likely to choose? Why? Check the approach you would prefer

- ☐ personal mentor, tutor, or consultant
- ☐ writing partner (you choose)
- ☐ writing workshop
- ☐ writing boot camp
- ☐ writing buddy program
- ☐ loosely organized research writing group
- ☐ support group

_____

_____

Which of these supports are available to you? If a search for these supports is not fruitful, are you prepared to take things in your own hands to make one happen?

Resources

Aitchison, C., & Guerin, C. (Eds.). (2014). *Writing groups for doctoral education and beyond*. Routledge.

Albert, T., & Wager, E. (2003). *How to handle authorship disputes: A guide for new researchers*. The COPE Report. https://publicationethics.org/sites/default/files/2003pdf12_0.pdf

Faulkes, Z. (2018). Resolving authorship disputes by mediation and arbitration. *Research Integrity and Peer Review, 3*, 12. https://doi.org/10.1186/s41073-018-0057-z

Fleming N. (2021). The authorship rows that sour scientific collaborations. *Nature, 594*(7863), 459–462. https://doi.org/10.1038/d41586-021-01574-y

Johnson, J. (2017). Writing by the book, writing beyond the book. *Composition Studies, 45.2*, 55–72.

Morton, P. G. (2021). Publishing in professional journals: A guide for getting started. *Nursing Education and Science*. http://www.nes.fdmz.hr/images/articles/nes-morton.pdf.

Redelfs, A. H., Aguilera, J., & Ruiz, S. L. (2019). Practical strategies to improve your writing: Lessons learned from public health practitioners participating in a writing group. *Health Promotion Practice, 20*, 333–337. https://doi.org/10.1177/1524839919838398

Sarnecka, B. W. (2019). *The writing workshop: Write more, write better, be happier in academia*. Self-published.

Sharifi, C., & Buccheri, R. K. (2020). Selecting a journal for your manuscript: A 4-step process. *Journal of Professional Nursing: Official Journal of the American Association of Colleges of Nursing, 36*(1), 85–91. https://doi.org/10.1016/j.profnurs.2019.06.003

Sword, H. (2017). *Air & light & time & space: How successful academics write*. Harvard University Press.

Tivis, L., & Meyer, D. (2018). Operation innovation: A writing workshop for nurses. *Nurse Leader*, *16*, 63–68. https://doi.org/10.1016/j.mnl.2017.10.004.

von Isenburg, M., Lee, L. S., & Oermann, M. H. (2017). Writing together to get AHEAD: An interprofessional boot camp to support scholarly writing in the health professions. *Journal of the Medical Library Association: JMLA*, *105*(2), 167–172. https://doi.org/10.5195/jmla.2017.222.

Weiss, B. D., Stillwater, B. J., Aldulaimi, S., Cunningham, J. K., Gachupin, F.C., Koleski, J., Shirai, Y., Denny, L., Pettit, J. M., & Freeman, J. (2022, July 1). Writing support group for medical school faculty—a simple way to do it. *Teaching and Learning in Medicine*, 1–8. https://doi.org/10.1080/10401334.2022.2092114

References

American Psychological Association. (2020). *Publication manual of the American Psychological Association* (7th ed.). https://doi.org/10.1037/0000165-000

DeMeyer, E. S., & DeMeyer, S. (2018). Mentoring the next generation of authors. *Seminars in Oncology Nursing*, *34*, 338–353. https://doi.org/10.1016/j.soncn.2018.09.002

Fleming, L. W., Malinowski, S. S., Fleming, J. W., Brown, M. A., Davis, C. S., & Hogan, S. (2017). The impact of participation in a research/writing group on scholarly pursuits by non-tenure track clinical faculty. *Currents in Pharmacy Teaching and Learning*, *9*, 486–490. https://doi.org/10.1016/j.cptl.2016.12.004

Haas, S. (2014). Pick-n-mix: A typology of writers' groups in use. In C. Aitchison & C. Guerin (Eds.), *Writing groups for doctoral education and beyond* (pp. 30–47). Routledge.

Johnston, J., Wilson, S., Rix. E.F., & Pit, S. (2014). Publish or perish: Strategies to help rural early career researchers increase publication output. *Rural and Remote Health*, *14*, 2870. https://doi.org/10.22605/RRH2870

Noone, J., & Young, H. M. (2019). Creating a community of writers: Participant perception of the impact of a writing retreat on scholarly productivity. *Journal of Professional Nursing: Official Journal of the American Association of Colleges of Nursing*, *35*(1), 65–69. https://doi.org/10.1016/j.profnurs.2018.07.006

Northridge, M. E., Holtzman, D., Bergeron, C. D., Zambrana, R. E., & Greenberg, M. R. (2015). Mentoring for publication in the *American Journal of Public Health*. *American Journal of Public Health*, *105 Suppl 1*(Suppl 1), S14–S16. https://doi.org/10.2105/AJPH.2014.302543

Orman, K. S., Mancuso, M. P., Ceballos, K., Makic, M. F., & Fink, R. (2016). Mentoring clinical nurses to write for publication: Strategies for success. *American Journal of Nursing*, *116*, 48–55. https://doi.org/10.1097/01.NAJ.0000482966.46919.0f

von Isenburg, M., Lee, L. S., & Oermann, M. H. (2017). Writing together to get AHEAD: An interprofessional boot camp to support scholarly writing in the health professions. *Journal of the Medical Library Association*, *105*(2), 167–172. https://doi.org/10.5195/jmla.2017.222

CHAPTER 5

What Do I Need to Know About the Professional Journals I'm Considering?

Can I Draft a Manuscript and Then Look for a Journal Later?

This would not be advised. Journals differ greatly in terms of editorial policy, the type and length of papers they will accept, the format and typical number of references they expect, and so on. This chapter will address important ways journals differ so that you can consider the best journal for your manuscript. If after reading the chapter you still have two to three journals you think would likely be interested in your manuscript, then keep these in mind as you write and finalize your decision later. Sometimes, in the later stages of writing, one realizes that the manuscript has been drafted in such a way that it is better suited for one journal than another.

How Do Journals Differ?

What Are Predatory Journals?

Predatory journals have also been called pseudo-journals, fake journals, deceptive journals, and opportunistic journals and described as a threat to science because "they undermine its integrity … quality and credibility" (Oviedo-Garcia, 2021, p. 406). These journals are usually known for their lack of quality because they may not edit the manuscripts sent to them despite poor grammar or spelling. A marketing email that I received from one of them contained this line by itself, "Journal are processing to assign a DOI number." Another one's web page listed reviewers under "Reviewer's."

They may claim to have a genuine peer-review system in place but provide no details about it. They may say they have an editorial board but then don't identify the members. One that I came across provided only an email address for submission of manuscripts; the full name of the editor was not available. Typically, these are "journals" only in the name they use in their frequent spam solicitations. Primarily, they exist to make money for their publishers.

How do you identify a predatory journal? They are always open access, and authors must pay to publish their works in them. The fees may be less than $100 or much, much larger. Some of these journals charge separate fees for a "fast-track review." Predatory journals have title names created to sound similar to older, more established journals. They may drop or add "studies" to their title or insert "research." The journal's name often includes "international" to attract manuscripts from a larger market.

A definite characteristic is the breadth of disciplines across which they accept manuscripts. This is in marked contrast to most professional journals whose scope is restricted to a specialized area. One predatory journal accepts articles ranging from interior design to law, philosophy, gender studies, archaeology, and public administration. A recent revision of their web page added "social welfare" and "religious studies."

Predatory journals may advertise they are indexed in legitimate academic databases such as MEDLINE and the Cumulative Index to Nursing and Allied Health Literature (CINAHL) when in fact this is not true" (Oermann et al., 2020), and they may report "fake index factors with names such as 'global Index factor' instead of the accepted Journal Impact Factor" (p. 12). They may also explain why impact factors aren't the best method for evaluating their journal.Be leery of any journal that is not affiliated with a professional association or, at least, is not well-known to your colleagues. It should have a mailing address and identify the editor and members of the editorial board on its website.

What makes predatory journals especially attractive to inexperienced authors is that they promise high acceptance rates, a lightning-fast review and response (e.g., 7 days), and a rapid turn-around time for getting the manuscript in print. If a predatory journal has a peer-review process at all, the quality of the reviews could be "questionable" or completely lack any editorial review or copyediting—promoting the "propagation of errors" (Forero et al., 2018).

If after the previous discussion you still have questions about a journal you are considering, you might want to consult *Beall's List of Potential Predatory Journals and Publishers* (Beall, 2021). Or even better, read the first paragraph of Pearson's (2017) piece about a nurse who paid an open-access fee but lost her money. Her emails and phone calls went unanswered. She also couldn't find members of the editorial board to contact on Google Scholar.

The following is a checklist of characteristics usually associated with predatory journals modified from the international initiative Think. Check. Submit. (2023).

Checklist 5.1 of Predatory Journal Characteristics

- ☐ The title can be easily confused with another, potentially misleading.
- ☐ Ridiculously wide scope of interests.
- ☐ False claims of being indexed in major databases.
- ☐ No publisher address or contact information other than the submission link. The publisher's name should be displayed on the website along with the address, telephone number, and email addresses.
- ☐ It spams researchers with emails inviting submissions unrelated to expertise.
- ☐ Advertises rapid processing from submission to publication.
- ☐ Poor or nonexistent editing of articles (e.g., poor spelling and grammar).
- ☐ Article processing charges (APC; which may or may not be fully revealed).
- ☐ Editorial board may not be listed, have nonexistent members, or those without specialization.
- ☐ Lack of information on the peer-review process, short review time, or guaranteed acceptance.

Other considerations for determining the trust that can be placed in a purported professional journal were also mentioned by Think. Check. Submit (2023) and include the following:

- ☐ No mention of the publisher belonging to the Committee on Publication Ethics.
- ☐ Journal not listed in the Directory of Open Access Journals (DOAJ).
- ☐ The open-access journal is not listed in the Open Access Scholarly Publishers' Association (OASPA).
- ☐ The publisher doesn't mention having a license policy.
- ☐ The publisher doesn't allow you to retain the copyright of your work.
- ☐ Articles may not be indexed or archived in a commonly used database.
- ☐ Publisher doesn't use permanent digital identifiers.

If you find yourself answering "yes" to the majority of the characteristics in the checklist, you are likely looking at a predatory journal. Think. Check. Submit. (2023) also asks two fundamental questions that should not be overlooked.

1. Have you read any articles in the journal?
2. Was it easy to discover other papers in the journal (e.g., three issues back)?

Although the checklist does a great job of giving readers clues to help recognize predatory journals, the scoundrels behind these journals have continued to evolve like a malevolent virus, and you may find that they may *show* names of editorial board members or reviewers, but they may be minimally involved in reviewing manuscripts. These journals also may state certain peer-review policies that don't really take place. Heck, they may even claim that they have a low acceptance rate (e.g., 38% or so) when actually they accept every paper that is paid for. Realize that the websites of predatory journals will mimic more established journals. There is no substitute for the old maxim of "buyer beware." Don't believe everything you read. Look for evidence before sending money.

What Are the Characteristics of Legitimate Journals?

By contrast, legitimate journals usually have been around a goodly number of years. You can usually tell this by the number of volumes associated with the journal. As you can see in Table 5.1, despite wars, economic hard times, editorial changes, and developments within professions, a sample of some of the best-known American journals have been in existence not just in the last 5 or 10 years, but many decades. These journals, by and large, are known to have rigorous peer-review processes that they explain, as well as specific instructions to authors for preparing manuscripts. In these journals, manuscripts are typically professionally edited and formatted.

Typically, in social science journals, there is no fee associated with publishing a paper, and not every paper is accepted. (In other fields, legitimate journals may charge publication fees.) Long-established journals are often associated with professional associations and may publish their acceptance rates—as we'll see later in this chapter. They also tend to have high impact factors, which is one way to estimate the quality of the journal.

What Are Impact Factors?

Impact factors represent the number of citations that are associated with articles published in the journal during the preceding year divided by the "citable items" published in the journal in the two preceding years (SCI Journal, n.d.). Generally, the higher the impact factor, the stronger the reputation of the

TABLE 5.1 Some of the Oldest American Journals in Selected Fields

Journal Title	Year Established	Current Volume # (2022)
New England Journal of Medicine	1812	387
American Journal of Psychiatry	1844	179
American Journal of Nursing	1886	123
American Journal of Psychology	1887	135
American Journal of Sociology	1895	128
Psychological Bulletin	1904	148
Social Work	1948	68
Journal of College Counseling	1998	24

journal. However, one should compare journals within one's discipline, as the consideration of what might be an "excellent" or average impact factor can vary widely across disciplines.

All things considered, aiming for higher impact journals can improve the visibility that a publication will obtain, as it will likely be cited more often than a lower impact journal. If you are an assistant professor, colleagues looking over your body of work after several years will note if you are publishing in the more prestigious journals with higher impact factors or if the preponderance of your publications are in journals with lower impact factors. This kind of comment may be expressed to you by a kind-hearted colleague or noted in a letter that is less supportive of your promotion and awarding of tenure. You may not always need to worry about what other faculty will think about your choice of professional journal to publish in, but in competitive departments, it could be a consideration. The trade-off is that more prestigious journals with higher impact factors are likely to have higher rejection rates.

Table 5.2 shows the differences among a selected set of journals using impact factors from Web of Science and Scopus. The actual impact factors vary in the table, as Scopus started archiving in 1994 and Web of Science goes back much further. Unless you are in an extremely competitive field or institution, journal rankings may not mean a whole lot to you. After all, there are over 28,000 science journals (https://www.scijournal.org/) How many do you think can crowd into the top 20 slots?

Placing a paper in a journal with a higher impact factor means you are also placing the paper in a stronger journal that has a higher ranking in the database of journals. You can look up this data (and other information about each journal) by going to https://www.SCIjournal.org. The website states that impact

TABLE 5.2 Impact Factors of Selected Journals (March 2023)

Journal Name	Impact Factor (Web of Science)	Impact Factor (Scopus)	Web of Science Ranking
Addictive Behaviors	3.913	4.152	3173
Children & Youth Services Review	2.393	2.634	6517
Criminal Justice & Behavior	2.8	2.777	5384
Drug & Alcohol Dependence	4.492	4.283	2410
International Journal of Eating Disorders	4.861	6.102	2103
Journal of Abnormal Psychology	6.673	6.542	1067
Journal of Personality	5.117	5.396	1895
Psychological Assessment	5.123	5.56	1887
Psychological Bulletin	17.74	21.28	169

factors are frequently used as a proxy for the relative importance of a journal within its field, with journals with higher impact factors deemed to be more important than those with lower ones.

What Are Acceptance/Rejection Rates Like in Professional Journals?

A paper by Herbert (2020) exploring the 2017 journal acceptance rates for 2,371 journals published by Elsevier has these findings:

- Acceptance rates ranged from 1% to 93% with an average of 32%.
- The largest journals tend to have lower acceptance rates compared to smaller journals, but the range ran between approximately 10% and 60%.
- There was virtually no relationship between the age of the journal and acceptance rates.

- While journals with the very highest citation rates "tend towards lower acceptance rates," there was "no clear relationship between journal citation impact and acceptance rate" (p. 4).
- "Gold open access journals tend to have higher acceptance rates than other journals" (p. 6). [Note: The "gold open access" is associated with open-access journals charging an article publishing charge, which then gives the author the right to share the article anywhere they choose once it has been published, and the author can keep the copyright of the work postpublication. It can also be licensed with minimal restrictions on how people can use it.]
- "Low acceptance rates are demonstrated typically by very large, very old, and very high impact journals, as well as those that are not 'gold open access'" (p. 9).

We all know that journals have rejection rates, and using the Herbert average finding, we can assume a manuscript we write should have one chance in three of being accepted. It's not bad to believe that. However, the acceptance/rejection rate will depend very much on the discipline and the particular journal in question.

The American Psychological Association (APA) publishes over 90 journals every year and provides rejection rates for those submitting to one of its journals in the *American Psychologist* (APA, 2022). Journals published by APA Divisions (e.g., School Psychology) in 2021 had an average rejection rate of 65%. APA journals not associated with a specific division (e.g., *Psychological Review*) had an average rejection rate of 69%. When "out-of-scope" manuscripts (not appropriate for the journal) were included, 73% of received submissions were rejected. If you are thinking about submitting to a psychological journal, the data provided by APA allows you to see the number of manuscripts received by each of its journals and the number accepted—that way you can see how many others against which you are competing. (However, you may not want to look at that data; it probably won't build your confidence.)

Learn what you can about the journals you are considering. Examine the journals' impact factors. Make a note of their rejection rates if you can find that information. Study the way authors of the published articles craft them. Compare the length of their pieces and the number of references they cite. Does it feel like your kind of journal? When you look at the references you will use in the manuscript you are writing, if several of them have been "recently published in a particular journal, that is a good indication" of the journal's interest in the topic and is a "good rule of thumb" for selecting possible journals (Healey et al., 2019, p. 41).

Why Is It Necessary to Consider the Journal's Audience?

The audience can be thought of as, "Whom do you want to talk to?" (Healey et al., 2019). Early in your decision to develop a manuscript, you must be clear on those you expect to be interested in reading your paper. Will it be educators and possibly teaching assistants (e.g., *Teaching of Psychology*)? Practitioners and applied scientists (e.g., *Sport, Exercise, and Performance Psychology*)? Or clinicians, administrators, researchers, policymakers, educators, and students (e.g., *Journal of Trauma Nursing*)?

Journals provide information to help the aspiring author to know about what kinds of manuscripts they hope to receive. For instance, the *Journal of Trauma Nursing (JTN)* has provided criteria used to evaluate manuscripts coming to them. Note in the following list its first criterion that if the topic of your paper isn't directly related to the focus of the journal, then it will be rejected as one of the *out-of-scope* submissions or *desk rejections* You can save yourself considerable time if you make sure your paper will at least be pertinent to the journal you are considering. Here are the six criteria used by *JTN*:

1. *Topic relevance.* Is the topic pertinent to contemporary trauma care?
2. *Study originality.* Is the study interesting, innovative, or novel?
3. *Study context.* Is the study framed with adequate breadth and currency of related literature?
4. *Knowledge advancement.* Does the study add, extend, or challenge what is currently known?
5. *Scientific strength.* Are the aim, design, data analysis, and conclusions aligned, reliable, and valid?
6. *Writing impact.* Does the writing communicate with impact, concisely, with continuity, and flow?

(Mikhail, 2021, p. 145)

How Useful Are a Journal's Author Guidelines?

Most professional journals publish a brief description of the kind of papers they would like to review. Such narratives are *extremely helpful* in assisting authors to assess if their manuscript will be a "good fit" with the journal they are considering. Here is the description of the type of papers *Addictive Behaviors* is seeking:

> *Addictive Behaviors* is an international peer-reviewed journal publishing high quality human research on addictive behaviors and disorders since 1975. The journal accepts submissions of full-length papers and short communications on substance-related addictions such as the abuse of alcohol, drugs and nicotine, and behavioral addictions involving gambling and technology. We primarily publish behavioral and psychosocial research, but our articles span the fields of psychology, sociology, psychiatry, epidemiology, social policy, medicine, pharmacology, and neuroscience. While theoretical orientations are diverse, the emphasis of the journal is primarily empirical. That is, sound experimental design combined with valid, reliable assessment and evaluation procedures are a requisite for acceptance. However, innovative and empirically oriented case studies that might encourage new lines of inquiry are accepted as well. Studies that clearly contribute to current knowledge of etiology, prevention, social policy, or treatment are given priority. Scholarly commentaries on topical issues, systematic reviews, and mini reviews are encouraged. We especially welcome multimedia papers that incorporate video or audio components to better display methodology or findings.
>
> Studies can also be submitted to Addictive Behaviors' companion title, the open-access journal *Addictive Behaviors Reports*, which has a particular interest in "non-traditional", innovative, and empirically oriented research such as negative/null data papers, replication studies, case reports on novel treatments, and cross-cultural research. (Addictive Behaviors, 2023)

Research on Social Work Practice provides this description of what would be considered appropriate topics for submission:

> *Research on Social Work Practice* is a peer-reviewed disciplinary journal devoted to the publication of empirical research concerning the outcomes of social work practice. Social work practice is broadly interpreted to refer to the application of intentionally designed social work intervention programs to problems of societal and/or interpersonal importance. Interventions include, but are not limited to, behavior analysis and therapy, psychotherapy or counseling with individuals, cognitive therapy, case management/care coordination,

education, supervision, practice involving couples, families, or small groups, advocacy, community practice, organizational management, and the evaluation of social policies. At least one author of a submitted article must be a professional social worker, and/or the interventions evaluated must have been provided by professional social workers.

The journal primarily serves as an outlet for the publication of:

1. Original reports of evidence-based evaluation studies on the outcomes of social work practice.
2. Systematic reviews or meta-analyses of the practice-research literature that convey direct applications (not simply implications) to social work practice. The only two types of systematic reviews considered for publication are:
    A. Systematic reviews of the evidence-based status of a particular psychosocial intervention or assessment method or
    B. Systematic reviews of different psychosocial interventions applicable to clients with a particular psychosocial problem.

The journal welcomes empirical research appropriately derived from a variety of etiological and intervention theories, as well as studies which focus on evaluations not based upon formal theoretical frameworks. Studies using diverse methodologies, such as group or single-system research designs, qualitative approaches, mixed methods approaches, and interdisciplinary works are welcome to be submitted. Replication studies *are* welcome, as are well-designed studies with negative findings or reports of treatment failures. Authors are encouraged to submit *only* articles of the highest quality for editorial review and possible publication. The submission of seriously flawed or marginal studies is discouraged. Reports of inferential statistics involving significant differences *must* be accompanied by suitable measures of effect sizes and their appropriate confidence intervals, and include a discussion of the practical impact indicated by these effects. (Sage Journals, n.d.)

> *One of the most important steps in selecting a journal is to ask yourself,*
>
> *"Does my manuscript fit the scope of the journal?"*
>
> Parrish (2022)

Should I Consider an Open-Access Journal?

The Directory of Open Access Journals (doaj.org) reports that there are almost 13,000 open-access journals, and the number seems to be rapidly increasing. What is confusing is that there also exist hybrid journals—established professional journals, which, for a fee, are also available as open access. Open-access journals make their publications available to everyone (no subscription is required); however, they require APC for manuscripts to be published. As of this writing (March 2023), *Frontiers in Psychology*, for instance, had an APC of $3,225 for original research articles and $2,020 for smaller case reports or brief research reports. It reported an 86% acceptance rate.

PLOS One began in 2006, and by 2022 had produced 17 volumes. *PLOS* journals have publishing fees that vary by journal title. *PLOS Global Public Health* started in October 2021 and has a fee of $2,100 (March 2023) for a research article, while *PLOS Medicine* (2004 start) had a fee of $6,300 (March 2023) for a research article. Open-access journals are often overly broad in their subject coverage. *PLOS One*, for example, describes itself as multidisciplinary and, often interdisciplinary." It accepts "research in over two hundred subject areas across science, engineering, medicine, and related social sciences and humanities" (PLOS One, n.d.). *PLOS One* reports a desk rejection rate of about 22% where the manuscript does not receive peer-review and an acceptance rate of about 48%.

In terms of impact factors, *PLOS One* weighed in at 3.24 (Web of Science) and 3.58 (Scopus) while *Frontiers in Psychology* was 2.99 (Web of Science) and 3.88 (Scopus). On its website, *PLOS One* says this about its impact factor, "Rather than relying exclusively on journal-level metrics such as the Impact Factor, PLOS offers individualized Article-Level Metrics reflecting the viewership, download rates, social sharing, and citations for each article we publish in real time, helping you illustrate the impact of your research." Open-access journals may not be indexed in mainline academic research databases like PubMed and Web of Science but instead may claim articles can be found in Google Scholar and little-known databases. You can search to see if the journal you are considering is found in the Web of Science Master Journal List by going here: https://mjl.clarivate.com/home.

A marketing device that some open-access journals use is their claim to get your manuscript published (online) within 20 days or less after acceptance. This is many times faster than most professional journals, which are not open access and which may take 6 to 8 months or longer for printed issues to come out. Some, however, will post articles electronically ahead of the print version.

I may be wrong, but I suspect a sizable proportion of the authors who submit to open-access journals have experienced a rejection, perhaps a harsh rejection, from a more established professional journal. That, in my opinion, does not suggest one should immediately sprint to the closest open-access journal and pound on its door. As I'll explain more in Chapter 14, a rejection almost always gives you an opportunity to learn from your failure, which provides the ability to revise and submit a stronger and more vibrant manuscript to another journal. You might even want to try submitting the manuscript as many as three times before considering a journal with an expensive article processing fee. Don't panic, you still have choices and options. If you are rich, then sure, go the open-access route and hope you won't have senior faculty rolling their eyes at your publication "success."

Despite the cautions raised about some of the open access journals, much greater acceptance of them is likely on the horizon. In August 2022 the White House Office of Science and Technology Policy released a memo to all federal agencies (known as the "Nelson Memo") recommending that they create or update their plans to allow greater public access to the research stemming from federal funds. More specifically, the memo is seeking "free immediate (without embargo) and equitable access to research that is federally funded and applies to peer-review publications and underlying scientific data" (https://guides.lib.umich.edu/open-research-and-scholarship/OSTP-memo#). In other words, federal agencies with more than 100 million dollars in annual research and development expenditures will have to submit plans for free access by the public to scholarly materials resulting from federally funded research. Universities and other organizations receiving research funds from the government can be counted on to respond in various ways but at least two paths seem clear. They may provide greater support to their faculty and researchers who publish in open access journals by paying some or all of the APC. Already, some journals are providing discounts or waiving fees for universities with subscriptions to their journals, who purchase blocks of e-books, or which have membership in certain consortiums, or specific site licenses. Another approach being discussed would require universities to create institutional repositories where the public could have free access to publications, book chapters, and possibly more material that previously was available only behind a paywall.

Given All the Considerations, How Do I Choose a Journal?

Most of us will want to publish in a journal that is respected for the quality of the articles that it publishes, one that has a good reputation, and perhaps might even be considered prestigious. We can arrive at a decision about those qualities by checking to see if it is indexed in established bibliographic databases and lists members of its editorial board and their university, hospital, or research affiliations. Sometimes you may be able to recognize nationally prominent individuals, or you may feel good when published lists of past reviewers have connections with notable institutions. Having a reasonable impact factor, a stable record of publishing, and a reasonable history of publishing (e.g., not a new journal in Volumes 2, 3, 4, or 5) are important considerations. The journal should also have a clearly stated peer-review process.

Consult your colleagues or university professors to secure their opinions about the reputation and quality of the journal you are considering. In some departments, it is important to shoot for the "top tier" journals in a discipline. In other areas, the absolute ranking is not so important as long as the journal is one frequently used by faculty and students in the discipline—one considered "major" or "respectable." This issue could be one that you want to check out with your writing mentor or with faculty who are actively writing and publishing in your department. Doctoral students "just beginning the journey of publishing" have been recommended to submit "to the middle level journals" (Stoilescu & McDugall 2010, p. 82), which may have lower rejection rates than top journals.

If you don't have any idea where to start with looking for a journal, look at the last several papers you have written (especially the ones where you got the best grades or positive encouragement). Which journal or journals did you end up referencing more than any of the others? That's a good place to start by investigating the journal's author guidelines and so forth.

What is research but a blind date with knowledge?

Will Harvey, American software developer and entrepreneur

While it cannot be denied that getting published in a small journal with a low impact factor is still a publication (and may make your parent(s) very happy), it may not advance your career or improve your chances for tenure. My advice is don't publish in brand new journals that are unknown to your faculty or colleagues. Place your manuscripts in the journals most familiar to faculty in your department or area.

Some journals publish many issues annually (e.g., *JAMA, the Journal of the American Association* is published 48 times a year) while smaller journals may publish monthly or only four times a year. A small number of issues each year may not be a concern if the selected journal is absolutely the best fit for your paper. However, if a new issue only comes out quarterly and they have a backlog of already accepted articles waiting to be published, how long would you be willing to wait to see your paper in print? Are there APC? If so, are there refunds if you later decide to withdraw the paper? The decision of selecting the best journal to receive your manuscript is often a complex one.

After completing the checklist below, you may discover that the journal you have in mind did not get 10 checks. Sometimes we have to negotiate which of the desired journal characteristics must absolutely be checked, and which would just be icing on the cake but aren't essential. For instance, that the journal be well respected is usually going to be an important consideration, but the length of time to see the paper in print may not be a deal-breaker. After doing your due diligence and learning all you can about the journal of interest, the best fit for your manuscript might be one that has a lower impact factor than

> **Checklist 5.2 Journal Selection Criteria**
>
> ☐ Is the journal published by a professional association or well respected by colleagues?
> ☐ Does the journal have a mailing address and identify the editor and members of its editorial board?
> ☐ Does the journal have a good impact factor?
> ☐ Does the journal have a reasonable rejection rate?
> ☐ Will the journal reach my desired audience?
> ☐ Will my manuscript fit under the journal's author's guidelines?
> ☐ Will the journal charge a fee that I am willing to pay?
> ☐ Will the journal meet my needs for respect/recognition or advancement as a faculty member?
> ☐ Is the length of time to see my paper in print reasonable?
> ☐ Is the journal indexed in standard academic databases?

another journal that seems a bit of a reach. Certainly, there is nothing wrong with trying to publish in a journal with a higher impact factor, but if you are just starting out with no prior experience, it might be best to be practical, to learn the ropes, and shoot for the stars with the next manuscript. Your mentor or writing coach may be able to help you think about the best journal given the perceived strength of your study.

> **Your Turn 5.1**
>
> If you had to decide right now, what three journals would you consider submitting your manuscript to?
>
> 1. _____
>
> _____
>
> 2. _____
>
> _____

CHAPTER 5   WHAT DO I NEED TO KNOW ABOUT THE PROFESSIONAL JOURNALS?   **89**

3. _____

_____

What do you need to learn about these journals? For instance, have you read their author guidelines? Do you have three to four articles from the journal that you've studied?

1. _____

_____

2. _____

_____

3. _____

_____

Who could you talk to who would be knowledgeable about the best journal for your manuscript?

1. _____

_____

2. _____

_____

3. _____

_____

Resources

Johnson, B., & Mullen, C. (2007). *Write to the top: How to become a prolific academic.* Palgrave, McMillan & Digital Printing.

Sharifi, C., & Buccheri, R. K. (2020). Selecting a journal for your manuscript: A four-step process. *Journal of Professional Nursing, 36,* 85–91. https"//doi.org/10.1016/j.profnurs.2019.06.003

Web of Science Master Journal List (https://mjl.clarivate.com/home).

The Master Journal List includes all journals indexed in Web of Science, including the complete list of journals in the Web of Science Core Collection (including Science Citation Index Expanded, Social Sciences Citation Index, Arts & Humanities Citation Index, and Emerging Sources Citation Index), Biological Abstracts, BIOSIS Previews, Zoological Record, and Current Contents Connect, as well as the Chemical Information Products.

References

Addictive Behaviors. (2023, July 9). *Author information pack.* https://www.elsevier.com/wps/find/journaldescription.cws_home/471?generatepdf=true

American Psychological Association (APA). (2022). Summary report of journal operations, 2021. *American Psychologist, 77*(5), 714–715. https://www.apa.org/pubs/journals/features/2021-statistics.pdf

Beall, J. (2021). *Beall's list of potential predatory journals and publishers.* Beall's List. Retrieved March 2023 from https://beallslist.net/standalone-journals/

Forero, D. A., Oermann, M. H., Manca, A., Deriu, F., Mendieta-Zerón, H., Dadkhah, M., Bhad, R., Deshpande, S.N., Wang, W., & Cifuentes, M. P. (2018). Negative effects of "predatory" journals on global health research. *Annals of Global Health, 84*(4), 584–589. https://doi.org/10.9204/aogh.2389

Healey, M., Matthews, K. E., & Cook-Sather, A. (2019. Writing scholarship of teaching and learning articles for peer-reviewed journals. *Teaching & Learning Inquiry, 7*(2), 29–50. Files.eric.ed.gov/fulltext/EJ1229209.pdf

Herbert, R. (2020, February 15). Accept me, accept me not: what do journal acceptance rates really mean? [ICSR Perspectives]. International Center for the Study of Research Paper No. http://dx.doi.org/10.2139/ssrn.3526365

Mikhail, J. (2021). Prevent rejection of your manuscript—read the author guidelines! *Journal of Trauma Nursing, 28*(3), 145–148. https://doi.org/10.1097/JTN.0000000000000582

Oermann M. H., Nicoll, L. H., Ashton, K. S., Edie, A. H., Amarasekara, S., Chinn, P. L., Carter-Templeton, H., & Ledbetter, L. S. (2020). Analysis of citation patterns and impact of predatory sources in the nursing literature. *Journal of Nursing Scholarship, 52,* 311–319. https://doi.org/10.1111/jnu.12557

Oviedo-Garcia, M. A. (2021). Journal citation reports and the definition of a predatory journal: The case of the Multidisciplinary Digital Publishing Institute (MDPI). *Research Evaluation, 30,* 405–419. https://doi.org10.1093/reseval/rvab020

Parrish, E. (2022). My manuscript was rejected: Why and what can I do? *Perspectives on Psychiatric Care, 58,* 437. https://doi.org/10.1111/ppc.13074

Pearson G. S. (2017). Avoiding predatory journals with "Think. Check. Submit." *Journal of the American Psychiatric Nurses Association, 23*(4), 239–240. https://doi.org/10.1177/1078390317716883

PLOS ONE. (n.d.). *Journal information.* https://journals.plos.org/plosone/s/journal-information

Sage Journals. (n.d.). *Research on Social Work Practice*: Submission guidelines. https://journals.sagepub.com/author-instructions/rsw

SCI Journal. (n.d.). *Check the latest impact factor.* https://www.scijournal.org

Stoilescu, D., & McDougall, D. (2010). Starting to publish academic research as a doctoral student. *International Journal of Doctoral Studies, 5*, 79–92.

Think. Check. Submit. (2023). *Journals.* https://thinkchecksubmit.org/journals/

CHAPTER 6

What Is the Peer-Review Process?

Peer-review is a set of screening activities that takes place within most professional journals. Reviewers "assess the quality, credibility, accuracy of the methods and conclusions, relevancy to the journal readership, and contribution to the existing body of knowledge (Foster, 2006)" (Parrish, 2021, p. 7). Reviewers appraise and decide whether a manuscript is well-written, original, coherent, cites key authors, acknowledges contemporary issues, uses appropriate methodology, contains an authentic analysis, and makes a potential contribution (Martín, 2016). Peer-review is, for most disciplines, a way to

> govern the production and dissemination of knowledge. Editors and reviewers evaluate manuscripts submitted to their journal, commonly focusing on the quality of the methods used, strength of arguments presented, and overall utility of the findings/content, which results in a determination about acceptability for publication. (Dunleavy, 2021, p. 556)

Köhler et al. (2020) have made a compelling case for peer-review to develop authors and their ideas—promoting "the dissemination of high quality, relevant, and rigorous work products" by evaluating "what constitutes a theoretical, practical, or methodological contribution" (p. 4). The authors argue that

> the role of peer-review goes beyond its important contribution to the creation of the best possible research design or the most appropriate execution of research. Peer-review is how we ensure the overall quality of our work, how we support each other, how we can push and constructively challenge each other to be truly innovative, how we can make sure that our work connects with and is relevant for others, and how we can drive impact and change that are appropriately targeted at the needs of different communities. Good peer-reviewing ensures that the proposed work appropriately extends and tests prior work, but also that our application of research in practice is

relevant and rigorous. An excellent peer-review can help authors to challenge their more conventional thinking to achieve new insights or to refine their arguments and evidence base. (p. 2)

Now that we understand its purpose and importance, we can examine what is involved in the peer-review process. Three sets of actors have roles: editors, reviewers, and authors. Let's look at each of these—one at a time.

The Editor's Role

Editors (or their assistants) are the first ones to encounter a manuscript sent to the journal from a hopeful author or team of authors. Editors have the initial responsibility of determining whether the submission complies with the published journal guidelines which address the desired format, word count, policies, and so forth. Editors have the first right of rejection, called a desk rejection. This action is taken if the manuscript is focused on a topic outside the scope of the journal, is formatted for a different journal, full of errors, makes unsupported claims, or is not written in a professional, academic style. When any of these issues are apparent, the manuscript will be rejected without going to any reviewer. The email sent back to the author may describe it as a "reject without review" (Gennaro, 2022). If a manuscript is going to be desk-rejected, this will typically happen very fast—generally within two weeks.

A study by Huisman and Smits (2017) looked at 3,500 author review experiences submitted to the www.scirev.sc website between 2013 and 2016. Immediate rejection slightly differed by field, averaging 10 days in medicine, 12 in public health, and 15 in psychology and social sciences. Desk rejections were reported by 16.3% of responders, with another 19.8% rejected after the first review round. After one or more review rounds, 60.8% were accepted. Only 1.2% were accepted without any peer-review process.

Submissions that "pass" the initial screening go on to the next step in the process. For the editor, this means looking at the journal's pool of reviewers and selecting several who are knowledgeable about the topic or have expertise in the methodological approach. Sometimes a reviewer with special skills may be sought or another author who has published extensively in that particular area. Journals vary in the number of reviewers they may routinely ask to read a manuscript.

Three reviewers allow for the editor to determine if there is concurrence among two reviewers. When the manuscript is controversial or complex, more than three reviewers may be sought. For instance, one reviewer might indicate that the author should make minor revisions, one reviewer might say it would be acceptable if a major revision was made, and a third might reject it as being an inappropriate submission and not harmonious with the journal's stated interest. Reviewers on the same manuscript can bring diverse perspectives and instead of agreement "draw the author's attention to different issues in the manuscript" (Martín, 2016, p. 692). While this may require some rewriting on the author's part, at least the authors know the manuscript was read—and strengthening the manuscript with reviewers' suggestions may help the article to be cited more times when published.

The Peer-Reviewer's Role

Once the reviewers have been identified, they are sent an email invitation containing the manuscript's title and abstract and asked if they would be interested in reviewing it. Reviewers may accept the assignment or decline it. If they accept the assignment, they are asked to provide a review within a set period such as 14, 21, or 30 days, depending on the journal. It is not unusual for reviewers to take longer than the time allowed. Reviewers are not paid for their efforts; they volunteer to review as a service to their profession or discipline. Reviewers give of their time because they enjoy learning and wish to keep abreast of new developments and approaches in their fields. Some may do it to add to their CVs.

Depending on the journal, most reviewers are likely to be faculty or researchers connected to universities; they may also be practitioners. Carefully reading and critiquing manuscripts is not "the day job" for reviewers, and they must shoehorn the editor's request into their already scheduled activities or responsibilities. Most journals do not provide training for their reviewers. However, it is common for journals to use rating scales for evaluating key components of manuscripts and producing overall ratings. Reviewers typically are established authors and may be known to editors or their editorial boards because of their publications, expertise, or special recognition received (e.g., being asked to be a special issues editor for another journal).

A problem that authors may not realize is that editors may have difficulty finding reviewers for a given manuscript (Yaffe, 2017, p. 577). Indeed, Martín (2016), editor of *Current Sociology*, says, "Finding referees is never easy" (p. 692). This, of course, explains why anxious authors puzzle over why it is taking so long to learn the fate of their submission. Editor Gennaro (2022) of the *Journal of Nursing Scholarship* has noted that fewer people were willing to review during the COVID pandemic and that the lack of adequate peer-reviewers "is exacerbated by the increase in manuscript submissions ... more than doubled" (p. 533).

Most journals use a double-blind review process—meaning that authors do not learn who the reviewers were, and reviewers do not learn the author's identity. Over my career, I have encountered one or two journals that, at the time, were single-blinded. This usually means that the author's identity was not hidden from reviewers. The single-blinded review can be criticized on the basis of prestige bias. That is, a reviewer might be inclined to positively review a manuscript coming from a prolific researcher or prominent university despite obvious shortcomings in a manuscript. Reviewers could also be more negative about manuscripts coming from individuals new to the discipline or from unremarkable universities. Does this happen? I believe so.

Reviewers make assumptions about who has written the piece. If they assume the author is a graduate student rather than a tenured professor, they may take the time to frame their remarks as a pedagogical moment—as opposed to simply pointing out the need for more detail or explanation. Making such an assumption might have resulted from newer faculty being under pressure to "publish or perish" and to produce articles that are not polished—"articles sent in for publication when they still clearly need several months of work" (Martín, 2016, p. 698).

Sometimes is easy to criticize peer-reviewers' assessments. Reviewers vary in the amount of time they spend reading manuscripts. Personally speaking, I have had reviewers whom I felt skimmed my paper instead of reading it carefully. A close reading would have answered some of the questions they posed on their comments back to me. Another issue is that some reviewers do not come to their task thinking that they should be constructive in their criticism. I've had reviewers who seemed unnecessarily critical and anything but objective. One even disparaged the findings of a strong statewide study conducted by a university's Survey Research Center directed by PhD sociologists. Of course, editors would prefer that their reviewers be competent, kind, fair-minded individuals, but even reviewers with impressive CVs can make poor reviewers. My guess is that every journal has a few of these and that editors may not drop them immediately even after a terrible job of reviewing but probably would simply send fewer manuscripts to them.

Going back to Huisman and Smits (2017) again, 19% of respondents reported a first response time about their manuscripts' outcome in less than a month. About a third of the authors had to wait 3 months or more, and 10% had to wait more than 6 months. Eighty-one percent of authors in the field of public health were informed within three months, but 60% of those in psychology, 50% of those in social sciences, and 53% in humanities. The total time taken on average to review the initial manuscript and subsequent revisions averaged 17 weeks for all fields but averaged 12 for medicine, 13 for public health, 20 for psychology, and 23 in the social sciences. Some journals are faster than the average, of course; however, it is pointless to sit and do nothing but wait for a response. One you have submitted a manuscript, start planning or writing another.

The Author's Role

When a sufficient number of reviews on a manuscript have taken place, the editor will pull together the comments from the two, three, four, or five reviewers and determine whether the piece should be published or not. If the decision is to reject it, generally this means the editor would not entertain any "second chance" at fixing or improving the manuscript. The author should simply move on to another journal with or without revising it—the author's decision to make.

If the editor and reviewers agree that the paper needs revision (e.g., that a particular theoretical framework should be added, or the literature review broadened or deepened, or that the piece currently is too long and words must be cut), then the author is notified by email (both rejection and acceptance notices also come by email). The language used with authors is usually tentative—not a promise to publish but contingent on the editor's approval of the strengthening or improvement made to the manuscript.) Here's an actual example my coauthor and I received. (Names disguised to protect the guilty.)

> **Emailed Editorial Response From Manuscript Submission: Example #1**
>
> Your manuscript entitled "ABC DEF GHIJ, KLMN OP QRST, UVWZYZ," which you submitted to *Professional Journal* has been reviewed. The reviewer comments are included at the bottom of this letter.
>
> The reviews are in general favorable and suggest that, subject to minor revisions, your paper could be suitable for publication. Please consider these suggestions, and I look forward to receiving your revision.
>
> When you revise your manuscript, please highlight the changes you make in the manuscript by using the track changes mode in MS Word or by using bold or colored text.
>
> Sincerely,
> *Editor*

The email letter from the editor can be even more cagey—as in the following second example. This example is a similar email from the same journal, with a different manuscript and a different editor. There seems to be a hint that the paper will be published, but it is not a wildly enthusiastic letter. Notice that no promise was made—one way or the other. This seems necessary as authors need to fully address reviewers' comments either directly, by responding to each or by revising the manuscript so that peer-reviewers and editors can evaluate the changes.

When minor revisions are suggested, the revised manuscript may not go back to reviewers a second time. However, when major revisions have been asked for, reviewers may be asked if they would wish to review the updated manuscript. New reviewers may also be appointed if some of the original reviewers decline to read the piece again.

> **Emailed Response from Manuscript Submission: Example #2**
>
> Your manuscript entitled "ABC DEF GHIJ, KLMN OP QRST, UVWZYZ," which you submitted to *Professional Journal* has been reviewed. The reviewer comments are included at the bottom of this letter.
>
> The reviewer(s) would like to see some revisions made to your manuscript before publication. Therefore, I invite you to respond to the reviewer(s)' comments and revise your manuscript.
>
> When you revise your manuscript, please highlight the changes you make in the manuscript by using the track changes mode in MS Word or by using bold or colored text.
>
> To start the revision, please click on the link below:

In a different year with a different journal, we received an emailed response from an editor that also makes no promises:

> Thank you for submitting your manuscript to *Different Professional Journal*. We have completed the review of your manuscript. A summary is appended below. While revising the paper please consider the reviewers' comments carefully. We look forward to receiving your detailed response and your revised manuscript.

I always take the reviewers' comments seriously and try to fully accommodate their suggestions. However, sometimes one must push back a bit because the reviewer is asking for something that isn't available—for example, when it was assumed that there were more unexplored items from the dataset. Or, when the reviewer asked for dates that events occurred in the lives of participants. Although two of the editors' emails made no promises of publication, all three papers were published. Authors should never view a reviewer's "offhand suggestion to make a fundamental change to the work ... as a promise of success" (Köhler et al., 2020, p. 7).

Most editors are very thorough in sharing every comment made by reviewers. The problem with that is one reviewer may compliment the author's handling of a section while another reviewer finds three things wrong with it. In such a case, you may want to contact the editor and ask how to handle the issue. Because you want to see your paper published, your tendency may be to try to address even the most trivial of concerns. However, if you feel that you can mount a good defense for not addressing a reviewer's comment, then do it.

The editor will review all of your revisions and perhaps agree with you. Don't go overboard with tackling every suggestion asking for revision or give the impression that the reviewer is an idiot. This would not be a formula for success.

When there are several reviewer comments requiring revision, number and identify the comment (e. g., Reviewer #1, Comment 4). Place these on the left side of a Word document and the on the right side of the page indicate how you addressed each comment (e.g., "Added two new sentences at the end of *Method* section"). Send the document showing how you have responded to the reviewers' comments back to the editor by email. Editors may also request that you use track changes and send along your revisions in the original document. Sometimes if your document is already close to the journal's word limit and only one of the reviewers requested some minor addition, you may be able to make a case for not responding to a comment that can't be handled without adding another 200 words. Don't be surprised if the editor writes back and asks if you can address the comment in 50 to 100 words.

When reviewers' comments are positive and there are no parts of the paper that trouble the reviewers, then the paper is accepted. In this case, the author may simply need to wait for the galley proofs to check, but if the journal doesn't supply galleys, then the author's work is done. One could then feel the project is safe and its future secure. Time to start a new one or finish polishing another draft.

Huisman and Smits (2017) reported that authors who received an invitation to revise and resubmit took on average 39 days to modify or revise their manuscripts but those in psychology and the social sciences tend to take longer (50 days) than those in medicine (38 days) or public health (29 days). Lastly, those who had their manuscripts accepted rated the peer-review experience much higher (4 on a 5-point scale) than those whose papers were rejected (ratings of 2.2).

> **Your Turn 6.1**
>
> Having read about the peer-review process, what questions have emerged? Consider making a list of these and having a conversation with your mentor or someone who is well published.
>
> List your questions:
>
> 1. _____
>
> _____

2. _____

_____

3. _____

_____

4. _____

_____

5. _____

_____

Alternatively, consult the journal or journals where you are considering sending your manuscript. Look to see what information the journal has posted about its peer-review process. Does this kick up any new questions?

_____

_____

_____

_____

What Is an Academic Writing Style?

An academic writing style is one that models objectivity. Think about when a bicyclist and pedestrian collide. As a witness, you are asked to provide a description of the event. Provide just the facts, not your impression or belief about who was guilty or at fault. Seeing the bicyclist suddenly swerve onto the sidewalk is a fact. Another fact might be the pedestrian had his eyes on his cell phone as he was walking. You might have had an impression about the speed the bicycle was traveling or about the health of the pedestrian who appeared ill and walked hesitantly. Perhaps you noticed a dog chasing a squirrel into the path of the bicycle. In other words, objectivity doesn't try to persuade or present only one side of things.

Presenting and examining evidence is very important in academic writing. One very noticeable characteristic of academic writing is its use of in-text citations or footnotes to provide readers with the specific sources of information being discussed.

If you are a researcher or investigator, it is fine to have a hypothesis, but check your text to make sure you are not showing bias or only one side of an argument. For instance, don't review and report only the literature that supports your position. Similarly, your interpretation and analysis of data must not ignore findings that do not support your argument or thesis.

A second characteristic of an academic writing style is that use of the first-person pronouns of "I" and "my" are typically avoided. Rather than saying in the active voice, "I distributed the survey form to all sections of students in Sociology 100 the first week of the semester," the passive voice is used most often. Thus, one might write, "Students in all sections of Sociology 100 were emailed the survey form during the first week of the semester."

Christensen et al. (2009) have observed, "Regular use of active voice improves readability of your manuscripts" but "passive voice is common in scientific writings because authors in this discipline like to put more emphasis on facts (the research) than on subjects (who does the research)" (p. 226). Passive voice is recognized by the use of such words as *was, were, have been,* and *by*. When reporting research, the data collection and analysis have already been completed, so the past tense is almost always used.

Depending on the journal, you will find some (e. g., qualitative) articles containing "we," "my," and "our," but even then, these terms are not used with the same frequency as found in personal letters or in agency memos and communications. The tone in academic writing is formal, not informal. You might consider its style more "studied" than laid back. It is not conversational and does not use slang or imprecise terms. You shouldn't say that you have a *small* sample without identifying the number in the sample or that participants received a *large* incentive—be precise and tell readers the value of the incentive. Was it $25 or $125?

Third, academic writing has a definite structure and organizational style. Articles are organized in a logical manner depending, in the social sciences, on whether they are quantitative or qualitative. As suggested in Chapter 2, one of the key decisions you must make in preparing a manuscript is to become familiar with the journal or journals to which you are likely to submit, as each journal tends to further impose its own unique style requirements. As you study a sample of recent articles, you will be able to determine the average length of the articles. Note the referencing style expected, and identify the average number of references cited. Similarly, you can see how many tables or figures are commonly found, all of this information can be helpful to you in drafting your manuscript.

If developing a quantitative research report, you'll be able to discover the usual template sections the journal articles typically contain (e.g., Introduction, Methods, Results, and Discussion [IMRAD]). Although, as we discuss in the next chapter, the sections in the IMRAD model can incorporate many different variations.

A fourth characteristic of academic writing is that brevity is generally preferred over verbosity. Depending on your college professors, you may have felt the need to stuff papers full of unneeded references for them to appear "scholarly" and long quotations to meet some assigned page length (e.g., 25 to 30 pages) at the end of the semester. However, especially in academic journals published in a paper format, space is precious and expensive. As you can see in Table 6.1 derived from various journals' Instructions to Authors, some journals are more restrictive of manuscript length than others.

TABLE 6.1 Journal Length and Selected Journals

Journal Title	Pages Should Not Exceed
Journal of Pain & Symptom Management	14 pages excluding*
Journal of Nursing Education	15 pages excluding*
Nursing Research	16 pages excluding*
Social Work	20 pages inclusive
Psychology of Violence	30 pages inclusive
Journal of Consulting & Clinical Psychology	35 pages inclusive

Note* excluded material = abstract, tables, figures, and references

George Choueiry (n.d.) provides precise information to answer the question, "How long should a research paper be?" Analyzing a sample of 61,519 full-text papers from PubMed for the years 2016 to 2021, he found the median length was 4,133 words or 16.5 pages (250 words per page). That figure is an average length and nothing magical. Half of the papers will be smaller and half longer. The best advice is to study a sample of articles from the journal you are considering and try to approximately reach that average for the particular article type. (Realizing, too, that the Instructions to Authors may express helpful guidelines.)

Should I Use Rare and Recondite Words to Impress Journal Reviewers?

This temptation, like the many times in life when we have gone astray by listening only to our own poorly reasoned plans, will not impress reviewers who are evaluating our efforts from afar. My freshman year in college,

I remember helping edit a dorm mate's paper for his English 101 course. As I labored to make sense of his sentences, which ran away from each other like trains passing each other in the night, instead of carrying the reader to the same destination, my friend added his own advice, "Work in nouveau riche into a sentence. Teachers love to see words like that in papers." I wish I knew what comments he got on that paper; unfortunately, I don't. As an educator who has read thousands of student papers, that term would have jumped out from his pages like a flashing blue light on a dark highway—the rest of his paper didn't use any other vocabulary that would have suggested the largess of his personal dictionary.

Don't give educators and reviewers the occasion to wonder if you deliberately consulted a dictionary looking for high-sounding words to convince readers of the astronomical level of your intelligence. Such tactics always rub me the wrong way. I prefer words actually used in conversation—don't make your reviewers leave your paper in order to look up unfamiliar terms. Here are a few examples of terms that would slow down or pause most readers:

> heterodox, apsidal, panegyrics, contrapuntal, vestigial, apotheosis, paroxysm, comity, deracinated, fissiparous, postprandial, jeremiad, asperity, portents, funambulist, mephitic, peregrination, cassoulet, modillion, hagiography, execrable, puissant, lapidarian, voluble, odium, tergiversation, objurgation, simulacrum, shibboleth, punctilious, peregrination, tendentious

Avoid using any pretentious or stilted terms. If you are writing for American audiences, terms like "whilst" and "amongst" will stick in the reviewer's throat like a chunk of stale French bread.

While there may be times when you have to use technical or terms known only to a scientific audience, there's nothing wrong with using simpler plain everyday words with which you are most familiar.

Here are two quotes about the use of "silver dollar words."

> *One of the really bad things you can do to your writing is to dress up the vocabulary, looking for long words because you're maybe a little bit ashamed of your short ones. This is like dressing up a household pet in evening clothes. The pet is embarrassed and the person who committed this act of premeditated cuteness should be even more embarrassed.*
>
> Stephen King, *On Writing: A Memoir of the Craft*

At seventeen years old, I'd developed a philosophy on big words that was no different than my philosophy on cologne. The more the better. ... I loved words—their sound, their power—without understanding or appreciating their precision, and this led to one jaw-dropping sentence after another.

J. R. Moehringer, *The Tender Bar: A Memoir*, pp. 168–169

What Is Swampy Writing?

Succinctly stated, swampy writing is any writing where reading a passage is like walking through a mucky swamp. The reader loses a boot in the mud and later sinks to her knees because key details are left out or because the organization, word use, structure, or grammar is deficient. Was that a snake over there? Did an alligator just glide under the water? The reader can't trust the writer's environment when walking in a swamp. Here are several examples:

Example #1. *Maine has low divorce rates like New York and Nevada.*

Reader's reaction: More details are wanted. Are these three among the states with the lowest rates in the nation? What are their actual rates? Since Maine and New York actually have very low rates of divorce while Nevada has a very high rate, grouping the three together makes no sense. Why compare these three states?

Example #2. *Foster parent recruitment has yet to link with the longevity of certification. Still, one recent study found that foster parent networks appear to be one of the most effective recruitment methods.*

Reader's reaction: Exactly what is the connection or link between recruitment of foster parents and longevity of certification—whatever that is? The reader needs to know more. Is the author saying there are few studies of the length of time foster parents serve that examine the methodology used to recruit them? Finally, doesn't the second sentence (without "Still") say everything the reader needs to know?

Example #3. *My philosophy of helping others and core values I hold grew from what experiences I have had growing up in Key West. I remember my introduction to family counseling vividly. Our professor explained things in terms we could understand—for example, what standing in someone else's shoes meant. I began to understand the difference between empathy and sympathy. I stopped rote learning and moved into meaningful learning in this introductory class. Upon that transformation, I soaked up instruction, theories, and models. My evolution into a middle school teacher materialized through the lens of systems,* *social cognitive, and psychoanalytic theory. Mirroring these paradigms for me addresses both social justice and dignity/worth of a person by providing a lens of empathy and motivation by students.*

Reader's reaction: Although the first sentence sounds as if we are going to learn the author's core values, the author has difficulty explicating them. Perhaps becoming an empathic person became a core value, but the author doesn't really say that. The author gets distracted again with the learning of various theories and models—some of which don't seem relevant. The reader has a loss of confidence in the author when they suggest that psychoanalytical theory helps address social justice issues and motivation. Would a middle school teacher draw upon such a theory in teaching? While reading the works of Freud and his later disciples might have influenced the teacher's core values, the reader is doing some significant head-scratching to try to figure out how and why that material might be relevant to one's core values. Finally, using the terms "evolution" and "materialized" brings conflicting images into one's mind. Evolution is generally thought of as a slow process—something that occurred over thousands of millions of years while for something to "materialize" conjures up Dr. Spock from Star Trek ("Beam us up, Scotty").

Example #4. *In classrooms across America, students find space to drive their learning process and engage in stimulating curriculum when instructors don't drive their learning with lectures but allow student-driven active learning of their own choosing. Wilson's theory provides this space for learners to take leadership for learning that will personally fit their tastes and learning style within the course and amplify their retention of knowledge.*

Reader's reaction: The term "space" in this paragraph is confusing. Is the author acknowledging that American classrooms are adequately spacious? Or is the author using "space" to mean something like a psychic or incorporeal place having nothing to do with the physical features of the room? The last line might have educators outraged. Was it intended to be provocative? Educators, of course, want to give students the space to learn (however that is meant), but to give students the authority to establish what they want to learn and how they want to learn it (e.g., only that which is palatable to their tastes) seems to be a dereliction of the educator's responsibility. If the author is proposing a radical rethinking of classroom leadership, it might have been helpful to start the sentence with a flag for the reader—perhaps something like, "While it may be controversial ..." Lastly, the words "learning" and "drive" or "driven" occur too many times in a little more than five lines. Too much repetition dulls the reader's interest in reading more of the author's work. The author could have minimized the repetition by using a thesaurus. Lastly, let's think about the phrase "amplify their retention of knowledge." The phrase is creative, but typically in the social sciences, we would discuss the benefit of an educational approach as increasing students' retention of specific classroom material. As stated, "knowledge" has no bounds and thus would be difficult to assess whether retention was improved.

All of us write swampy sentences from time to time. I have written my share, and you can be forgiven for that as well. However, writing for professional journals requires that you examine each of your sentences. Make sure they convey exactly what you intend so that no confusion is created, there is no overuse of terms or needless repetition, and needed details are supplied. Within paragraphs, sentences are organized so that the reader is gently guided down the road you want them to follow. Don't be naive like the Scarecrow in the Wizard of Oz. Use your brain!

Lest you think I'm overselling the importance of your writing, here are a few peer-reviewer comments from a manuscript of mine that was later published after revisions were made. (I thought the skull and crossbones were an accurate reflection of my sentiments.)

 "The first sentence of the abstract seemed out of place with the title of the article. It might be relevant to the findings; however, it might be best to keep the intro to the abstract a little broader."

 "See p. 5, row 38, a misplaced period."

 "p. 15, row 22, the use of 'etc.'"

 "p. 3, second sentence, there is a contraction 'weren't' that should be spelled out."

 "p. 11, the words 'stated' and 'mentioned' were used but only one is needed."

 "Check APA style for the block quote on p. 8."

If your command of good grammar might benefit from additional instruction, a quick self-test is found below for self-assessment. (I'm making no claims about the validity or reliability of these items. I listed a few items that pain me whenever I read them.)

While it is beyond the scope of this book to teach you everything that you could or should have learned about writing well, there are a few points that can be made quickly. The first two of these are from a writing checklist found in Hirschey et al. (2019), but the commentary is mine.

Writing Tips

📖 **A paragraph should have just one focus or theme.** For instance, if you are describing an urban setting where you are walking with a cacophony of buses and car horns and ambulances rushing past a busy intersection, let your sentences portray the scene. Don't slap on more sentences about ducking inside an apartment building, walking up three flights of stairs, and trying to open your apartment door, finding it unexpectedly a little tight requiring you to push with your shoulder to open it. That change of observation, setting, and activity could be a little jarring to the reader. New descriptions about the entrance of the apartment building, walking up the stairs and opening of the apartment door deserve a new paragraph or two. Don't try to juggle baseballs and scramble eggs at the same time.

📖 **It is often useful to guide the reader from one paragraph to the next with a sentence that provides a transition or a logical bridge.** For example, a sentence providing a transition from the noisy walk through the city could be something like, "Battered by the city's clamor, I was glad to reach my apartment building, and hurriedly stepped inside the quiet foyer." The next new paragraph can now discuss your struggles going up the stairs or trying to open your stuck door.

📖 **Pronouns are fine, but don't allow the reader to be confused about which he or they you are referring to.** For instance, "He was going to tell his supervisor about a new development in the case, but he was interrupted by a phone call." In this example, it is not clear whose phone rang. Was it the supervisor's or the other fellow's phone?

Grammar Self-Assessment

Can you identify the problems with the items below?

1. There own place to live was in a rural part of the county between the citizens of Port Washington, Red Bird, and Townson.
2. Societies norms and morales were largely responsible for the family becoming homesteaders in Alaska and living off the grid.
3. She had soul guardianship of the child but the court didn't see it that way.
4. Jake is a 15-year-old male whom entered the bar with an attitude.
5. After about a zillion arguments his wife threatened used physical restraints.
6. However, when doing that activity, Terry talked, and acted, in an inappropriate manner.
7. 9 times this month my spouse has watered the cactus on my desk, so I applied the hair dryer.

> 8. One cat had injured it's paw but run passed the officer and than up the tree.
> 9. "Sit in the chair, he said, or I won't read the newspaper to you."
> 10. While waiting to cross the street I witnessed two firefighters talking and waving their hands animatedly.

Explanations to Self-Assessment

1. Use "Their" not "There." Also, "between" is a comparison of two things, but three areas are noted. "Among" should have been used instead of "between."
2. "Societies" should be in the possessive case as in "Society's." Further, "morales" is not likely to be correct since it refers to the feeling of confidence in leadership, sense of well-being, and enthusiasm. In this example, the author might have been thinking of "morals." Also, the choice of "morals" makes the sentence hard to follow since a society would likely represent individuals with many different morals. A more common usage is the pairing of "norms and mores" to refer to traditional, societal, and cultural practices. Thus, one questions if the author not only had poor grammar but also a poor vocabulary.
3. "Soul" should be "sole."
4. It would be clearer to put a semicolon after "male," and to insert "he." The sentence would read: Jake is a 15-year-old male; he entered the bar with an attitude. "Whom" is not correct and feels swampy because we don't talk that way.
5. Here "to use" is easier to understand than "used." Also, "used physical restraints" sounds like old, not new restraints. Finally, "zillion" is not a term you would use in formal, professional writing.
6. Too many commas. Removing two of them would be better as in this example: However, when doing that activity, Terry talked and acted in an inappropriate manner. There is no sound reason for separating talked and acted with a comma. The additional commas slow the reader down. The point of the sentence is to say that Terry acted inappropriately so just get on with it. Now if she talked in a florid, word salad kind of way and walked hesitantly, and then stumbled, a case could be made for the use of another comma. The commas seem to be trying to do the heavy lifting when using additional descriptive terms would be helpful.
7. Two problems. First, a numerical value should not open a sentence. Spell it out. Second, the misplaced modifier makes it unclear whether the hair dryer was applied to the cactus, or to the spouse. It would be better to

prepare the sentence this way: "Nine times this month my spouse has watered the cactus on my desk, so I applied the hair dryer to the cactus."

8. Three problems here: "it's" is a contraction for "it is," while "its" is the possessive case meaning something belonging to the cat. Second the cat "ran" up the tree as a past tense of run; run is present tense. Third, "then" is what happened next, not "than" which is a comparative term. (Bill is taller than Ed.)

9. This is the correct way to punctuate the sentence: "Sit in the chair," he said, "or I won't read the newspaper to you."

10. The opening phrase is known as a dangling modifier. It sows confusion because it is unclear whether the narrator of the sentence was waiting to cross the street or the two firefighters. It would be better to write, "I witnessed two firefighters waiting to cross the street, talking and waving their hands animatedly."

Scoring:

10 Correct:	Amazingly good!
9 Correct:	Good to go!
8 Correct:	B+ Several things still to learn.
7 Correct:	Barely there. Use someone else to proofread for you.
6 Correct:	You may need to brush up in a positive, assertive way to learn what you don't know.
5 Correct	Not ready for prime time.

Your Turn 6.2

Congratulations if you have been told on several occasions that you write well. However, is there anything you could do to improve? Is there one thing you tend to do that detracts from your writing? Do you get in a hurry to be finished? Hate to proofread? Do you have a mindset that it is better to launch three so-so papers than to spend time creating one well-written paper?

_____

_____

_____

_____

What issue with your writing do you think you need to work on?

_____

_____

_____

_____

Do you need to talk with someone about identifying problems in your writing?

_____

_____

_____

_____

When might you talk with this person?

_____

_____

_____

_____

Your Turn 6.3

If you do not believe you have a good academic writing style, list three areas where you most need improvement:

1. _____
   _____

2. _____
   _____

3. _____
   _____

Now, list at least two places where you could get help to overcome any of the weaknesses you've identified. Have you looked for mentors or writing classes in your locality? If not, perhaps now is the time. Make a note of any that you may want to explore further.

1. _____
   _____

2. _____
   _____

Note:
_____
_____
_____

Resources

Bernoff, J. (2016). *Writing without bullshit: Boost your career by saying what you mean.* HarperCollins.

McCloskey, D. N. (2019). *Economical writing: Thirty-five rules for clear and persuasive prose* (3rd ed.). University of Chicago Press.

Sternberg R. J. (2018). The scientific work we love: A duplex theory of scientific impact and its application to the top-cited articles in the first 30 years of APS journals. *Perspectives on Psychological Science: A Journal of the Association for Psychological Science, 13*(2), 260–267. https://doi.org/10.1177/1745691617752690

Sword, H. (2012). *Stylish academic writing.* Harvard University Press.

Zinsser, W. K. (2006). *On writing well: The classic guide to writing nonfiction.* HarperCollins.

References

Choueiry, G. (n.d.). *How long should a research paper be? Data from 61,519 examples.* Quantifying Health. https://quantifyinghealth.com/length-of-a-research-paper/

Christensen, N. B., Sasaki, S., & Sasaki, K. (2009). How to write in the active voice. *International Journal of Urology, 16,* 226–226. https://doi.org/10.1111/j.1442-2042.2009.02271.x

Dunleavy, D. J. (2021). The cultivation of social work knowledge: Toward a more robust system of peer review. *Families in Society, 102*(4), 556–568. https://doi.org/10.1177/10443894211012243

Gennaro S. (2022). Helping the crisis in peer review. *Journal of Nursing Scholarship: An Official Publication of Sigma Theta Tau International Honor Society of Nursing, 54*(5), 533–534. https://doi.org/10.1111/jnu.12807

Hirschey, R., Rodgers, C., & Hockenberry, M. (2019). A program to enhance writing skills for advanced practice nurses. *Journal of Continuing Education in Nursing, 50*(3), 109–114. https://doi.org/10.3928/00220124-20190218-05

Huisman, J., & Smits, J. (2017). Duration and quality of the peer review process: The author's perspective. *Scientometrics, 113*(1), 633–650. https://doi.org/10.1007/s11192-017-2310-5

Köhler, T., González-Morales, M., Banks, G., O'Boyle, E., Allen, J., Sinha, R., Woo, S. E., & Gulick, L. (2020). Supporting robust, rigorous, and reliable reviewing as the cornerstone of our profession: Introducing a competency framework for peer review. *Industrial and Organizational Psychology, 13*(1), 1–27. https://doi.org/10.1017/iop.2019.121

Martín, E. (2016). How double-blind peer review works and what it takes to be a good referee. *Current Sociology, 64*(5), 691–698. https://doi.org/10.1177/0011392116656711

Parrish, E. (2021). Editorial: Peer review process. *Perspectives in Psychiatric Care, 57*(1), 7–8. https://doi.org/10.1111/ppc.12724

Yaffe, J. (2017) From the editor—on peer review: Improving the credibility of social work scholarship, *Journal of Social Work Education, 53,* 577–579. https://doi.org/10.1080/10437797.2017.1376953

Credits

IMG 6.1: Copyright © 2019 Depositphotos/nikiteev.
IMG 6.2: Copyright © 2012 Depositphotos/dvargg.

CHAPTER 7

How Do I Write the *Introduction* and the *Literature Review*?

As mentioned in the last chapter, it is common for articles in the social sciences to contain sections with the major headings of Introduction, Methods, Results, and Discussion (IMRAD)—at a minimum. Journals may also ask for a *Conclusions* section or other headings depending on the discipline. Sometimes after a short Introduction, the next heading will be Literature Review—giving the manuscript five sections (excluding the references). However, authors usually have a lot of freedom in choosing how to open and introduce their manuscripts, and a wide variety of headings are commonly seen. As a reminder, before submitting to any academic journal, it is important to study several articles from the journal where you plan to submit your manuscript. Read the journal's author guidelines and follow the style and headings typically used by their authors. Pay attention to the average length of the introductions in these articles as well as the overall length of the articles. You will probably note that some journals use the heading of Introduction while others don't. The *APA Publication Manual* (2020) notes that the heading is not needed "because the first paragraphs are understood to be introductory" (p. 47).

Whether you use the heading of Introduction (or any of the exact headings in the IMRAD template), you will be writing components of the IMRAD template in some form or other. As we will see later in the chapter, the IMRAD headings are often tweaked by authors. ("What's in a name? That which we call a rose by any other name would smell as sweet," William Shakespeare.) To be clear, you will need to reveal a problem, question, or issue, and then discuss the literature providing the context for your study, the method used to collect data for the study, your findings, and finish with a discussion of the implications or uses of your results. In other words, the major sections in your manuscript being prepared for a professional journal in the social sciences will closely resemble the component parts of the IMRAD template discussed in this and the following chapters.

What Goes Into an Introduction?

Let's think about how to introduce your topic by imagining this section as a solid block of ice. Got it? OK, now let's hand you a hammer and a chisel and pretend you want to sculpt something from the ice. What image do you want to give your audience? What would they be waiting to see? Note that both of the previous questions assume you have a reasonable idea of who your audience will be. If not, is there some way to obtain a little more information on them or to imagine them?

The aim of the *Introduction* section is to encourage your audience to take their seats while you explain the context or back story that helps to give shape to the frozen block. Coincidentally, it is likely the same story that gave rise to your interest in a particular topic or research question. In some ways, it is like viewing a video trailer or preview of a movie. You want to hook potential readers' interest in the topic so that they stay with you. (We'll examine ways to catch and reel in your readers later in the chapter.)

Briefly, the Introduction explains what the paper is about. When writing for journals in the social sciences, you also want to indicate why the topic or research question is important and what contribution your paper will make. For instance, do you have data that will advance a theory or challenge existing notions?

Drotar (2009), editor of the *Journal of Pediatric Psychology*, has written,

> Reviewers need to understand and appreciate the question that is being addressed in the research in order to appreciate its significance. For this reason, the primary research question needs to be clearly described and derived from previous research, theory, and/or clinical practice.
>
> ... [Authors] need to convince reviewers that their research not only addresses a relevant, important question in the field of pediatric psychology but does so with innovative methods, theory, and/or findings that advance the state of science. Moreover, it is highly desirable that research also has significant relevance to clinical care in the field of pediatric psychology and/or public health. (pp. 1–2)

In the Introduction, you may wish to quickly describe how your project draws upon or builds upon previous studies. You won't be able to go into exhaustive detail, but can mention the most salient or related research. (Later, in the *Literature Review* section, you can go into more depth highlighting the major studies that relate.)

What goes into the Introduction? Ahlstrom and Wang (2020) have sketched an outline for introductions for those submitting manuscripts to "management and IB" (international business) and "related social science fields" that authors might find useful. They state the introduction is generally about five to seven paragraphs or two to three pages. These authors suggest the research question be stated as "early as possible" in the "first paragraph, and if possible, in the first sentence" (p. 4).

Their recommendation is that the first and second paragraphs provide a *"mini literature review"* (p. 4) to show that there is a need for further study of the topic or question. These paragraphs "situate the paper in the past literature" (p. 8) and briefly summarize the most relevant research establishing the gap in our knowledge about the topic or question.

In the third paragraph, they advocate describing "what the current paper is proposing" and in the fourth paragraph describing where the "motivation for the paper comes from ... and the limits of previous research and also recent calls for research on this topic" (p. 4)

Paragraph five presents a brief "mini methods" description of the study that is to follow. Paragraph six would contain "a brief summary of contributions to theory, empirical evidence, and research design ... (which is expanded on later in the *Discussion* section)" (p. 4).

I'm not a big fan of formulaic approaches but believe that the type of journal, type of article, and author's writing style may not always fit the tight Introduction guidelines proposed by Ahlstrom and Wang (2020). For instance, Kallestinova (2011) suggests, "The Introduction should not be long. Indeed, for most journals, this is a very brief section of about 250 to 600 words" (p. 187). Silvia (2015) suggests that the "standard Introduction" might be six or more pages with headings and subheadings (p. 105). I looked at a handful of articles in the social sciences and quickly estimated the length of the Literature Review and Introduction combined in these studies constituted about 20% of the papers (counting the reference pages). However, I'm not pretending that was a fair or representative sample. Because you have examined (or studied!) several articles in the journal to which you are submitting, you will have obtained possibly even more valuable data than discussed here and observed how other authors have presented their introductions.

Faber (2012) cautions,

> Possibly the most common mistake is to write a long introduction. This may stem from different factors, but apparently the most common is that sometimes articles are derived from theses where relatively lengthy literature reviews are not uncommon. After a bitter struggle to craft a beautiful literature review, authors tend to become infatuated with the quality of their text, and feel the urge to share it with others. ... The rule of thumb to determine section length is that it should not exceed 10% of the total article word count. (p. e133)

Lamanauskas (2019) has discussed a slightly different way to think about writing the Introduction. He writes, "In general, the introduction has to answer the fundamental problem—why has the research/study been undertaken?" (p. 688). It follows that one must then describe the available information, describing what is known about the problem and then moving to what is not known. He recommends moving from general information on the topic or problem to more specific facts. He continues,

> As a rule, the introduction ends with a clear formulation of the research aim and question(s). Thus, the introduction usually presents researchers' brief overview of what is supposed to be solved during the reported original research. (p. 690)

Personally, I don't believe there is a fixed rule about whether the research question or problem must be presented in the first or the last paragraph of the Introduction. The way I think about this is that authors have a wide net for capturing readers (and reviewers). As an author, my task is to make my Introduction as interesting as possible. How can you do that? Here are several ways you might attract or entice readers.

How Do I Engage the Reader Early On?

1. Starting the Introduction With a Question or a Problem

One of the most effective approaches to writing an Introduction is to pose a question or a problem. This might be a question in your field that many readers have pondered. The question might also involve the effectiveness of an intervention, a fresh way of looking at an old problem, or the results of a recent survey of clients that explored information they withheld from their therapists.

To present this idea to you, I thought of this analogy: Imagine a friend or coworker is having a party and asks you to come. You agree to attend, even though you are pretty sure that you will know only one or two other people attending. To keep from being miserable, you are prepared to have to introduce yourself to other people so that you can engage in conversation with them. Where do you start? What do you say?

According to some social media advice, a safe question to ask is, "Where are you from?" If the location is close by, you might find that you, too, have family or friends who live there, or perhaps even had a flat tire there on the interstate. If they are from a city you know nothing about, your follow-up question might be, "What do you like most about it?" That question allows you to build connections about the parks where one might walk or jog, art museums, theaters, philharmonic orchestras, and the like.

Asking questions of those at a party is a way to create interest and grounds for conversation. Questions provide a platform or foundation for more expansive conversation. Similarly, presenting questions to readers is a great way to entice those who come across your title, abstract, or article to read it.

Several excerpts showing this approach are provided next. The excerpts will come from mostly quantitative articles and a few from qualitative articles appearing in a variety of social science journals. To comply with "fair use" of copyrighted materials, these excerpts are approximately 200 words in length or about two paragraphs. Readers who desire to see the paragraph ahead or below the presented material are provided with the full reference for consulting that work themselves.

Here are the excerpts:

The Problem Appearing as the First and Second Sentence in the Introduction

> Burnout is a hot topic in today's workplace, given its high costs for both employees and organizations. What causes this problem, and what can be done about it? (Maslach & Leiter, 2017, p. 160)

The Problem Appearing in the First Paragraph (as Well as in the Title)

> As the United States surpasses 28 million COVID-19 cases and 515,000 deaths as of March 4, 2021, many healthcare workers continue to be overloaded by work associated with caring for COVID-19 patients. Burnout among healthcare workers is not a newly recognized crisis [1], and is associated with higher rates of anxiety, depression, and substance abuse [2]. (Prasad et al., 2021)

It is common for articles appearing in journals to provide numerical data showing the extent of the problem—as can be seen in the next excerpt from Renner et al. (2023).

> Children who experience various forms of family violence are at an increased risk for a wide array of health problems and academic challenges when compared to children not exposed to family violence. In federal fiscal year 2019, Child Protective Services (CPS) agencies in the U.S. received an estimated 4.3 million referrals of alleged child maltreatment involving approximately 7.9 million children (USDHHS, 2021). Of these, an estimated 656,243 unique children were the substantiated victims of abuse and neglect. These data also show that 84.5% of children experienced a single maltreatment type, with 10.3% having experienced physical abuse.

In their lifetime, 16% of children are exposed to psychological or emotional intimate partner violence (IPV) and 17.9% are exposed to physical IPV (Hamby et al., 2011). Data on children's exposure to a sibling's physical abuse are largely unavailable; yet, there is evidence to suggest that when one child in a family is physically abused, other children are not (Hamilton-Giachritsis & Browne, 2005). Results from a national sample of 1467 children, ages 2–17, revealed that 7.2% experienced physical abuse and 2.8% were exposed to the physical abuse of a sibling (Finkelhor et al., 2009). (p. 2511)

The Question Appearing in an Abstract
The Late Iron Age has traditionally been portrayed as an age of swords, Celtic-patterned shields, and bronze cauldrons, a time of warfare, banquets, and raids, mostly starring male warriors. But what do we know about the rest of the population, especially women? Is it possible, based on the same data, to uncover an alternative narrative that includes women? (Liceras-Garrido, 2022, p. 396)

The Question Appearing in the Abstract
In order to gain a granular view of the relationship between mindfulness training and cognition, we report on the following: 1) What do we know? How does mindfulness affect cognition? (Vago et al., 2019, p. 143)

The Question Appearing in the Abstract
There exists wide variation in the way children respond to toxic stressors in their lives. Some children appear to be relatively unaffected, while others develop a variety of psychological, behavioral, and physical consequences. What is the explanation for this phenomenon? (Hornor, 2017).

Whether the question appears in the abstract or early in the Introduction, its presence sets the stage, so to speak, and guides the reader through the author's presentation of the germane background material. The question is the glue that binds the sentences and paragraphs together in the Introduction. If there are studies or facts that don't directly relate in some way or another to the Introduction, then they don't belong there. Stay true to your topic and cut the fluff!

2. Starting the Introduction With a Controversy
This approach is similar to posing a question early in the Introduction or abstract, but you make statements demonstrating the squabbles or debates.

Readers may become engaged because they have previously taken one side of a dispute but would like to hear what the opposition now has to say. Or, they may have heard about an unsettled issue within the field or profession and now want to learn more about it. The topic could be one that students are bringing into university classrooms or one from this week's news.

The controversy could involve the lack of evidence or the quality of evidence that has been used to support a prevailing theory or therapeutic approach. You, as author, can assume the role of sleuth in the Introduction and sift through the controversial studies on the topic contributing to a confusing tapestry. When you can provide the clarity to straighten out a perplexing case or situation, your article stands a chance of getting lots of citations! Here are several excerpts showing this approach:

A Controversy Appearing in the Introduction

Contradicting the view that emotional reactions foster irrational and maladaptive behavior, research reveals that emotional experiences can play a key role in facilitating constructive behaviors on societal threats (Brosch, 2021; Fessler & Haley, 2003; Smith & Mackie, 2016; Yang, 2000). Previous research on emotional reactions related to climate change has focused chiefly on assessing emotional reactions related to climate change at a broad level. As we explain below, this literature has suffered from largely inconsistent results. (Geiger et al., 2021)

A Controversy Appearing in the Introduction

There has been a long-standing ethical debate on the appropriateness of self-disclosure and transparency in therapy. Cashwell and colleagues[1] define therapist self-disclosure as the "verbal sharing by the counselor of personal revelations or information to the client." The literature demonstrates both benefits and risks of self-disclosure. (McDonald et al., 2022, p. 263)

A Controversy Appearing in the Abstract

As environmental movements rage, how to handle nuclear power plants has become a hotly contested issue globally. While concerns about nuclear power plants are warranted, nuclear power plants may play a crucial role in climate change discourse. In this context this study examines the connections between individuals' perceived environmental threats and their perceptions of the environmental threats posed by nuclear power plants (perceived nuclear threats). (Lim & Moon, 2021)

A Controversy Appearing in the Introduction

Scholars have long documented the positive effects of social support on mental and physical health outcomes and longevity [1]. Pain is one such health outcome that is known to be affected by supportive responses from others [2], and much of the recent literature has focused on either operant based (e.g., pain reinforcing) and/or empathic responses (e.g., responses that validate another's emotional experience). Yet, other theory-based responses may affect pain and quality of life, and knowledge of these behaviors may contribute to behavioral medicine treatment development. (Pester et al., 2020, p. 280)

A Controversy Appearing in the Introduction

The United States is engaged in an ongoing national policy debate about how best to address serious mental illness (SMI) ... A major controversy among leading mental health experts and advocates is whether drawing public attention to an apparent link between SMI and violence, a strategy shown to elevate public stigma toward people with SMI, is the best way to increase the public's willingness to invest in improving the mental health system or whether alternative, nonstigmatizing messages are equally effective ... There is also debate over which types of mental health services should receive additional investment. A key point of controversy in this debate is whether society should invest in expanding mandatory versus voluntary treatment approaches. (McGinty et al., 2018, pp. 185–186)

If you find it difficult to get started, to find the "perfect" opening, you would do well to follow the advice of Dorothy Bradbury who advised in a small monograph in 1972, "Do not waste time finding an ideal opening. If it does not come easily, use the best one you can think of at the moment and change it later. Get under way. ... Many times you will find a good opening simply by crossing out the first paragraph or so" (p. 10).

> You may not write well every day, but you can always edit a bad page. You can't edit a blank page.
>
> Jodi Picoult, American writer with 40 million books in print

Figuring out how to start your Introduction may not come easy. (I'm reminded of the First Noble Truth of Buddhism: life involves suffering.) You might struggle, you might make many false starts, but give yourself permission to forego perfection. Any draft can be improved. Blank pages not so much. Make a start, even if it feels meager and unsophisticated. Tomorrow you may have an insight for a brand-new way to begin or improve today's effort. Writing is hard work, but success will never come from a portfolio of blank pages. You are not alone if you feel it is difficult. Lots of graduate and doctoral students have been quietly defeated, as well as more faculty than you might expect, because just getting started is so challenging.

In the old days before automatic transmissions in cars, when they wouldn't start, you could get a pal or two to push the car until it was rolling, and the driver inside would pop the clutch, and the car would often magically roar to life. I don't know of anyone who pushes a car anymore to start it—probably because that doesn't work with automatic transmissions. Perfectionism is like pushing a car today to start it. It doesn't often work. Perfectionists are their own worst enemies. Be a realist, a draft is what you are creating. No journal editor is going to be critically rejecting your first draft. You can draw lines through sentences, shuffle their order, throw out the ones you don't like—all with no consequences or reflection on your intellect. Write a draft Introduction, not a perfect one.

One can always make the time to revise a document that is mostly complete. You can find time to change up the Introduction, to shorten the Literature Review or Discussion. What you will never find the time to do is to make it perfect. Accept that most of the things we write in our lifetime could be edited to make them more elegant, more exquisite in high heels and pearls. Don't let "perfect be the enemy of good." Most articles don't have to be perfect—they only have to be good enough to please the peer-reviewers and editor. Don't wear the burden of perfectionism around your neck like an ox yoke. Give it up. Breathe the fresh air of freedom to rewrite and revise—even if the first effort is as bland as unsweetened oatmeal.

> *The thing I have to do as I write, and that God permits me to do, is that I have to be willing to fail.*
>
> Mary Karr, professor of English, poet, and memoirist

What Is Unacceptable Content in the *Introduction* Section?

Table 7.1 is not original from me but is a paraphrased excerpt taken from Lamanauskas (2019, p. 691) with additional content I added. It is self-explanatory.

Kallestinova (2011) tidily sums up what is needed in the Introduction. She says to "establish the territory,"

> place your research in context and highlight the importance of your research topic. By finding the niche, you outline the scope of your research problem and enter the scientific dialogue. The final move, "occupying the niche," is where you explain your research concisely and highlight your paper's significance. (p. 186)

TABLE 7.1 Unneeded Content in the *Introduction* Section

Don't Do This	Explanation
Fill the Introduction with quotations	Use only an exceptional or remarkable quotation if needed, seldom use more than one
Fill the Introduction with references	Use only directly applicable studies that present or set up your problem/question
Don't try to teach new concepts, introduce long definitions	Keep the Introduction simple, easy to follow
Resist the urge to make the research question(s) overly complicated	The research question should be clearly stated (fewer words are better)
Don't assume the reader understands how your study is unique	Plainly state how your study is different from others in this vein
Explore rabbit holes along the way, making the Literature Review too broad and including studies not directly related	Draw upon the weighty and compelling studies; it is not necessary to identify every study ever written on the topic
Cut and paste the *Literature Review* section from your thesis into the current manuscript	Keep the Literature Review lively, don't kill the reader's interest by forcing them to wade waist-deep through prior studies

How Do I Develop a Literature Review as Part of the Introduction?

Before you can begin writing the Introduction, it is most helpful to have conducted a literature search. Not knowing the cutting-edge investigations into your topic and past investigative efforts is like being in a dark room without a flashlight as you try to find the light switch. You benefit from knowing what others have concluded, questions still unresolved, and suggestions for future research. If you can masterfully weave some of this information into your Introduction, you will seduce many readers and reviewers into reading your article. There isn't a specific formula for doing this weaving; each author's Introduction can and should be different from others.

The field you are in will generally guide you to the literature database to use. For instance, in the medical field, you would probably rely on PubMed or Medline, but CINAHL was developed specifically for nursing literature. You might want to supplement your search with EMBASE to pick up more international research and the Cochrane Library. There are many, many specialized databases, and a consultation with a research librarian can save you time. Not all databases are equal—their specialization might not bring the large net that you wish because their holdings are considerably smaller than a vast database such as Web of Science—a favorite of mine.

A research librarian can help you from being smothered by thousands and thousands of hits when your net is too large. For instance, don't do a subject search on a broad topic like mental illness or schizophrenia because you need to be much more specific about what you want to know. Who fits the profile of patients or individuals you want to study? Are they being treated with a certain medication or psychotherapy or counseling approach? You must target your population or problem and focus like a laser pointer. If your capture net is too small, however, you could end up with very few articles. In that case, you could expand the age range a bit, look for similar treatment approaches, or open up the years selected for the search. For instance, instead of looking for studies only in the last 5 years, broaden your search to the last 10 or 15 years.

If you are still having difficulty, Knopf (2006) advises to look for other literature reviews, or systematic reviews, or mega-analyses with these terms in the search box (but not all of them at once.) You can also look for recent dissertations on the topic to see what they have revealed in the way of found literature. In all of the relevant studies, be sure to check the references those authors cite. One advantage of the Web of Science is that it allows you to see how many times each relevant article in the database has been cited, and then you can open these articles up and read them electronically.

Your literature search should (hopefully) indicate that there is a gap in the literature, an area that has not previously been well explored—thus justifying your research question and study.

How Do I Write the Literature Review?

After you have drafted the *Introduction*, the *Literature Review* section generally follows. Let's start by thinking about how we can begin this part of our manuscript. Note, however, that sometimes the Introduction contains the Literature Review without a clear division between the two. You are particularly likely to see this approach in brief reports and when the literature on a topic is relatively shallow.

If you began your Introduction with a problem, controversy, or question, it would be logical to give some historical background. For example, you might want to present information about when the problem was first discovered or when the controversy has most recently come to attention. Usually, there are classical or salient studies that should be noted. If you've already supplied that information, that's fine. However, if there are other studies that have made a substantial contribution to an understanding of the problem, or attempts to resolve it, you may want to acknowledge these in the *Literature Review* section. Depending on the point you are trying to get across, you may want to identify the date of the original paper on the topic and then recognize any important developments—including current applications and what authors have said about it recently.

When you discover decades of literature on the problem, there could be too many studies or articles to cover without the Literature Review growing to an unacceptable length. Keep your focus on the most salient or pertinent studies. You are *not* obligated to review every paper that has been written on a topic. Avoid trying to give every detail or nuance. Your task is to discuss briefly and summarize studies that are directly relevant to your investigation or paper.

You don't need to mention every unorthodox or unusual theory that has come into existence. For instance, in 1818, John Cleves Symmes published a circular declaring his theory that the earth is hollow, habitable within, and open at the North Pole 4,000 miles across and at the South Pole open at 6,000 miles across. He lectured about his ideas and in 1824 held a benefit for an expedition to travel to the North Pole to confirm his theory but the funding was never secured. "His theory was widely met with ridicule" (Suess, 2023). Similarly, you might also not want to bring up studies that have weak methodology, small samples, or are less than rigorous.

In this piece of the manuscript, try to show that you are knowledgeable of (perhaps even the master of) the literature on a key theory, phenomenon, problem, intervention, or topic. Don't spend 15 minutes searching in Google Scholar and feel that you have conducted a thorough search. Separate the wheat from the chaff. When you are finished, you should have both current and somewhat older studies. Don't focus on just one end of the spectrum. Survey all of the pertinent studies, if possible.

Seldom is it necessary to bring in quotations; they are rarely seen in this section of the manuscript. What is important is that you do not lose the reader's interest. Keep the readers' eyes on the gap in the literature, how little we know on the topic. Lead them to see how your study can fill the gap, or at least supplement our knowledge or expand our thinking. After reading the Literature Review, readers should be well-informed about your rationale for conducting the study.

Here are a few other tips:

- Don't present a laundry list of studies in a serial fashion, one right after the other. Find a way to group them by their methodology, findings, theoretical school, more recent or older studies, etc. If possible, "synthesize the literature, gain a new perspective on it, and clarify what has been done and still needs to be done" (Boote & Beile, 2005, p. 7).

> - Try to be objective and balanced. Do not deliberately leave out a study with findings just because it doesn't support your hypotheses or assumptions. (An exception could be made here if the study is terribly flawed.)
> - Particularly if you are writing about interventions, readers will want to know how many studies show positive and or negative findings.
> - Readers will want to know about the quality of evidence available in the studies. Were the methodologies strong or weak, the findings mixed? Did you find agreement in conceptualization and uniform operationalization of key dependent variables—or was there a great deal of variation making it difficult to compare findings?

Authors usually position their research questions at the end of their Introduction and Literature Review. Here is one example from Wilke et al.'s (2019) study "Predictors of Early Departure Among Recently Hired Child Welfare Workers." This excerpt is the first paragraph under the heading "Current Study," and a second paragraph describes the CPS in Florida.

> Much has been discovered regarding job turnover among child welfare workers, with attention to individual worker characteristics, organizational efforts, and responses to job conditions. Yet little is known about factors that affect the timing of departure, especially among newly employed workers. As conceptualized by organizational psychologists, the integration of new employees is a developmental process in which employees socialize within their new roles and become embedded within the organization (Allen et al., 2010; Bauer & Erdogan, 2011). This framework informs our investigation of the correlates of departure during the early employment of child welfare workers. We aim to answer the following two questions: (1) How do early leavers differ from workers who remain on the job? and (2) What factors influence early departure among child welfare workers? While known correlates of employee turnover are likely to be salient with new employees, based on Bauer and Erdogan's (2011) developmental framework, we anticipate that unique factors will influence worker adjustment and retention during their first six months of employment in child welfare. (p. 190)

Here is a second example of the research questions coming at the end of the *Introduction* and *Literature Review* sections in a study previously cited by Renner et al. (2023) entitled "Academic Outcomes Among Children Who Experienced or Were Exposed to Physical Abuse." This paragraph comes after five paragraphs in the Introduction.

Current Study

The scant publications focused on the effects of exposure to child physical abuse almost exclusively attend to behavioral outcomes, namely externalizing and internalizing behaviors. In this study, we explored school attendance and academic achievement over time among children who experience different forms of family violence, with a specific focus on child physical abuse.

Through this study, we sought to answer three research questions:

1. Do school attendance and achievement patterns differ for children who were involved with CPS due to alleged physical abuse compared to their peers who were not involved in CPS?
2. Do school attendance and achievement patterns differ for children who were allegedly physically abused compared to children who were exposed to alleged physical abuse?
3. Does exposure to IPV explain differences in attendance and achievement outcomes among children who are involved with CPS?

We anticipated that CPS involvement would be associated with both decreased school attendance and decreased academic achievement, compared to no CPS involvement. We did not pose specific hypotheses regarding whether direct or indirect child physical abuse would be most salient for children in the sample. This decision was largely due to the lack of available research on exposure to child maltreatment of a sibling and how this type of victimization may influence academic outcomes. (p. 5)

[Note: Two sentences discussing the covariates employed in the study were not included due to trying not to exceed the "fair use" standard.]

A third example comes from a qualitative study by Jurewicz et al. (2022) entitled "Social Relationships, Homelessness, and Substance Use Among Emergency Department Patients." This excerpt is a portion of the third paragraph under the heading of Introduction.

As part of a broader study to develop ED-based {Emergency Department} homelessness prevention interventions, we conducted qualitative interviews with ED patients who had recently become homeless. In a prior paper, we described ED patients' pathways to homelessness [24]. The current analysis expanded upon some findings from our prior work and ultimately provided an in-depth examination of social relationships as they relate to substance use and homelessness that was not previously described. In particular, qualitative interviews offered the opportunity to study how social relationships helped or hindered the stress of being newly homeless and the role of substance use. We examined the following questions:

1. What role do social relationships play in precipitating and/or ameliorating homelessness in study participants who use drugs and alcohol?
2. How do study participants view the connection (if any) between their substance use and their social relationships? (pp. 574–5)

Although addressing literature reviews in a small sample of 12 doctoral dissertations, Boote and Beile (2005) have noted that "the best literature reviews were thorough, critical examinations of the state of the field that set the stage for the author's substantive research projects" (p. 9). May it be that yours does the same.

Your Turn 7.1

Let's think about drafting your Introduction and/or Literature Review. Do the articles you have read for the journal that you will submit to (the models) usually have an Introduction that includes the Literature Review or are there separate headings?

_____

_____

_____

What would you be most comfortable in writing for your manuscript?
a) A one-heading Introduction
b) Two headings: Introduction and Literature Review

_____

_____

Will you place your research questions or purpose at the end of one of the choices above, or do you prefer the "Current Study" approach?

Your Turn 7.2

Develop a first draft of the Introduction and/or Literature Review. Don't worry about getting every sentence perfect for now. Just let your thoughts flow about what a reader needs to understand. Why is the problem or question of interest, and what makes your study unique? What contribution does it make?

Once you have finished the draft, try to look at it as a reader or reviewer might. For instance, think about these three questions:

☐ Is enough detail provided, or does it feel you were too brief?

(continued)

☐ Does this front section contain many more references than the article models you have examined? Is this draft too long? Does it need to be shortened?

☐ When discussing various interventions, theoretical perspectives, and findings from other studies, are you fair and objective, or do your favorites get all of the applause?

Your Turn 7.3

When you are relatively happy with your draft of the Introduction or the Literature Review, give it to your writing colleague, mentor, or so on, to receive their feedback.

When you received the feedback, did anything surprise you? Were you aware of any weaknesses that your chosen reviewer also identified?

What will you do to strengthen the draft?

References

Ahlstrom, D., & Wang, L. (2020). Getting a good start on your research: Writing up the paper's introduction. *International Journal of Higher Education Management, 6*(2). https://doi.org/10.24052/IJHEM/V06N02/ART-1

American Psychological Association. (2020). *Publication manual of the American Psychological Association* (7th ed.). https://doi.org/10.1037/0000165-000

Boote, D. N., & Beile, P. (2005). Scholars before researchers: On the centrality of the dissertation literature review in research preparation. *Educational Researcher, 34*(6), 3–15. https://doi.org/10.3102/0013189X034006003

Bradbury, D. (1972). *Some principles of good writing.* National Association of Social Workers.

Drotar, D. (2009). Editorial: Thoughts on improving the quality of manuscripts submitted to the *Journal of Pediatric Psychology*: Writing a convincing introduction. *Journal of Pediatric Psychology, 34*, 1–3.

Faber, J. (2012). How to write the introduction of a scientific article. *Journal of the World Federation of Orthodontists, 1*(4), e133. https://doi.org/10.1016/j.ejwf.2012.11.002

Geiger, N., Swim, J. K., Gasper, I. K., Fraser, J., & Flinner, K. (2021). How do I feel when I think about taking action? Hope and boredom, not anxiety and helplessness, predict intentions to take climate action. *Journal of Environmental Psychology, 76*, 101649. https://doi.org/10.1016/j.jenvp.2021.101649

Hornor, G. (2017). Resilience. *Journal of Pediatric Health Care, 31*, 384–390. https://doi.org/10.1016/j.pedhc.2016.09.005

Jurewicz, A., Padgett, D. K., Ran, Z., Castelblanco, D. G., McCormack, R. P., Gelberg, L., Shelley, D., & Doran, K. M. (2022). Social relationships, homelessness, and substance use among emergency department patients. *Substance abuse, 43*(1), 573–580. https://doi.org/10.1080/08897077.2021.1975869

Kallestinova, E. D. (2011). How to write your first research paper. *The Yale Journal of Biology and Medicine, 84*(3), 181–190.

Knopf, J. (2006). Doing a literature review. *PS: Political Science & Politics, 39*(1), 127–132. https://doi.org/10.1017/S1049096506060264

Lamanauskas, V. (2019). Scientific article preparation: A comprehensive introduction. *Problems of Education in the 21st Century, 77*(6), 688–694. https://files.eric.ed.gov/fulltext/EJ1267931.pdf

Liceras-Garrido, R. (2022). A perspective on late Iron Age women in the Iberian Northern Meseta. *European Journal of Archaeology, 25*(3), 396–415. https://doi.org/10.1017/eaa.2022.1

Lim, J., & Moon, K.-K. (2021). Can political trust weaken the relationship between perceived environmental threats and perceived nuclear threats? Evidence from South Korea. *International Journal of Environmental Research and Public Health, 18*, 9816. https://doi.org/10.3390/ijerph18189816

Maslach, C., & Leiter, M. P. (2017). New insights into burnout and health care: Strategies for improving civility and alleviating burnout. *Medical Teacher, 39*(2), 1–4. https://doi.org/10.1080/0142159X.2016.1248918

McDonald, M., Rappaport, A., & Bates, A. (2022). How do I work with fertility loss as a pregnant therapist? A case study and discussion about pregnancy self-disclosure in the oncology setting. *Journal of Psychosocial Oncology, 40*(2), 263–266. https://doi.org/10.1080/07347332.2021.1951423

McGinty, E. E., Goldman, H. H., Pescosolido, B. A., & Barry, C. L. (2018). Communicating about mental illness and violence: Balancing stigma and increased support for services. *Journal of Health Politics, Policy and Law, 43*, 185–228. https://doi.org/10.1215/03616878-4303507

Pester, B. D., Cano, A., Kostecki, T., & Wurm, L. H. (2020). How do I help my partner in pain? Partners' helping behaviors are linked to lower pain and greater perceived validation during an experimental pain task. *Annals of Behavioral Medicine, 54*, 280–290. https://doi.org/10.1093/abm/kaz047

Prasad, K., McLoughlin, C., Stillman, M., Poplau, S., Goelz, E., Taylor, S., Nankivil, N., Brown, R., Linzer, M., Cappelucci, K., Barbouche, M., & Sinsky, C. A. (2021). Prevalence and correlates of stress and burnout among U.S. healthcare workers during the COVID-19 pandemic: A national cross-sectional survey study. *EClinicalMedicine, 35*, 100879. https://doi.org/10.1016/j.eclinm.2021.100879

Renner, L. M., Piescher, K. N., & Mickelson, N. L. (2023). Academic outcomes among children who experienced or were exposed to physical abuse. *Journal of Interpersonal Violence, 38*(3–4), 2510–2533. https://doi.org/10.1177/08862605221101185

Silvia, P. J. (2015). *Write it up: Practical strategies for writing and publishing journal articles*. American Psychological Association.

Suess, J. (2023, January 8). Capt. Symmes and his ridiculed theory reside in Hamilton. *The Cincinnati Enquirer*, 8A.

Vago, D. R., Gupta, R. S., & Lazar, S. W. (2019). Measuring cognitive outcomes in mindfulness-based intervention research: A reflection on confounding factors and methodological limitations. *Current Opinion in Psychology, 28,* 143–150. https://doi.org/10.1016/j.copsyc.2018.12.015

Wilke, D. J., Rakes, S., & Randolph, K. A. (2019). Predictors of early departure among recently hired child welfare workers. *Social Work, 64*(3), 188–197. https://doi.org/10.1093/sw/swz020

CHAPTER 8

How Do I Write the *Method* Section for My Manuscript?

What Basic Information Should the *Method* Section Provide?

The *Method* section has two purposes: "to provide enough information to allow the reader to judge the merit of the study and its conclusions, while also laying out a blueprint for the study to be replicated in the future" (Fox & Jennings, 2014, p. 137). A study's blueprint is its design. The *Method* section of a quantitative article must explain the design of the study. This approach can be direct and involve, for instance, a subheading of "Design." Another common approach is to use the four general subheadings that focus on specific aspects of the design:

>   Participants
>   Procedure
>   Measures
>   Data Analysis

In many ways, writing the *Method* section may seem easier than writing the Introduction because you basically will be discussing the design of your study and there are guidelines (subheadings) to assist in that effort. However, the journal, the type of article, the target audience, and the author's judgment about how to best present relevant material all shape the final decision on which subheadings to use. Although you may encounter journals that are rigid in the format they require, authors typically have freedom in the choice of headings they apply in the *Methodology* section. That is why it is important to decide early which journal you are preparing the manuscript to fit. Once that decision is made, you can then study three or four current issues of the journal or articles similar to the one you are planning on writing so that your manuscript conforms to the journal's style. (You may have heard this three times by now. Could it be that important?)

Further, those who are planning to submit quantitative manuscripts to psychology journals will especially want to review the *APA Publication Manual* (APA, 2020) or the article by Appelbaum et al. (2018) "Journal Article Reporting Standards for Quantitative Research in Psychology: The APA Publications and Communications Board Task Force Report." Those who are considering developing a qualitative, mixed-method, or meta-analysis type of manuscript should examine the Levitt et al. (2018) article "Journal Article Reporting Standards for Qualitative Primary, Qualitative Meta-analytic, and Mixed Method Research in Psychology: The APA Publications and Communications Board Task Force Report." Both articles provide much greater specificity than the more generic, broader social science framework presented here. The APA standards are often referred to as Journal Article Reporting Standards Quantitative Research Design (JARS-Quant) and Journal Article Reporting Standards Qualitative Research Design (JARS-Qual).

When starting to write your *Method* section, consider the questions that you might want answered as a reader of a study's design. Wouldn't you want to know if the authors will be conducting an experiment or a survey? If reporting a survey, did it employ a probability or a convenience sample? Were the participants a special subset of a population? A purposeful sample? What instruments were used to collect the data? What were the settings and locations where the data were collected?

This shouldn't be a lengthy list of questions. *Method* sections are not usually the longest part of a manuscript. The Applebaum et al. (2018) article contains a nice table showing topics you may want to address when discussing the design in your study.

As in the previous chapter and in this one and the following chapters, excerpts from mostly quantitative articles and a few from qualitative articles appearing in a variety of social science journals will be shared to show the wide variety in style and presentation. To comply with "fair use" of copyrighted materials, these excerpts are approximately 200 words in length or about two paragraphs. Readers who desire to see the paragraphs ahead or below the presented material are provided with the full reference for consulting that work themselves. The following two excerpts show how authors presented their designs.

Design

Here is an excerpt from a study entitled "Evaluating Seeking Safety for Women in Prison: A Randomized Controlled Trial" written by Tripodi and his colleagues (2019). Under the major heading of "Method," they applied the subheading "Design."

Design

This study employed an RCT design with an intended treatment-to-control allocation of 1:1 in order to meet the specific aims and test the hypotheses. A certified Seeking Safety facilitator delivered the intervention to the treatment group (two groups of Seeking Safety), and the control group did not receive Seeking Safety but continued treatment as usual. Treatment-as-usual programming included residential substance abuse, psychological services, mindful meditation, group intervention, and/or anger management. The treatment-as-usual programming does not include gender-responsive and trauma-focused interventions. Most women participated in treatment-as-usual programing before this study was implemented. Two members of the research team administered the scales at posttest and again 4 months after the intervention ended. The research team members who collected posttest and follow-up data did not know whether the women were in the treatment group or in the control group. (p. 282)

In the Tripodi et al. (2019) article, the authors followed the "Design" paragraph with other paragraphs under the subheadings of "Sample," "Recruitment and Screening," "Procedures," and "Measures."

In the same journal, a separate set of authors did not use the "Design" subheading but instead informed readers of the group research design used and under that heading incorporated their procedures. The authors, Young et al. (2022), entitled their article "Feasibility of Self-Guided Online Cognitive Behavioral Therapy for University Students During COVID-19."

One Group Pre–Posttest Design

A one group pre–posttest design with convenience sampling was adopted. This iCBT project was promoted to the university students who were studying a master program in counseling at a local university through emails and online class announcements. Those university students who gave their consent to participate in this research project were allocated to use the self-guided iCBT. Subjects were eligible to participate in this study if they: (i) aged between 18 or above years old; (ii) were currently studying a master program in counseling at a local university in Hong Kong; (iii) were accessible to any computer and smart phone; and (iv) had given informed consent. Outcome measures were assessed with standardized assessment tools at baseline (t1) and within 2 weeks after completing all the online modules of the self-guided iCBT (t2).The ethical considerations of this study were evaluated and approved by the Research Committee of the Hong Kong Baptist University. Written informed consent were obtained from all participants on the day of pre-treatment assessment. Data were collected between January 2020 and June 2021,and two cohorts of university students at a local university joined in the research. (pp. 899–900)

The authors' second paragraph under the *Method* section gave the time period of the data collection and the number of students in each of the two cohorts. The other subheadings under *Method* employed by the authors of this article were "Subjects' Characteristics," followed by "Outcome Assessment Tools," and then "Design of the Intervention."

Authors Wahler et al. (2022) in their article "Changing Public Library Staff and Patron Needs Due to the COVID-19 Pandemic" developed a paragraph under their major heading of "Method" to give a context and overview and then used two additional subheadings "Patron Survey," "Staff Survey," and to provide further details (but were not reproduced below).

Methods

A needs assessment of the Allen County (Indiana) Public Library system was conducted by the Indiana University School of Social Work in late 2020 and early 2021. This is a large library system with 14 branches located in a metropolitan area of a Midwestern state. The needs assessment consisted of a staff survey and a patron survey and was originally conducted to examine psychosocial needs of library patrons from the perceptions of both staff and patrons. Because of the timing of the surveys in November of 2020 (staff survey) and February of 2021 (patron survey), questions about COVID-19 were included to examine how the pandemic had impacted patrons' needs and staffs' job duties. Because of the focus of this article, only data from the COVID-related questions of the staff and patron surveys are included in this analysis. Procedures for both surveys were considered exempt by the university's Institutional Review Board since the original data collection was done for program improvement purposes rather than research and no identifying information was collected. (p. 51)

When writing the *Method* section, keep in mind that readers, peer-reviewers, and the editor are expecting to learn about the generalizability of the findings. Give good attention to contextual details about the population of interest, the construction of the sample, how participants were recruited, the setting, and what information was collected. (It might help to consider the who, what, when, where, and why journalism questions.) This information would be necessary for anyone wanting to replicate your study.

Participants

The way participants were recruited or selected is important to describe in the *Method* section, and many authors provide this information under the subheading of "Participants." Your readers will want to know who these participants are. How was the sample in your study composed? What decisions were made relative to excluding or including participants? Of those eligible for participation, how many or what percent chose not to participate?

Under this subheading one normally describes the demographic characteristics of the sample (e.g., sex, ethnicity, age), and any other specific characteristics (e.g., sophomore and juniors in high school English classes). You will need to disclose the final size of the sample or samples (if there is more than one). If you have more than one sample, you should discuss how similar or dissimilar they are, especially if different processes were used to construct the samples (e.g., if one sample was randomly selected from a larger population creating a probability sample and the other was a small nonprobability convenience sample). How were the samples formed or developed? Similarly, it is important to report the number of participants responding (the achieved sample) as well as the number invited to participate (the intended sample) so that response rates can be computed. Specific journals may expect a report on the study's power. Also, indicate the dates associated with the data collection.

The *Participants* subheading may include a brief description of the design to explain how the participants were collected, as we will see next in the Studts et al. (2019) article entitled "Fatigue and Physical Activity: Potential Modifiable Contributors to Parenting Sense of Competence."

> *Participants*
>
> Participants were recruited from a university-based pediatric primary care clinic waiting room. Eligible participants were age 21 years or older, able to read and write English, and the parent (or other primary caregiver) of a child between the ages of 3 and 5 years. Parents of children with developmental delay, autism, or debilitating neurological conditions were excluded. From November 2012 through March 2014, a trained research assistant approached all parents in the clinic waiting room on various days of the week and screened them for eligibility. Eligible parents were invited to

participate, and those who were interested and willing provided written informed consent. A total of 195 parents participated in the parent study, with a 94% response rate among potential participants who were screened as eligible. In cases in which there were two or more eligible children in a household, parents were asked to select the eligible child with the most recent birthday, to minimize selection bias. For the current study, analyses included only female primary caregivers with complete data for measures of parenting sense of competence, child behavior problems, fatigue, and physical activity level (N = 137). Participants will be referred to as "mothers," although 9% were related in other ways to the target child (i.e., grandmothers, stepmothers, foster parents, and kinship caregivers). (pp. 2902–2903)

This one long paragraph was followed by a *Procedure* section of two paragraphs, a *Measures* section of six paragraphs, and then the *Results* section.

An example of participants from a qualitative study comes from "'Home Is Where Your Root Is': Place Making, Belonging, and Community Building among Somalis in Chicago" (Magan & Padgett, 2021).

Study Participants

A total of 15 in-depth interviews were conducted with Somalis who arrived in the United States through U.S. refugee resettlement programs. All study participants met the eligibility criteria, including that they self-identified as Somali, were admitted to the United States with refugee status, had been living in the United States for a minimum of five years, were at least 18 years of age, and were current residents of Chicago or its surrounding suburbs. Participant recruitment began in February 2017 at an East African community center. A snowball sampling method was used for recruitment of participants who were not affiliated with the center. As highlighted in Table 1, the participants were 10 men and five women between the ages of 19 and 70. The smaller number of female participants reflects their limited presence at the initial site of recruitment and in public spaces. In addition, several women showed interest in the study but did not meet the inclusion criteria of holding refugee status on entering the United States. (pp. 103–104)

While this paragraph is relatively short, the authors provide additional information on the participants' age, gender, initial place of resettlement, years in the United States, and occupation in their Table 1. Magan and Padgett (2021) also used two other subheadings ("Interviews" and "Data Analysis") to further expand the detail under their "Method" heading.

In the next example, participants are discussed along with the procedure in the same heading. The title of the article by Webster et al. (2019) is "Brief Report: Sex Differences in Substance Use, Mental Health, and Impaired Driving Among Rural DUI Offenders."

> Sample and Procedure
>
> A purposive sample of 118 individuals convicted of driving under the influence was recruited from three rural counties in Kentucky. Study eligibility included (a) being at least 18 years old, (b) convicted of DUI within the past 12 months in one of the three counties, and (c) residing in the same county in which they were convicted. Ninety percent of participants were recruited from district court houses in person immediately following their DUI conviction, while the remaining 10% were recruited through flyers posted throughout the community. DUI conviction information was verified through court records for participants responding to flyers. Eligible and interested participants completed a one-time, 90-minute confidential research interview with a trained interviewer either in person (61%) or over the telephone (39%). Participants' responses were protected by a federal Certificate of Confidentiality, and they received $25 for their participation. All study procedures were approved by the University Institutional Review Board. (p. 405)

Webster et al. (2019) follow their *Sample and Procedure* section with the additional subheadings under "Method of Measures" and "Analytic Plan."

Procedures

This major subheading refers to the procedures used to collect the data. For example, were participants emailed questionnaires or personally interviewed? If pretests and posttest were employed, where were they administered, and when? This section needs to be detailed enough that readers can understand how the data were collected and if there were any situations that might have resulted in unplanned bias in the study. You don't have to write a manual; however, be succinct without losing any critical details.

Hearn et al. (2022) in "Counselors' Attitudes Toward Psychedelics and Their Use in Therapy" describe their survey of counseling professionals in one long paragraph under the subheading "Procedures."

Procedures

This study was part of a broader project, which included the current study designed to explore counselors' attitudes toward psychedelics and their use in therapy, as well as a confirmatory component designed to the roles of religiousness and spirituality in predicting these attitudes. To be eligible for participation, respondents had to be over the age of 18 and self-identify as a member of the counseling profession in the United States, including masters' and doctoral students, professional counselors, and counselor educators. Recruitment took place between August and September of 2020 and was intended to target practicing counselors, counselor educators, and counseling students. We contacted licensing boards in all 50 states to request email lists of counselors and received lists from Ohio and Wyoming. During this time, we posted an initial call for participants on CESNET (http://www.cesnet-l.net/), emailed 500 randomly selected counselors once from the lists provided by Ohio and Wyoming state boards, and sent an email to 344 CACREP-approved masters' program faculty chairs requesting they distribute the survey among faculty and students. We repeated our call on CESNET and emailed an additional 500 randomly selected counselors 1 and 2 weeks after initial recruitment began to minimize overrepresentation from professional counselors. After these procedures, we received 250 responses and 223 complete surveys. We then ceased data collection because the priori power analysis used to design the confirmatory component of this project suggested we needed 141 participants to detect medium effects using $\alpha = 0.01$. (p. 367)

Again, various subheadings may be used as in the following example by Franz et al. (2022) in their article "Digital Bibliotherapy as a Scalable Intervention for Suicidal Thoughts: A Randomized Controlled Trial." After their subheading of "Participants," they used "Trial Design" to explain their randomized controlled trial.

Trial Design

Five hundred twenty-eight participants were randomized into either the treatment (n = 266) or waitlist control (n = 262) condition and provided data. As described in greater detail below, during the 14-day trial period participants in the treatment condition read one suicide narrative per day and responded to daily surveys assessing constructs of interest, while participants in the control condition completed daily surveys only. A total of 293, treatment condition n = 150 [56.4%]; control condition n = 143 [54.6%], participants responded to a 2-week follow-up survey. After the follow-up period, participants originally assigned to the waitlist control condition received the treatment, i.e., crossover; n = 194 [74.0%] participants provided data. Baseline group-level characteristics are presented in Table 1. Participants were compensated by being entered into a raffle for one of two $250 checks. Participants were eligible for the raffle if they completed at least 75% of the daily surveys, and each eligible participant was given one entry into the raffle for each survey response they provided. All trial procedures were approved by the Harvard University Institutional Review Board (IRB19-0843). (p. 628)

Under their "Procedure" heading, Pachankis et al. (2022) used the subheading of "Recruitment and Screening." After that, they also used the following subheadings: "Study Design" and "Training Intervention."

Recruitment and Screening

All study procedures were approved by the Yale University Human Subjects Committee and preregistered on clinicaltrials.gov (Record NCT04559698). From September to October 2020, we recruited participants through an online flyer emailed to listservs of mental health providers working at CenterLink-affiliated LGBTQ community centers. CenterLink is an international nonprofit organization consisting of over 270 member LGBTQ community centers in the U.S., Canada, Australia, China, and Uganda. The study trainers also held an informational webinar in October 2020 to offer mental health providers at CenterLink-affiliated LGBTQ community centers the opportunity to learn more about the LGBTQ-affirmative CBT training and this study. Participants completed a brief online screener on Qualtrics to confirm the following eligibility criteria: (a) Age 18 or older; (b) fluent in English; (c) licensed or unlicensed mental health provider (e.g., clinical/counseling psychologist, predoctoral psychology intern, counselor, martial and family therapist, social worker, crisis counselor, third-year or greater graduate practicum student/extern in a mental health training program); and (d) currently practicing in or formally affiliated with a CenterLink-affiliated LGBTQ community center, confirmed by a CenterLink director. All mental health providers received emails confirming their eligibility to participate in the LGBTQ-affirmative CBT training. (p. 586)

Measures

Measures is the subheading that describes the instruments used to collect your data. If they are previously published and validated measures, then you would identify the original study (author, year) briefly describing their reliability and validity (the psychometrics), how many items they contained, and the response set. Typically, two or three items from the instrument are presented to help the reader grasp the presentation style. If you have created original instruments to measure a behavior, attitude, or knowledge, then you will probably need to give more information about how the items were created, examined, tested, and so forth—in addition to internal consistency coefficients, factor analyses, or other forms of validity (e.g., test-retest).

Parnaby and Broll (2020) follow that convention in their article, "After 10-7: Trauma, Resilience and Satisfaction with Life Among Retired Police Officers." [Note: The police radio code 10-7 indicates "out of service."]

> Measures
>
> *Dependent variable.* Rather than inferring participants' well-being on the basis of self-reported symptoms, participants subjectively assessed their global well-being (Diener et al., 2009). Police retirees' satisfaction with life was measured using Diener et al.'s (1985) well-validated Satisfaction with Life Scale (SWLS). The SWLS is a general measure of life satisfaction that consists of five items measured on a seven-point scale, with higher scores indicating greater life satisfaction ($\alpha = 0.876$). Sample items include "In most ways, my life is close to ideal" and "If I could live my life over, I would change almost nothing."
>
> *Independent variables.* In total, two exogenous variables were used to capture different dimensions of trauma exposure. Weiss et al.'s (2010) Critical Incident History Questionnaire (CIHQ) measured experiences of on-the-job trauma. The CIHQ is a 34-item index of cumulative exposure to traumatic incidents among police officers that captures common (e.g., encountering the body of a deceased person) and rare (e.g., making a mistake that contributed to the injury or death of a colleague) experiences, with higher scores indicating exposure to more traumatic incidents ($\alpha = 0.905$). Traumatic experiences unrelated to policing were measured using the Brief Trauma Questionnaire (BTQ; Schnurr et al., 1999). The ten-item BTQ provides a complete assessment of the traumatic exposure diagnostic criteria (Criteria A) of the DSM-5. Sample events measured include having been seriously injured in a car accident and

fearing for one's life as a result of a life-threatening illness. Higher scores indicate exposure to more traumatic incidents. (pp. 232–233)

[Note that this study used a third measure, a 37-item Resilience Scale for Adults, which was discussed in a paragraph following the excerpt above.]

In their 2022 study, "Self-Care Skills to Prevent Burnout: A Pilot Study Embedding Mindfulness in an Undergraduate Nursing Course," Burner and Spadaro use two different instruments described in two paragraphs.

Measures

There were two outcomes for this pilot: stress and self-care. The authors anticipated a reduction in stress and an increase in self-care, and were also interested in the relationship, if any, between the two. To measure stress, the 10-item Perceived Stress Scale (PSS) (Cohen, 1994; Cohen et al., 1983) was chosen to evaluate how participants rate stress in response to various life situations over the past month. Items are measured on a five-point Likert scale ranging from 0 (never) to 4 (very often), and four items are reverse scored. Then scores are summed, with higher scores indicating higher levels of psychological stress (Cohen & Janicki-Deverts, 2012). Internal reliability of the PSS as measured by Cronbach's alpha varies from 0.78 to 0.91 (Cohen & Janicki-Deverts, 2012). The PSS was selected because of its ability to measure stress over a recent timescale and its high reliability and validity.

Self-care was measured using the 33-item Mindful Self-Care Scale (MSCS). The MSCS (Cook-Cottone & Guyker, 2017) assesses six factors: physical care, supportive relationships, mindful awareness, self-compassion and purpose, mindful relaxation, and supportive structure. Items are scored on a Likert scale according to behavior frequency over the past week: never (0 days), rarely (1 day), sometimes (2–3 days), often (4–5 days), and regularly (6–7 days) with only one item reverse scored. The MSCS is scored by summing the subscale means with higher scores correlated with higher total self-care behaviors. Cronbach's alpha of the MSCS is 0.89 (Cook-Cottone & Guyker, 2017). The MSCS was selected because it measures aspects of mindfulness as well as self-care. (p. 4)

Worthy et al. (2020) also report using two measures in their article, "Relationships Among Nursing Deans' Leadership Styles and Faculty Job Satisfaction Levels."

Measures

To explore research question 1, the Multifactor Leadership Questionnaire 5x-Short (MLQ-5x) instrument was used to measure the leadership style of the nursing deans. Developed by Bass and Avolio (1993), it operationalizes the FRL model constructs of laissez-faire, transactional, and transformational leadership styles. The MLQ-5x is a 45-item questionnaire with nine subscales:

> Five items in the transformational scale: idealized attributes, idealized behaviors, inspirational motivation, intellectual stimulation, and individual consideration.
> Three items in the transactional scale: contingent reward, management-by-exception (active), and management-by-exception (passive).
> One item in the laissez-faire scale.

The higher the scores are on individualized consideration and motivation factors (5-point Likert scale, ranging from 0 [*not at all*] to 4 [*frequently, if not always*]), the more the leader displays transformational leadership behaviors (Cronbach's a = .93; the nine subscales ranged from .74 to .90).

To explore research question 2, The Minnesota Satisfaction Questionnaire (MSQ) was used to measure faculty job satisfaction. In this 20-item short form developed by Weiss, Dawis, England, and Lofquist (1967), data are captured using a 5-point Likert scale ranging from 1 (*very dissatisfied*) to 5 (*very satisfied*). A higher score on the MSQ represents a higher level of job satisfaction. The 20 questions were categorized into three subscales: general satisfaction (two questions; α = .93), intrinsic satisfaction (e.g., being challenged by your work, recognition, responsibility; 12 questions, α = .88), and extrinsic satisfaction (e.g., monetary compensation, awards, fringe benefits; six questions, α = .87). (p. 70)

Data Analysis

This component in your *Method* section may be the briefest of them all, as it addresses your analytic strategy and inferential statistics used. Although, more complex analyses tend to require longer descriptions—especially if there might be some questions about the statistical procedures used. However, the *APA Publication Manual* (2020) suggests that authors "do not review basic concepts and procedures or provide citations for the most commonly used statistical procedures" and that authors should "assume readers have a professional knowledge of statistical methods" (p. 87). If missing data is an issue, readers will want to know how it was addressed. Effect sizes will often be expected, as well as the power and precision of samples.

Three examples are provided—one from a qualitative journal and two from a quantitative journal.

Wahman et al. (2022) have published a qualitative article entitled, "'No Intervention, Just Straight Suspension': Family Perspectives of Suspension and Expulsion"

> *2.7. Data Coding and Analysis*
>
> The procedures for data coding and analysis occurred in several steps. First, data were transcribed using a paid transcription service. Second, using the constant-comparison method and open and axial coding, researchers identified codes, categories, and themes that emerged from the data. Third, the first and second authors separately completed line-by-line coding of the transcript to uncover underlying meaning of participants' experiences. Line-by-line coding was completed using paper and pen, as well as Microsoft Word. By highlighting important quotes from participants' experiences, codes were developed. Fourth, the individual codes were then grouped into categories and synthesized into six themes. Next, common themes were analyzed to identify meaningful patterns and/or categories. Discrepancies in data codes were reviewed and discussed until consensus was reached. In addition, triangulation techniques were employed to compare our findings to existing literature. Finally, to establish reliability, operational definitions were created to define themes. The first author and a graduate student in Public Health coded 30% of the data and 90% agreement was reached. Reliability was calculated by dividing the total number of agreements by the number of agreements plus disagreements and multiplying by 100. (p. 4)

The excerpt from the Ruff et al. (2022) article "Preliminary Examination of A Home Within Psychotherapy with Clients with a History of Foster Care" provides an example of quantitative data analysis from a series of conducted interviews.

> *4.3. Data Analyses*
>
> Preliminary analyses included a descriptive summary of the sample, examination of the distribution of the outcomes, screening for outliers, and examination of missing data. We then used general linear models, estimated with SPSS (version 26), to examine change in the study

outcomes. Outcomes included therapist reports of their client's mental health and social functioning including depression, anxiety, conduct problems, perpetration of aggression/violence, peer relationship problems, and cohabitation relationship problems. One repeated measures analysis of variance (ANOVA) model was specified for each outcome and each model specified a within-subject time factor, defined with two variables, the baseline and exit measure of the outcome. Models also adjusted for effects associated with the client's baseline age and length of treatment. The within-subject time factor was evaluated to determine whether significant changes were observed in the outcomes from baseline to exit. We provide eta-square (η^2) estimates, following the convention 0.01 small, 0.06 medium, and 0.14 large (Cohen, 1988), as an effect size measure for change in the study outcomes. To protect against Type-I errors, we report, and interpret for statistical significance, the Benjamini-Hochberg false discovery rate adjusted p-value (Benjamini & Hochberg, 1995).

The third data analysis excerpt comes from Ickes et al. (2020) in their article entitled "Truth® Ads, Receptivity, and Motivation to Use or Quit Tobacco Among College Students."

Data analysis

Descriptive statistics (means and standard deviations or frequency distributions) were used to summarize sociodemographic characteristics of the study sample. Repeated measures analysis of variance (RM ANOVA) was used to compare receptivity across the four ads; post hoc comparisons were accomplished using the Fisher's least significant difference pairwise method. Generalized estimating equation (GEE) modeling was used to compare motivation to use/quit tobacco across the ads. Multiple linear regression models assessed relationships between sociodemographic characteristics and receptivity to each ad. Logistic regression determined associations between sociodemographic characteristics and motivation to use/quit tobacco for each ad. All data analysis was conducted using SAS, version 9.4, with an alpha level of 0.05 throughout. (p. 368)

Do I Have to Use the Subheadings Typically Used in the *Method* Section?

Readers, I suspect you have noticed that under the "typical" subheadings of *Participants, Procedures, Measures,* and *Data Analysis* authors creatively used various other subheadings to communicate some aspect of the methods they employed. Don't let these variations on a theme trouble you. As these excerpts show, there is no single "correct way" to describe the component headings under the *Method* section. In this small sample of articles, *Participants* as a subheading often was combined with terms like "Recruitment" and "Procedure" and contained important information about the study. Remember to always be familiar with the journal where you are planning to submit your manuscript as exceptions to the "no single correct way" statement will surely be discovered. Indeed, Fox and Jennings (2014) have written, "The methodology section is often tailored to the unique features and individual needs of the study and the intended audience" (p. 138).

The good news from this sample of articles is that what seems to be most important is the clarity of the description in one's subheadings. Perhaps editors are happy to see the creativity in the subheadings as long as they flow naturally from the organization of paragraphs supporting a topic. To conclude this chapter and refresh your memory, here are the variations found in the 15 articles where excerpts were taken (Table 8.1):

TABLE 8.1 Listing of Subheadings Found in a Sample of Articles' Method Section

Participants
Demographic Characteristics
Sample
Sample and Procedure
Sampling and Recruitment
Study Participants
Study Participants and Recruitment
Study Procedure and Sample
Subject Characteristics
Procedures
Data Collection Procedures
Interview Procedures
Recruitment and Screening
Trial Design
Measures
Instrument Selection and Development
Measures
Outcome Measures
Study Outcomes
Data Analysis
Analysis
Analytic Plan
Analyzing the Focus Group Data
Data Coding and Analysis

Scientists ... proceed by common sense and ingenuity. There are no rules, only the principles of integrity and objectivity, with a complete rejection of all authority except that of fact.

Joel H. Hildebrand, winner of virtually every major prize in the field of chemistry, except the Nobel Prize

CHAPTER 8 HOW DO I WRITE THE *METHOD* SECTION FOR MY MANUSCRIPT? **147**

Your Turn 8.1

Don't be overwhelmed by the demands of the *Method* section. Instead, focus on writing one component at a time. Once you've studied the journal in which you plan to submit and several articles of the type you plan to write, then begin drafting whichever section first that you believe to be easiest. [*Note: Feel free to replace the suggested subheadings that follow with any that you believe work better for your manuscript.*]

Participants

1. Draft a paragraph or two section describing the *Participants* in your study.

   Reread it two or three times, revising as necessary.

   _____

   _____

   _____

Procedure

2. Draft the *Procedure* section describing your data collection steps.

   Reread it two or three times, revising as necessary.

   _____

   _____

   _____

Measures

3. Draft the *Measures* section describing the instruments used in your study.

   Reread it two or three times, revising as necessary.

   _____

   _____

(continued)

Data Analysis

4. Draft the *Data Analysis* section describing what statistical or qualitative procedures you used to interpret your collected set of data.

   Reread it two or three times, revising as necessary.

When you are pleased with your *Method* section, give it to a colleague or mentor for feedback.

Make any necessary changes.

References

American Psychological Association (APA). (2020). *Publication manual of the American Psychological Association* (7th ed.). https://doi.org/10.1037/0000165-000

Appelbaum, M., Cooper, H., Kline, R. B., Mayo-Wilson, E., Nezu, A. M., & Rao, S. M. (2018). Journal article reporting standards for quantitative research in psychology: The APA Publications and Communications Board task force report. *American Psychologist, 73*(1), 3–25. https://doi.org/10.1037/amp0000191

Burner, L. R., & Spadaro, K. C. (2022). Self-care skills to prevent burnout: A pilot study embedding mindfulness in an undergraduate nursing course. *Journal of Holistic Nursing: Official Journal of the American Holistic Nurses' Association*, 8980101221117367. https://doi.org/10.1177/08980101221117367

Fox, B., & Jennings, W. G. (2014). How to write methodology and results section for empirical research. *Journal of Criminal Justice Education, 25*(2), 137–156. http://dx.doi.org/10.1080/10511253.2014.888089

Franz, P. J., Mou, D., Kessler, D. T., Stubbing, J., Jaroszewski, A. C., Ray, S., Cao-Silveira, V. B., Bachman, S., Schuster, S., Graupensperger, D., Alpert, J. E., Porath, M., & Nock, M. K. (2022). Digital bibliotherapy as a scalable intervention for suicidal thoughts: A randomized controlled trial. *Journal of Consulting and Clinical Psychology, 90*(8), 626–637. https://doi.org/10.1037/ccp0000752

Hearn, B. G., Brubaker, M. D., & Richardson, G. (2022). Counselors' attitudes toward psychedelics and their use in therapy. *Journal of Counseling & Development, 100,* 364–373. https://doi.org/10.1002/jcad.12429

Ickes, M. J, Butler, K., Wiggins, A.T., Kercsmar, S., Rayens, M. K., & Hahn, E. J. (2020). Truth® ads, receptivity, and motivation to use or quit tobacco among college students. *Journal of American College Health, 68*(4), 366–373. https://doi.org/10.1080/07448481.2018.1549559

Levitt, H. M., Bamberg, M., Creswell, J. W., Frost, D. M., Josselson, R., & Suárez-Orozco, C. (2018). Journal article reporting standards for qualitative primary, qualitative meta-analytic, and mixed method research in psychology: The APA Publications and Communications Board task force report. *American Psychologist, 73*(1), 26–46. https://doi.org/10.1037/amp0000151

Magan, I. M., & Padgett, D. K. (2021). "Home is where your root is": Place making, belonging, and community building among Somalis in Chicago. *Social Work, 66,* 101–110. https://doi.org/10.1093/sw/swab007

Pachankis, J. E., Soulliard, Z. A., van Dyk, I. S., Layland, E. K., Clark, K. A., Levine, D. S., & Jackson, S. D. (2022). Training in LGBTQ-affirmative cognitive behavioral therapy: A randomized controlled trial across LGBTQ community centers. *Journal of Consulting and Clinical Psychology, 90*(7), 582–599. https://doi.org/10.1037/ccp0000745

Parnaby, P., & Broll, R. (2020). After 10-7: trauma, resilience, and satisfaction with life among retired police officers. *Policing: An International Journal.* https://doi.org/10.1108/PIJPSM-07-2020-0125

Ruff, S. C, Linville, D., Clausen, J. M., & Kjellstrand, J. (2022). Preliminary evaluation of a home within psychotherapy with clients with a history of foster care. *Children and Youth Services Review, 143,* 106674. https://doi.org/10.1016/j.childyouth.2022.106673

Studts, C. R., Pilar, M. R., Jacobs, J. A., & Fitzgerald, B. K. (2019). Fatigue and physical activity: Potential modifiable contributors to parenting sense of competence. *Journal of Child and Family Studies, 28*(10), 2901–2909. https://doi.org/10.1007/s10826-019-01470-0

Tripodi, S. J., Mennicke, A. M., McCarter, S. A., & Ropes, K. (2019). Evaluating seeking safety for women in prison: A randomized controlled trial. *Research on Social Work Practice, 29*(3), 281–290. https://doi.org/10.1177/1049731517706550

Wahler, E. A., Spuller, R., Ressler, J., Bolan, K., & Burnard, N. (2022) Changing public library staff and patron needs due to the COVID-19 pandemic. *Journal of Library Administration, 62*(1), 47–66. https://doi.org/10.1080/01930826.2021.2006985

Wahman, C. L., Steele, T., Steed, E. A., & Powers, L. (2022). "No intervention, just straight suspension": Family perspectives of suspension and expulsion. *Children and Youth Services Review, 143,* 106678. https://doi.org/10.1016/j.childyouth.2022.106678

Webster, J. M., Staton, M., & Dickson, M. F. (2019). Brief report: Sex differences in substance use, mental health, and impaired driving among rural DUI offenders. *American Journal of Addiction, 28*(5), 405–408. https://doi.org/10.1111/ajad.12920

Worthy, K., Dawson, R. M., & Tavakoli, A. S. (2020). Relationships among nursing deans' leadership styles and faculty job satisfaction levels. *Journal of Nursing Education, 59*(2), 68–75. https://doi.org/10.3928/01484834-20200122-03

Young, D. K. W., Carlbring, P., Ng, P. Y. N., & Chen, Q. J. (2022). Feasibility of self-guided online cognitive behavioral therapy for university students during COVID-19. *Research on Social Work Practice, 32*(8), 898–911. https://doi.org/10.1177/10497315221087904

CHAPTER 9

How Do I Write the *Results* Section?

Should I Be Concise or Lengthy in Drafting This Section?

In this portion of the manuscript, the author will share with the reader the findings stemming from the purpose of the study and its research questions or hypotheses. To say this a bit more formally, you will be presenting the results of your research as a thoughtful, organized summary based on your statistical or other analysis of the data. According to Fox and Jennings (2014), "The main objective of the results section is to present and neutrally describe the analytical output and findings from the study, but not yet interpret them" (p. 138). The interpretation of the data—that is, the implications, uses of the findings, nuances, and explanations of why the data revealed what they did—are addressed in the *Discussion* section.

Over the years, I have had students miss this next point, although most readers should recognize it. Your task is not to discuss the *raw data* item by item or respondent by respondent (the exception might be in a small qualitative study), but rather like a parent robin, your role is to find the tasty morsels and begin digesting the earthworm before sharing it with those back in the nest.

In writing this part of your paper, it is better to be succinct—at least in your first draft, and then to go back and fill in the needed details. Don't start off thinking that you must burden the reader with every minuscule finding down to the subatomic level. Readers don't want to know about all the extra statistical procedures you conducted unrelated to your research questions. Sometimes when our original hunches don't pan out with statistically significant findings, it is tempting to conduct a "shotgun" or broad sweep of variables with our statistical software in an effort to find something—anything—that we can report as significant. The trouble comes when these findings are not directly connected to our original research question(s). Journal reviewers can usually detect these detours and will make comments regarding the purpose of the study. Not every finding has to be significant at .05. Insignificant findings can be important to report, too—as when they show that the intervention being studied didn't work.

It may feel overwhelming to start the *Results* section when you have multiple dependent variables or analyses to report—especially if you are trying to be concise. Three strategies to consider for addressing this issue:

1. Don't believe that every finding is equally important. They are not all equal. Some results are much more important (e.g., central to the purpose of your study) than others. These should receive most of your attention. What findings were you most pleased to discover?
2. Make a list of findings that you feel you must report by research question. You can discuss these in the same chronological order as they appear in your manuscript. Or, as you look at the findings associated with each question, did you conduct more analyses with one question than with others? If so, that will involve more complex reporting. Do you want to get it out of the way first, or address the questions with simpler results first? An argument could be made for either approach. If you have multiple research questions, you might want to organize your findings in terms of those that have definite implications or significant findings that you will be discussing more in the *Discussion* section and those that won't get much coverage in that section. If your *Results* section becomes much too long, give yourself permission to edit it to a more appropriate size after the first draft.
3. Start off by being as succinct as possible. What are the essential things you must report from your manipulation and examination of the data? Consider making a series of bullet points about the results of your analyses, then go back and expand with details that are missing and still needed. The *APA Publication Manual* (2020) recommends providing the statistical data (e.g., F ratios, t values, degrees of freedom, significance level, confidence intervals, effect sizes), but you should also explain the findings in everyday English for those who are not statisticians. If not addressed in the *Method* section, be sure to explain whether high mean scores indicate a high level of that concept or the reverse (as sometimes occurs). If descriptive data are shown in a table, there is no need to spend much space discussing it again in the narrative.

What Is the Problem With Providing Unnecessary Information?

The case for being succinct and not providing information overload can also be stated as three points:

First, most readers only want to know what was most important and interesting, and usually, what were the statistically significant findings. While findings that don't support hypotheses can be of strong interest to some readers, many readers only want to know about the results you identify as statistically significant—making them the "celebrities" of the study—the important findings. What are the important findings? These are the ones that make you want to grab your phone and call your partner or mother, and proudly gush, "Guess what I found today?" What are the findings that stand out or give you a sense of having confirmed something you believed or hoped you would find?

Second, journals—especially print journals—have space limitations because publishing a journal is expensive; the more pages you require to present your results, the greater the cost to the journal. Editors and reviewers will sometimes flatly reject manuscripts that are overly long and don't conform to the general page guidelines. Don't detour yourself and get off the path you planned to follow earlier in your manuscript.

Given a great data set, many researchers will conduct analyses on new questions that arise during the exploration of the data. Suppress your urge to report on these—put them aside for another paper. The longer your list of research questions or hypotheses, the longer your manuscript, and possibly the less interest you will have from readers, editors, and peer-reviewers. Most readers don't want to wade through waist-deep (and mind-numbing) minutia from all the computations you have conducted.

Third, greater clarity is often achieved when the writer is succinct and direct. Of course, you will know more about the jots and tittles of your data than almost all of your readers, that's okay—just realize you don't have to tell everything you know. Ask yourself if it is about as important to the reader as learning you skinned your knee one summer as a third grader; it's like getting stuck with a long-winded conversationalist who isn't interesting and never allows an interruption. If you are evaluating an intervention, get to the point. Make sure the reader exits your paper knowing that it did—or didn't make a difference. If the practitioners in your survey feel that they need additional continuing education on some emerging issue, don't camouflage your main results by throwing unrelated SPSS analyses into their path. Focus the reader on your main or central findings. Help readers to have a takeaway grasp of the meaning of your results—one they will retain after they quit reading the article.

Where Do I Start?

In the *Results* section, you are only describing the output of the analyses conducted, "No interpretation or extended discussion of the results is needed" (Fox & Jennings, 2014, p. 146). The *Discussion* section is where you can expand your thoughts about the implications and applications of the findings, as well as explain the limitations of the study. Start with the main, central findings—not incidental or secondary findings. Conventional wisdom suggests one should show the reader the forest before identifying individual trees. Guide the reader through the forest. While this is your adventure, you don't want to lose your reader by identifying every tree's species, genus, family, order, class, and phylum. Your path through the data should be clear and not require a GPS device or satellite cell phone. Don't mistake an animal's path through the forest for your well-marked (written) trail.

In this section, report the relevant results relating to your questions or hypotheses. Don't "cherry-pick" and present only the results that are supportive of your hypotheses. You need to be transparent and also present findings that do not support your hypotheses or theories.

Bem (2004) advises that a result should be stated and then its statistical significance "but in no case should you ever present a statistical test alone without interpreting it substantively" (p. 9).

How Do You Structure the *Results* Section?

Generally, the first segment of the *Results* section is to provide greater detail on the sample of participants. If the *Method* section didn't explain how they were recruited, then do it here. Describe their sociodemographic characteristics. This is necessary because the proposed sampling design may not have worked optimally and failed to identify participants with the desired characteristics. Does your sample resemble those reported in similar studies or are they different somehow? Are they older or younger, or a unique group? If they are unique, describe how they are different. Are any groups over or under-represented in your sample? Data showing the participants' ages, educational level, marital status, years employed, and so forth can often best be quickly digested in a table rather than in not-exciting-to-read paragraphs. Other results may also be best presented in a table as well.

If you have conducted a survey, be sure to report the response rate. The reader will want to know what proportion of possible participants provided data.

Empirical articles usually contain statistical analyses in their results sections. Whether you are writing for a psychological journal or not, you may want to refer to the JARS-Quant in the *APA Publication Manual* (2020). Many different approaches can be used to analyze the data, "no one approach is uniformly preferred as long as the method is appropriate to the research questions being asked and the nature of the data collected" (p. 87). This manual is useful for determining how much detail to incorporate in the description of the statistical model and information to include from inferential statistical tests and about confidence intervals, effect sizes, etc. Explanation of most statistical procedures is not needed, as it is assumed that "readers have a professional knowledge of statistical methods" (p. 87). Problems with statistical assumptions not being met, missing data, and other data issues should be reported. "Do not hide uncomfortable results by omission" (p. 86).

While you may be quite competent with massaging data and presenting numerical values that are meaningful to you and your team, remember that not all of your readers may have your level of statistical competence. Here is a guideline suggested by Bem (2004): "There is, however, no such thing as a pure results section without an accompanying narrative. You cannot just throw numbers at readers and expect them to retain them in memory until they reach the discussion. In other words, write the results section in English prose" (p. 7). Similarly, Silvia (2015) notes, "a Results section should read well and make sense even if the numbers were stripped out. A simple way to get a compelling Results section, in fact, is to write it without the numbers, revise the next until it sounds right, and then plug in the statistics" (p. 125).

> *Without data you're just another person with an opinion.*
>
> Edwards Deming, statistician. Best known for Total Quality Management

As has been done previously in this book's earlier chapters, excerpts have been provided of *Results* sections from several articles to show the reader how other writers have structured their findings.

The first example comes from Taylor et al. (2022) in an article entitled "Racial/Ethnic Variation in Family Support: African Americans, Black Caribbeans, and Non-Latino Whites." This is a quantitative study drawing upon the National Survey of American Life-Reinterview with a sample of 3,483.

RESULTS

Table 1 presents the distribution of sample characteristics and the study variables. The average age of the sample is 44 years and respondents have roughly 13 years of education and an average annual income of $42,000. Women comprise 58% of the sample and 47% of respondents are married/cohabiting, 25% are never married, while roughly a quarter of the sample are either separated, divorced or widowed. Regionally, more than half of respondents reside in the South, 20% in the Northeast, and roughly 13% reside in both the North Central and West regions. Half of the sample are non-Latino Whites (54%), 43% are African American, and 2% are Black Caribbean (all percentages are weighted). Mean levels of receiving assistance in the four areas (transportation, chores, finances, and illness) range from 2.43 (illness) to 3.12 (chores). Mean levels for providing assistance range from 2.21 (illness) to 2.84 (finances). The average level of family contact is 6.04 (at least once a week) and subjective family closeness is 3.64 (fairly close). Comparisons by race and ethnicity reveal that non-Latino Whites and Black Caribbeans have more years of formal education and are also more likely to be currently married than African Americans. Black Caribbeans had the highest average income ($52,480) and African Americans had the lowest ($35,281). There were no racial/ethnic differences in family contact or subjective family closeness, but African American and Black Caribbeans received and provided support more frequently than non-Latino whites. (pp. 1009, 1012)

Note that Table 1 (not reproduced here but running to more than a page and a third) presents a great deal of information on the socio-demographics of the participants, even though the text description runs almost to a full page. Sometimes this cannot be avoided. However, in the text of the article, the authors avoided repeating the statistically significant differences found when the groups presented in the table were compared using chi-square and F tests. In other words, the previous text is not a verbatim account of everything in the table.

The next paragraph in the article begins by speaking about Table 2—which is a regression analysis of four measures of instrumental support by race and ethnicity. The authors explain the comparison categories. The next paragraph presents and interprets the results of the regression analysis. Subsequent paragraphs summarize the information contained in Tables 2, 3, and 4.

After the characteristics of the participants in the sample have been communicated, authors typically begin to describe the findings from their statistical procedures and analyses on the major variables. One straightforward approach to this reporting is simply to follow the order of the research questions or hypotheses previously listed for the reader.

How Many Tables Are Too Many?

Note that while tables can save you from writing a lot of verbiage, use restraint and don't overdo it. Tables require a lot of space in manuscripts, and if it is necessary to have more than three or four tables, you might want to look through issues of the journal to see if the journal has published papers with as many tables as you are considering. Also, check the journal's Author's Guidelines to see if any limitations to the number of tables are identified there. (Admittedly, sometimes analyses can require lots of tables.)

Always make your tables conform to the standards expected by the journal. The *APA Publication Manual* (2020) can be consulted for the appropriate format and instructions for tables but also check the journal's Author Guidelines to be sure. The placement of the tables depends upon the journal you have selected. They can be embedded in the text or come at the end of the manuscript.

The next excerpt from Nilsen et al. (2022) entitled "Sleep in Adolescence: Considering Family Structure and Family Complexity" presents a one-paragraph description of those involved in the study with more details in their Table 1. The authors then go straight to the findings from their research questions.

> The first research question considers how sleep patterns vary by family structure and family complexity. Across all weekday and weekend sleep parameters, adolescents in JPC [Joint Physical Custody] had similar estimates to peers in nuclear families (all ps > .05). On weekdays, significantly shorter sleep duration (15–18 min) and later bedtimes (5–8 min) were observed in single- and stepparent families compared with nuclear families. Adolescents in single-mother and stepfamilies also had significantly higher sleep deficit (about 22 min) and slightly lower sleep efficiency. On weekends, later bedtimes and rise times (about 20 min) were observed for adolescents in single- and stepparent families. Only adolescents in stepparent families had significantly lower sleep duration (9 min) ...
>
> The second research question focused more specifically on sleep problems. The Baseline model in Figure 1 shows the bivariate associations between family structure, family complexity, and sleep problems. Living in JPC was associated with a higher risk of oversleeping and significantly higher risk across most sleep outcomes. ...
>
> The third research question focused on whether family SES (Model 2) and symptoms of depression (Model 3) attenuated the association between family structure, family complexity, and sleep problems. As a general pattern, introducing these covariates to the analyses only partly reduced the associated risk of sleep problems by family structure and family complexity, suggesting that these variables explained a small part of the differences between the groups. (pp. 1161, 1163)

In the Nilsen et al. (2022) article, three tables and two figures were part of the *Results* section.

The model of presenting findings in the order of the research questions is also followed in the qualitative article, "Friend, Foe, or Forget 'Em? The Quality of LGBTQ Adult Sibling Relationships" by Reczek et al. (2022). The following excerpt is an overview of the findings. At the end of this paragraph and excerpt, the authors then go into more detail, presenting subthemes and statements from participants.

Results

In response to our first research question, we found three primary ways LGBTQ adults characterize their sibling ties: solidary, conflictual, and tangential. First, respondents see siblings as solidary (n = 39), wherein the quality of the tie is high and the sibling has a positive impact through emotional, practical, and at times financial support and connection or support of their LGBTQ identity (including mitigating parents' anti-LGBTQ rejection); all sibling types identified in the data (i.e., full, step, half, chosen) were characterized in this way. Second, respondents framed their sibling relationships as conflictual (n = 52), wherein the adult sibling tie is of low quality and has a strong negative impact due to a sibling's problems, rejection of the respondents' LGBTQ identity, and conflicts within the family system; full siblings are characterized in this way, and transgender and gender expansive respondents more often categorized siblings as conflictual. Third, respondents described tangential (n = 58) ties, wherein relationship quality is absent as the sibling tie is emotionally, practically, and geographically distanced, because siblings have their own families, or because a close bond was never formed; full, step, and half siblings were characterized in this way while chosen siblings were not. Cisgender respondents, but very few transgender or gender expansive respondents, described siblings as tangential; bisexual respondents more often characterized siblings as tangential than solidary or conflictual. (pp. 422–423)

In the Reczek et al. (2022) article, the authors did not discuss their participants in the first part of the *Results* section but at the end of their *Methods* section where they refer readers to Table 1 containing categories describing those who were interviewed for the study.

In the qualitative article by Campbell et al. (2022) entitled "I Have to Hold It Together: Trauma in Law Enforcement Couples," the authors do not have multiple research questions, only one, "What is your lived experience, as a couple, of the impact of traumatic stress on your relationship?" (p. 1598). Thus, their findings are not presented in a serial fashion, one research question after another. The following excerpt is the first paragraph of their *Results* section. Subsequent paragraphs expand upon the three major themes they found and contain illustrative quotations "that highlight areas of agreeance and divergence within the couple's experience" (p. 1602).

Results

Three themes emerged that captured the essence of LE {Law Enforcement} couple experiences: (a) the stressful nature of the LE profession, (b) the impact of traumatic stress on the couple's relationship, and (c) protective factors and resilient coping characteristics. Couples described the stressful nature of the LE profession, including job demands, expectations of police culture, community relationships, and exposure to work-related traumatic events. Couples described exposure to a range of physically threatening ... and psychologically threatening traumatic events (e.g., the death of a fellow LEP, witnessing a suicide). Individual experiences of posttraumatic stress symptoms were determined by the type of work-related traumatic event (e.g., physical traumatic events or psychological traumatic events). After a traumatic event, couples experienced the impact of trauma in areas of communication, parenting, quality time, and commitment. Although relational impacts were an inevitable result of traumatic stress, LE couples reported that they activated resilient coping characteristics centered around intentionally processing the emotional distress of the LE profession, sharing with other LE couples, prioritizing time as a couple, and attending therapy. LE couples described how they purposefully activated resilient coping characteristics when they recognized the detrimental impact of less resilient coping strategies (e.g., LEP "shutting down" emotionally and disengaging from the couple relationship, leading the LEP spouse feeling resentful toward the LEP). Couples described how enacting resilient couple characteristics enabled them to create meaning out of their experiences with traumatic stress and ultimately offset its impact. (p. 1602)

What Other Suggestions Are There for Writing the *Results* Section?
- Double-check your calculations; make sure you incorporate the latest results, not an earlier version that was inaccurate. Verify that the numerical values in your tables agree with your narrative.
- Don't overgeneralize. Remember that data coming from a sample might have severe limitations and may not be representative of a whole population or even of other groups.
- If you are using sophisticated statistics, you might be well-advised to have someone who is knowledgeable about that type of procedure to read your written interpretative narrative. If you are doing

- simpler correlational analyses, you can't claim a causal relationship. Don't use the term "proof."
- If you have conducted bivariate analyses, don't overdo them and report too many of these. Be aware of possibly inviting in a Type I error.
- Tables are a good way to present complex data. Before creating a table, however, consider whether it is necessary. Fewer tables are generally better digested than multiple tables. When you have tables reporting data, don't duplicate and report every detail again in your narrative. Summarize and present what is most important.
- Since you have already conducted the analyses, make sure that you have used past tense all the way through this section.
- Don't get in such a big hurry that you fail to do a close reading of your final draft from start to finish.
- "Do not review basic concepts and procedures or provide citations for the most commonly used statistical procedures. If, however, there is any question about the appropriateness of a particular statistical procedure, justify its use by clearly stating the evidence for the robustness of the procedure as applied" (APA, 2020, p. 87).
- If you need help in deciding how much of the technical stuff to include in this section (e.g., the magnitude or value of the test statistics, a rounded p value, or the exact p value), particularly if writing for a psychology journal, consult the *APA Publication Manual*.
- Always try to find an article presenting an analysis or data the way you are considering in the journal to which you are planning to submit. The "model" might prevent you from making a mistake like reporting percentages without identifying the number of cases involved, and so forth.
- When you have conducted multiple analyses, even though you present the results separately, it can be a good idea to briefly remind the reader of the key findings at the end of the *Results* section. However, when the findings are very specific and each can be addressed in a short paragraph, overall summaries may not be required—particularly in short articles. See, for instance, Miller et al. (2018) "Self-compassion among child welfare workers: An exploratory study." The authors present results under the subheadings of self-compassion scores, group differences, relationships for professional variables, and significant predictors each in single paragraphs before launching into the *Discussion* section. You can also see this in the Wahler et al. (2022) article discussed in the last chapter.

Your Turn 9.1

Draft your *Results* section by describing the participants in your sample. See if you can keep this description to about a paragraph. However, if you are examining the data by several key independent or predictor variables (e.g., age group, employment status, marital status), try your hand at creating a table in the format used by the journal and then write a summary paragraph. When you are satisfied with the draft, have a colleague, writing companion, or mentor review it and provide you with feedback.

_____

_____

_____

_____

Your Turn 9.2

Now it is time to begin presenting your findings. Let's begin by starting with your first research question or hypothesis. What did you find? See if you can summarize your findings in one or two paragraphs per question or hypothesis. (No fair writing 350-word paragraphs.) Then, at the end, summarize what you have learned in this study based on the data—no implications or speculation.

_____

_____

_____

_____

Once you have completed this draft and have addressed all research questions or hypotheses, then read it carefully to see if you need to add any important details or if you need to be less detailed. Once you have read this draft three or four times, have a colleague, writing companion, or mentor review it and provide you with feedback.

_____

_____

_____

_____

References

American Psychological Association (APA). (2020). *Publication manual of the American Psychological Association* (7th ed.). https://doi.org/101037/0000165-000

Bem, D. J. (2004). Writing the empirical journal article. In J. M. Darley, M. P. Zanna, & H. L. Roediger III (Eds.), *The compleat academic: A career guide* (185–219). American Psychological Association. https://psychology.yale.edu/sites/default/files/bemempirical.pdf

Campbell, A. R., Landers, A. L., & Jackson, J. B. (2022). I have to hold it together: Trauma in law enforcement couples. *Family Relations, 71*, 1593–1618. https://doi.org/10.1111/fare.12661

Fox, B., & Jennings, W. G. (2014). How to write methodology and results section for empirical research. *Journal of Criminal Justice Education, 25*(2), 137–156. http://dx.doi.org/10.1080/10511253.2014.888089

Miller, J. J., Lee, J., Benner, K., Shalash, N., Barnhart, S., & Grise-Owens, E. (2018). Self-compassion among child welfare workers: An exploratory study. *Child and Youth Services Review, 89*, 205–211.

Nilsen, S. A., Bergström, M., Sivertsen, B., Stormark, K. M., & Hysing, M. (2022). Sleep in adolescence: Considering family structure and family complexity. *Journal of Marriage and Family, 84*(4), 1152–1174. https://doi.org/10.1111/jomf.12844

Reczek, R., Stacey, L., & Dunston, C. (2022). Friend, foe, or forget 'em?: The quality of LGBTQ adult sibling relationships. *Journal of Marriage and Family, 84*(2), 415–437. https://doi.org/10.1111/jomf.12821

Silvia, P. J. (2015). *Write it up: Practical strategies for writing and publishing journal articles*. American Psychological Association.

Taylor, R. J., Skipper, A. D., Cross, C. J., Taylor, H. O., & Chatters, L. M. (2022). Racial/ethnic variation in family support: African Americans, Black Caribbeans and non-Latino Whites. *Journal of Marriage and the Family, 84*(4), 1002–1023. https://doi.org/10.1111/jomf.12846

Wahler, E. A., Spuller, R., Ressler, J., Bolan, B., & Burnard, N. (2022). Changing public library staff and patron needs due to the COVID-19 pandemic. *Journal of Library Administration, 62*, 47–66. https://doi.org/10.1080/01930826.2021.2006985

CHAPTER 10

How Do I Write the *Discussion* Section?

What Is the Purpose of the *Discussion* Section?

The purpose of the *Discussion* section is to provide the reader with the interpretations and explanations of your findings. The APA (2020a) delivers this description:

> The Discussion is your opportunity to evaluate and interpret the results of your study or paper, draw inferences and conclusions from it, and communicate its contributions to science and/or society. ... In the Discussion section of a research paper, you should evaluate and interpret the implications of study results with respect to your original hypotheses. It is also where you can discuss your study's importance, present its strengths and limitations, and propose new directions for future research. In other types of papers ... the Discussion is where to summarize the key points or themes in your paper and reflect on previous statements and their broader connections.

How Do I Start the *Discussion* Section?

Start by summarizing the key points or themes in your study. This is what Silvia (2015) calls the "recap," and he advises authors, "In one or two paragraphs review the animating ideas from your introduction and summarize what you found" (p. 140). Again, this is a summary, not a detailed listing of every result or SPSS computation produced by your analysis, but your major and most salient findings. This summary should make clear whether your findings generally "support or nonsupport the hypotheses or answer the questions you first raised in your introduction" (Bem, 2004, p. 9). The same advice is also given in the *APA Publication Manual*: "Open the Discussion section with a clear statement of support or nonsupport for all hypotheses, distinguished by primary and secondary hypotheses" (APA, 2020b, p. 89). It is okay if your study does not have secondary hypotheses or if you have research questions instead of hypotheses. Heck, your study might just have a simple purpose.

You may feel that if readers actually did more than simply glance at the *Results* section, then beginning with a summary shouldn't be necessary. However, as a longtime educator, I know that many students (and perhaps many professionals as well) simply skip to the *Discussion* section to begin their serious reading. This saves them quite a bit of time and prevents struggling with all the tricky statistical maneuvers the study's authors presented in their tables. Thus, the summary is really quite important.

If your analyses were primarily statistical, translate the results into language accessible for students or others who may not have the same grounding or understanding of the numerical results. Keep your focus on the results that you have just finished outlining in the previous section. Don't bring in new findings that didn't appear earlier. If your findings are ambiguous or mixed, then you should offer an explanation.

Next, thoughtfully address the implications, the utility, of your findings. For instance, what do all the statistical probabilities of $p < .001$ actually mean or suggest for a practitioner? While the *Results* section concentrated on the question, *"What results have been obtained?,"* the focus of the *Discussion* section is on answering the questions, *"What is the importance of the results? What is the implication of the results obtained?"* (Lamanauskas, 2021, p. 6).

Hess (2004) has noted,

> No one has thought as long and as hard about your study as you have. As the person who conceived, designed, and conducted the study, the meaning of the results and their importance seem obvious to you. However, they might not be so clear for the person reading your paper for the first time. One of the purposes of the discussion is to explain the meaning of the findings and why they are important. ... Even if your findings are provocative, you do not want to force the reader to go through the paper multiple times to figure out what it means; most readers will not go to that effort and your findings will be overlooked, disregarded, and forgotten. (p. 1239)

Sayer et al. (2015) in an article entitled "Randomized Controlled Trial of Online Expressive Writing to Address Readjustment Difficulties Among U.S. Afghanistan and Iraq War Veterans" follows the advice given by Bem (2004) provided earlier, discussing the major findings and the evidence for support.

Discussion

Our primary hypothesis was partially supported. Writing expressively about the transition to civilian life was more effective than writing factually about veterans' issues in reducing physical complaints, anger, and psychological distress, but not more effective than factual writing in reducing PTSD symptoms, reintegration difficulty, social support, or life satisfaction. Expressive writing was more effective than no writing in reducing PTSD symptoms, anger, distress, reintegration problems, and physical complaints, and more effective than no writing in improving social support. It was not more effective than no writing in improving life satisfaction. Effects remained when we added baseline mental health treatment to the models. Consistent with Frattaroli's 2006 meta-analysis, the magnitude of the between group differences was small and expressive writing was equally effective for female and male veterans. (pp. 387–388)

Six paragraphs later, Sayer et al. (2015) encapsulate the implications of the research in a single paragraph.

Taken together, findings indicate that online expressive writing, a simple, resource-efficient intervention that can be implemented online without clinician involvement, may be a promising strategy for improving symptoms and functioning among combat veterans who experience reintegration difficulty. Attrition and small effect sizes should be considered in light of this intervention's low cost and accessibility. A better understanding of the mechanisms by which writing confers health benefits, which are currently poorly understood, may lead to strategies to magnify the beneficial effects of writing. (p. 389)

Should I Compare My Study's Findings to Previous Studies?

Yes, this is a good idea as it frames a context for the reader. Note that Sayer et al. (2015) in the first excerpt compared their findings to those of a meta-analysis by Frattaroli (2006). This helps to establish the credibility of your own study. Address the importance and implications of your findings, and compare your findings with those of comparable or related studies where possible.

Questions to consider: Are your findings similar to those of other studies? Do they boost the support for a novel hypothesis or theory? If they conflict with other studies, is it because of different instrumentation or methodology, a smaller or less representative sample? What explanations can you provide? Make sure the reader understands how your study is distinct from others or similar to them.

Here is another excerpt where the authors make a comparison to a previous study. This passage comes from an article entitled "Preventing Suicide Among Working-Age Adults: The Correlates of Help-Seeking Behavior." Ko et al. (2019) also quickly summarize their findings in the first paragraph of the *Discussion* section and then link their findings to previous research.

> *Discussion*
>
> Being male, being nonwhite, being employed full-time, having lower levels of mental health needs, and not having health insurance were associated with not seeking help. The present results also demonstrated the stages in which these factors affected help-seeking behavior among working-age adults.
>
> Working-age men with suicidal ideation are less likely to seek help than women of the same age group, and this gender disparity in help-seeking appears to start at the first stage of help-seeking: problem recognition (OR = 0.43–0.50). Results support a previous study using the NSDUH, [National Survey on Drug Use and Health] which demonstrated low mental health service utilization among men with suicide risk.[12,13,15] Recent study further reported that among suicidal adults who did not receive mental health treatment, men were less likely to feel the need for treatment.[14] Similarly, in this study, men were less likely to be found at a later stage in the help-seeking pathway, even with the same level of need, indicating a need for efforts to increase public awareness to increase help-seeking among men. (p. 5)

Should I Address Any Issues or Flaws in My Study?

Yes, but with a caveat. Issues or flaws in your study are known as limitations and are often addressed in the *Discussion* section. Limitations exist when the planned data collection procedures or potency of the intervention are affected—usually by something outside of the researcher's control. These are really important for the reader to know. For instance, in the previously cited Sayer et al. (2015) study, the authors state that while the study design called for participants to write 20 minutes a day on four different days, a sizable proportion of those in the expressive writing condition did not complete four writing sessions and thus did not get the full dose of the intervention.

When the design or methodology is compromised after the study begins, you have an obligation to report that. However, don't elevate minor issues into gigantic ones. For instance, in an email survey of several hundred people, if 15% bounce back because of flawed addresses, that is worth mentioning as a limitation. On the other hand, if you use surface mail for a survey of 100 former employees from your agency and two or three are returned for bad addresses, that is not of such magnitude as to be a limitation. (Although, it is fine to mention in the *Results* section that you achieved such a high response rate.)

Most quantitative research studies contain, toward the end of the *Discussion* section, a paragraph or so describing the limitations of the study. Don't worry about admitting to having a minor glitch. Most studies have something of this nature. Silvia (2015) suggests this strategy, "If you are aware of problems, get in front of them—don't make the reviewers ask you to discuss them. ... Sweeping your flaws under the bed never works. ... At the same time, don't go on and on about it. Readers use length as a cue to importance, so spending most of your discussion bemoaning your flaws and foibles sends the wrong message" (p. 146).

In this next brief article, we will see how the authors, de Moor et al. (2021), handle the limitations in their study entitled "Employment Outcomes Among Cancer Survivors in the United States: Implications for Cancer Care Delivery." You might notice that in this example the subheading "Limitations" was not used in the article. In fact, the article is a brief one (four pages) and uses no headings at all.

> These findings should be considered in the context of some limitations. Newly diagnosed survivors and those with advanced disease or more lethal cancers are underrepresented in household surveys. Thus, our study likely underestimates the impact of cancer on employment. MEPS [Medical Expenditure Panel Survey] does not capture cancer stage or treatment modality, so we were unable to explore employment outcomes by these factors. Because of the small sample size for most cancers, we were also unable to fully explore sociodemographic differences in employment at the level of individual cancer types. However, this study provides population level data about the prevalence of cancer-related employment changes in the United States, which complements previous work. (p. 642)

In a much longer article (22 pages) by Greenberg and Dillman (2023), the limitations are also situated in the *Discussion* section without a subheading. The following excerpt is taken from "Mail Communications and Survey Response: A Test of Social Exchange versus Pre-suasion Theory for Improving Response Rates and Data Quality."

A significant limitation of this study is that we did not have the budget to conduct cognitive interviews with respondents or other residents of the region about how they perceived the different design and communication elements of the survey. Focus groups with residents from the region, for example, may have been able to tell us if the design and communication elements were having the intended or the opposite effect. Therefore, we are left to mostly speculate on whether our operationalizations of pre-suasion (i.e., establishing privileged moments through magnetizers, mystery, etc.) were perceived as such from respondents. Further, we cannot be certain that some of the temporal aspects of Cialdini's theory were received in the intended order. Cialdini is explicit about the importance of creating a privileged moment (i.e., emphasizing the moment of influence just before asking a respondent to respond). While we assume people received the incentive and read the letter in full, the self-administered mode makes it hard to prove that ordering was received in the intended order. For example, potential respondents may have only skimmed sections of the letters—therefore missing what was intended to create a privileged moment. (pp. 19–20)

Should I Include Suggestions for Future Research?

In the *Discussion* section, many quantitative studies also include a brief passage making suggestions regarding the direction that future researchers may want to take who are investigating the same problem or using the same general approach. This can be a good way to make the best of any nagging issues encountered in your study. By providing ideas about how to reduce the attrition of respondents or stimulate interest in participation or recommending any number of possible ways to improve studies similar to yours, you'll sound experienced—giving the reader confidence in you and your study—and simultaneously help other researchers avoid the same problem(s) in their studies.

The danger and rewards of providing future research suggestions are these: First, Silvia (2015) recommends keeping the focus on the strengths of your study and says, "The worst way to do this is to compare your dowdy project to a sexy one that you'll probably never do" (p. 150). Don't review your study so critically that almost everything could be improved. Don't beg reviewers to reject your manuscript simply because of the things you learned in the process of conducting your study. A long laundry list will be treated just like a pile of sweaty gym clothes on the floor. Ugh. Who wants to be around all of that?

However, If you can make a substantive and pertinent suggestion or two that will benefit other researchers, your efforts may be rewarded by an increased number of citations. Silvia (2015) also notes there are "good times and places for describing future studies," such as when you have discovered "some intriguing new problems" (p. 150).

If your suggestions for future research include something you are seriously planning on doing in your next study, I see no reason to give that away to readers. Simply put, if you place these ideas in print and your article is quickly published, there is the possibility that someone else could move on to those suggestions before you. If you can make recommendations for a better way to study, measure, or improve some process, in a more generalized fashion that doesn't give others a head start on where you are heading, then go for it.

There's no firm rule on whether the paragraph on future research should come before or after limitations, but I generally like to see the limitations of one's study acknowledged first.

In the article by Macke et al. (2019) entitled "Outcomes for Black Students in Team-Based Learning Courses" a "Limitations" subheading is used, but future research is also addressed as well.

Limitations

There are several limitations to this study. First, no actual classroom observations were made. Actual observations may have provided a clearer picture of how peer interactions occur within the TBL pedagogy. Next, the low number of Black students in this study may have influenced the statistical tests. Only large effect sizes could be detected (Cohen, 1992), and the risk of making a Type II error is inflated. Next, there was no control for interactions outside of class. Peer evaluation scores may have been influenced by interactions outside the classroom environment. Finally, we assume that the instructors were all utilizing proper TBL techniques. There may be pedagogical fidelity issues resulting from instructors interpreting and using TBL differently. In response to these limitations, future research should include larger, more ethnically and geographically diverse samples. In addition, future studies should collect data that attempt to explain the findings from this study. These studies could involve either survey research or qualitative interviews or focus groups. One such future study may consider using TBL groups that consist predominantly of Black students to examine whether the trend in peer evaluation scores remains the same. This would help shed light on whether the lower peer evaluation scores are a result of being in the minority or the result of racial stereotyping. (p. 82)

You will find *Discussion* sections with the subheading "Limitations" used as well as those without. This is one of the topics that authors must decide for themselves. Limitations may be brief, but they also can be rather long. (Several examples I found at approximately 400 words were too long to wholly use as an excerpt without violating the fair use standards). When a good case can be made for a lengthy limitations description, then their own subheading makes sense.

Should I Have a "Conclusion" Subheading in My *Discussion* Section?

The answer to this question is that it depends. It depends on the journal where you are submitting and whether that is part of their standard template of expected manuscript components. Having a "Conclusion" heading allows readers (probably the same ones who just read your abstract) to skip to that part of your article and enlighten themselves with little effort. You might also get double duty out of it by using several of the same sentences in your abstract. It also formally concludes your article because what follows after the *Conclusion* are the references.

As seen in the next excerpt from Costa et al. (2022) "Microaggressions: Mega Problems or Micro Issues? A Meta-Analysis," conclusions do not have to be very long.

> CONCLUSION
>
> Much has been written about microaggressions in recent years, and a great deal of controversy surrounds the subject. This meta-analysis examined the relations between microaggressions and psychological well-being, physical health, job outcomes, and positive and negative coping, and it also examined what factors affected these relationships. We found that microaggressions were negatively associated with psychological well-being, physical health, and job outcomes and they were positively associated with positive coping. Typically, these effects did not depend on the type of microaggression being studied, the year in which the study was conducted, the publication status of the study, the occupation of the sample, or whether only members of stigmatized groups were included. Thus, microaggressive behaviors are detrimental across most individuals and contexts, and additional policies need to be implemented and actions taken to identify and reduce their prevalence. (p. 150)

Lawrence and Adebowale (2022) in "Adolescence Dropout Risk Predictors: Family Structure, Mental Health, and Self-Esteem" also had a brief, one-paragraph conclusion.

Conclusion

> Adolescence is a unique stage that predetermines the future of everyone who is fortunate to pass through it to the next stage of adulthood. Any behavior not checked during this stage will be difficult to control. Therefore, some of the behaviors that are allowed during childhood should be checked during adolescence to prevent abnormal behavior in adulthood. Several studies have confirmed that dropouts are less likely to perform expected behaviors to achieve their own serious development. This study established that family structure, mental health, and self-esteem were potent risk predictors of high school students' dropout risk among school-going adolescents. According to the finding of the study, family structure was the most risk factor, followed by mental health and self-esteem. Hence, the family structure is very crucial if the upsurge of school dropout that is bedevil the society will be reduced to bearable level or eradicated. (p. 131)

Note that the Lawrence and Adebowale (2022) article used separate headings for "Discussion of Findings," "Conclusion," "Implications of Findings," "Recommendations," and "Limitations." This was not a requirement of the journal; however, it makes it easy for the reader to zero in on the section quickly. In writing a draft of a *Discussion* section, use of these subheadings may help the author to stay focused. (They could be removed at the final draft stage.)

Authors Tracy et al. (2020) created the heading "Summary and Future Directions" for their article entitled "Cancer-Work Management: Hourly and Salaried Wage Women's Experiences Managing the Cancer-Work Interface Following New Breast Cancer Diagnosis."

> Summary and future directions
>
> Hourly wage women in our study were somewhat more likely than salaried wage women to report challenges managing cancer and work. ... Hourly wage women were also more likely than their salaried counterparts to leave their jobs altogether due to the demands of cancer treatment. Our study is the first we are aware of to examine differences in cancer-work management by job type–hourly vs salary. The differences that emerge indicate that at least at the beginning of treatment, the types of workplace supports that are beneficial differs between the two groups. Because hourly wage women were more likely to take unpaid time off and leave their job altogether, cancer treatment may put this group at a higher risk of financial stress over the course of treatment.

> Future research is needed to better understand the influence of occupational conditions on employment and cancer decision making of breast cancer survivors, financial stress and wellbeing, and employment outcomes. This study sets the foundation for future multi-variate analysis to examine direct and in-direct effect of job conditions on these stated outcomes. Data from the EMPOWER study will allow for this type of exploration and possibly form the basis for a larger study of cancer-work management among breast cancer patients in hourly and salary jobs. Likewise, understanding the interplay between the physical demands of cancer treatment, job conditions, and other factors that influence cancer-work management (e.g., provider supports) could help to identify key areas for interventions that might ease challenges experienced by survivors managing cancer and work. (pp. 14–15)

To wrap this section up, you have seen again how authors generally follow along using the traditional headings but at the same time have the freedom to devise subheadings that make sense organizationally in their particular manuscript. Yes, some journals have guidelines or templates that they expect to be followed using their defined headings. My guess, and I have no real data to support this, is that most journals are not terribly rigid in the actual headings or subheadings that authors use to identify the sections of their manuscripts.

What Questions May Arise When Writing the *Discussion* Section?

This last bit is a summary, but in case you missed one or more, here are points made in the chapter:

- You may wonder how many limitations should be mentioned. Conventional wisdom is that your *Limitations* section should not be longer than your Results. [That's a joke!] However, you really don't want to beat your own study into the ground. Mention the major issues, such as when samples don't turn out as expected, but as Bem (2004) advises, "Do not dwell compulsively on every flaw!" He says one should not make a "tortured attempt" to explain "every hiccup in the data" (p. 10).
- Those who wish to replicate your study do need to know about any major difficulties or challenges affecting the research design, data collection, and so forth. Your efforts should be transparent. Presenting study limitations is an ethical responsibility that supports

- the proper interpretation and generalization of the study's findings (Ross & Zaidi, 2019).
- When your study has several major limitations, you may want to follow that section by pointing out the strengths or contributions of your study (despite the flaws). I liked the way Macke et al. (2019) stated in the second paragraph of their Limitations, "Despite these limitations, this study still makes a valuable contribution to health literature" (p. 82). Don't be shy about stating the uniqueness of your findings or new ways of understanding the phenomenon being examined.
- Is making future research recommendations a cop-out? Not at all. Every study will have some limitations, and often in the course of a study, you will find a better way to measure, a different perspective or technique that could be useful for any of those conducting research in the same vein. New questions may also arise. Notice how many times future research or studies was mentioned (three times!) in the excerpt by Macke et al. (2019). Does it matter whether you call it future directions or future research? Probably not.
- *Discussion* sections may or may not contain subheadings; however, as an author, you need to keep in mind the points suggested in the quotation from the *APA Publication Manual* at the beginning of this chapter.

How Can I Be a Writing Mentor to Myself?

There are times in writing when you must put aside your most fervent hope or desire for publication. This may become apparent to you as you write the *Discussion* section. How so? Well, you have already collected the data, organized and written the *Introduction and Literature Review* sections, and finished the *Methods* section with no negative comments from your writing buddy or coauthor. However, in trying to find a way to discuss the clinical or practical implications of your findings, you draw a blank. You come to that godforsaken place because your primary research questions yielded nothing worth talking about. Your experimental approach didn't work. Even though you ran numerous analyses with different variables, there was nothing to hang your hat on. Even your mentor or writing partner sees little value in continuing with the existing findings. What do you do in that situation?

Four possibilities exist to salvage your work. You could separate the literature review from the rest of the paper, possibly expand it and try to reconfigure just that part of it into a different manuscript. Or you could try to find a conference where you have 10 to 15 minutes to present your study and where the focus might be more on your original intervention and how you developed it than on its trial or pilot study. The third option is to walk away, to not invest any more time in a manuscript that is not very likely to ever be published. A fourth approach is to swallow some of your pride and convert the draft into a "lessons learned" paper where you spend more time outlining what went wrong and suggest ways this topic can be better investigated in the future. (See the following textbox for examples of this type of writing.)

> *There is no such thing as failure. It's a life lesson for future.*
>
> Invajy (self-improvement blog)

You become a mentor to yourself when you are able to forget the work you have already put into it and objectively assess whether the weaknesses outweigh the strengths of the manuscript. It is possible to do this by thinking of yourself as a mentor and a colleague or student brings a manuscript (the very one in your computer) to you and asks your opinion regarding the possibility of it being published. If you have nothing of statistical, practical, or clinical significance to say, if you can't think of any implications you can honestly make, the best thing to do is to let it go. Be the mentor you would want. Before giving up, however, consult some others you trust. No need to rush to judgment. Perhaps put the manuscript aside for several days and consider it again?

Examples of Lessons Learned Articles

Douds, A. S., & Hummer, D. (2019). When a veteran's treatment court fails: Lessons learned from a qualitative evaluation. *Victims & Offenders, 14*(3), 322–343. https://doi.org/10.1080/15564886.2019.1595248

Flynn J. M. (2020). Mistakes made and lessons learned: A mid-career pediatric orthopaedic surgeon's journey to sustain energy and avoid burnout. *Journal of Pediatric Orthopedics, 40 Suppl 1*, S16–S21. https://doi.org/10.1097/BPO.0000000000001488

Hutchinson, K. (2018). *Evaluation failures: 22 tales of mistakes made and lessons learned*. SAGE Publications.

Kilburn, M. R., & Cannon, J. S. (2015). Home visiting start-up: Lessons learned from program replication in New Mexico. *Journal of Primary Prevention, 36*, 275–279. https://doi.org/10.1007/s10935-015-0392-5

Wells, T. (2020). Lessons learned from Georgia's 2010 Olmstead Settlement: The good, the bad, and the limitations of a Justice Department Olmstead Settlement. *Journal of Legal Medicine, 40*(1), 45–52. https://doi.org/10.1080/01947648.2020.1731334

Your Turn 10.1

Try your hand at drafting a *Discussion* section for your manuscript. When you have finished writing it, let it sit for a day or two so that you can read it again "cold." Revise as you read it the second time. If you are not happy with it, put it aside for another day. When you are finished revising, give it to your coauthor, mentor, or writing buddy for feedback.

_____

_____

_____

Overall, do you agree with the feedback? If you are not pleased with some of the comments, are you being too protective and defensive? Can you try to consider the criticisms objectively without taking them personally? Is there a second person you can consult?

_____

_____

_____

References

American Psychological Association. (APA). (2020a). APA style: Discussion phrases guide (7th ed.). https://apastyle.apa.org/instructional-aids/discussion-phrases-guide.pdf

American Psychological Association. (APA). (2020b). *Publication manual of the American Psychological Association* (7th ed.). https://doi.org/10.1037/0000165-00

Bem, D. J. (2004). Writing the empirical journal article. In J. M. Darley, M. P. Zanna, & H. L. Roediger III (Eds.), *The compleat academic: A career guide* (pp. 185–219). American Psychological Association. https://psychology.yale.edu/sites/default/files/bemempirical.pdf

Costa, P. L., McDuffie, J. W., Brown, S. E. V., He, Y., Ikner, B. N., Sabat, I. E., & Miner, K. N. (2022). Microaggressions: Mega problems or micro issues? A meta-analysis. *Journal of Community Psychology, 51*(1), 137–153. https://doi.org/10.1002/jcop.22885

de Moor, J. S., Kent, E. E., McNeel, T. S., Virgo, K. S., Swanberg, J., Tracy, J. K., Banegas, M. P., Han, X., Qin, J., & Yabroff, K. R. (2021). Employment outcomes among cancer survivors in the United States: Implications for cancer care delivery. *Journal of the National Cancer Institute, 113*(5), 641–644. https://doi.org/10.1093/jnci/djaa084

Greenberg, P., & Dillman, D. (2023). Mail communications and survey response: A test of social exchange versus pre-suasion theory for improving response rates and data quality. *Journal of Survey Statistics and Methodology, 11*, 1–22. https://doi.org/10.1093/jssam/smab020

Hess, D. R. (2004). How to write an effective discussion. *Respiratory Care, 49*(10), 1238–1241.

Ko, J., Frey, J. J., & Harrington, D. (2019). Preventing suicide among working-age adults: The correlates of help-seeking behavior. *Inquiry: A Journal of Medical Care Organization, Provision and Financing, 56*, 46958019850979. https://doi.org/10.1177/0046958019850979

Lamanauskas, V. (2021). Writing a scientific article: Focused discussion and rational conclusions. *Problems of Education in the 21st Century, 79*(1). https://doi.org/10.33225/pec/21.79.04

Lawrence, K. C., & Adebowale, T. A. (2022). Adolescence dropout risk predictors: Family structure, mental health, and self-esteem. *Journal of Community Psychology, 51*(1), 120–136. https://doi.org/10.1002/jcop.22884

Macke, C., Canfield, J., Tapp, K., & Hunn, V. (2019). Outcomes for black students in team-based learning courses. *Journal of Black Studies, 50*, 66–86. https://doi.org/10.1177/0021934718810124

Ross, P. T., & Bibler Zaidi, N. L. (2019). Limited by our limitations. *Perspectives on medical Education, 8*(4), 261–264. https://doi.org/10.1007/s40037-019-00530-x

Sayer, N. A., Noorbaloochi, S., Frazier, P. A., Pennebaker, J. W., Orazem, R. J., Schnurr, P. P., Murdoch, M., Carlson, K. F., Gravely, A., & Litz, B. T. (2015). Randomized controlled trial of online expressive writing to address readjustment difficulties among U.S. Afghanistan and Iraq War veterans. *Journal of Traumatic Stress, 28*(5), 381–390. https://doi.org/10.1002/jts.22047

Silvia, P. J. (2015). *Write it up: Practical strategies for writing and publishing journal articles.* American Psychological Association. https://doi.org/10.1037/14470-000

Tracy, J. K., Adetunji, F., Al Kibria, G. M., & Swanberg, J. E. (2020). Cancer-work management: Hourly and salaried wage women's experiences managing the cancer-work interface following new breast cancer diagnosis. *PloS One, 15*(11), e0241795. https://doi.org/10.1371/journal.pone.0241795

CHAPTER 11

How Do I Write Abstracts That Hook the Reader?

Why Is Information on Writing the Abstract This Far Into the Book?

The simple answer is that I find it probably the most difficult part of the manuscript to write. It has to be succinct and make terrific points while summarizing and trying to interest the reader in reading more. To be completely honest, when drafting a manuscript, I'm not always sure what implications the findings will have until I get to the Discussion section. At least, I don't give that part a great deal of thought in the early part of the paper when I'm still writing the Introduction or checking to make sure that my survey of the literature was good enough. Maybe some writers can draft the abstract before going to the other sections, but I can't and don't.

What Is the Purpose of an Abstract and How Important Is It?

"The purpose of an abstract and a title are to encourage readers to read the rest of the paper, or in the case of a potential conference submission, to have a paper accepted for a presentation" (Grech, 2022, p. 51). Its importance should not be underestimated, as editors' and peer-reviewers' first impressions of your submission can be affected by the adroit or gauche handling of your abstract (Grech, 2022). Editors often send out abstracts to potential referees to determine their interest in reviewing the manuscript for their journal. The abstract offers a "window" into your manuscript and will likely determine whether the reader will want to invest their time in reading further or not.

Piedra (2022) argues that it is "perhaps the most important paragraph you will write in your paper. ... After the title of the paper, it will be the item most frequently read" (p. 475). Piedra, the editor of *Qualitative Social Work*, also suggests that a well-formed abstract can speed up the review process and improve an author's chances of getting published, while "a longwinded or opaque abstract might signal an unfocused paper, making it an unattractive time investment for reviewers, who respond by declining their invitation to review" (p. 476). She cited an example of an author whose abstract was "lengthy and contained unnecessary information, which tends to deter probable referees" (p. 477) and asked the author to shorten it. Once that happened, the manuscript was then forwarded to reviewers.

How Do I Write a Good Abstract?

Pearce and Ferguson (2017) describe abstracts as "a written elevator speech" (p. 452). Elevator speeches are quick presentations where one has a brief amount of time (30 to 60 seconds) to "sell" or pitch an idea, topic, or paper so that others want to learn more about it. In the case of an abstract, the goal is for readers to become interested in reading more of the paper. The abstract must engage the reader and deliver an "enticing and relevant message" (p. 453). Freysteinson and Stankus (2019) assert, "The best abstracts tell a compelling story" (p. 107).

A "good" abstract should be clear and to the point with no wasted words. Tell what the study was about and what you learned. If it has unique aspects, is groundbreaking, or novel, you get extra points. A good abstract should stimulate a reader's interest, and one way to do this is with a title that suggests new knowledge, a question or issue they have not thought about before, or a controversy. Hartley (2017) has identified 13 types of titles, and we'll talk more about this toward the end of the chapter.

In the opening line or two of the abstract, authors often provide statistics about the extent of a problem to establish a rationale for exploring it. One might take another approach and show how long a problem has existed or the spectacularly failed attempts to solve it. Think about what captures your interest when you are reading abstracts. That's probably the path you should follow.

There are two basic types of abstracts. They can be *structured*, meaning that the journal has specific headings that the authors are expected to use to describe their papers and there are *unstructured* abstracts. It is a superb idea in your first draft to develop your abstract as if it were required to be a structured one. The good news about unstructured abstracts is that you can use the basic guidelines or headings occurring in structured abstracts but just don't incorporate the headings. For that reason, we are focusing only on structured abstracts. We'll see examples of these in this chapter, but first, let's dissect what goes into an abstract. Abstracts are brief, comprehensive summaries generally about 250 words or slightly longer. They are not usually optional but required by most journals (APA, 2020).

What Are the Parts of a Structured Abstract?

The structured abstract format of IMRAD stands for Introduction, Methods, Results, and Discussion (Pearce & Ferguson, 2017, p. 455). Because abstracts are short descriptions, the opening sentence is "the most important sentence" that can "illuminate the gap in the literature or the problem you were facing that motivated the desire or need for this project" (Freysteinson & Stankus, 2019, p. 108).

You might be wondering how a brief summary can be comprehensive enough to cover the whole of a manuscript. This is accomplished by identifying the abstract format that the journal you are planning to submit to uses and then composing a sentence or two that captures the essence of the purpose, method, findings, and conclusions or implications. Four or five headings in the abstract can give the reader the gist of what you have tackled in your manuscript. As you can see in Table 11.1, different journals and disciplines may prescribe slightly different headings in their structured abstracts. There are journals (e.g., *Qualitative Social Work*) that neither endorse a structured nor an unstructured format and also don't have a word limit.

While the abstract headings of "Introduction," "Background," "Purpose," or the "Problem" and "Objectives" may seem dissimilar, they actually overlap considerably. Describing the background of an investigation may be another way of discussing the nature of the problem that gave rise to an investigation. Similarly, the purpose of a study and its objectives can follow from a problem. Unless the targeted journal specifies particular headings, you ought to be able to select the headings that best allow you to comfortably present your study in a compelling way.

The heading "Method" or "Methods" seems to be common to all the structured formats. You may be able to manage the method in a single sentence (see Wilson et al., 2022 later in this chapter), or you may need several sentences to present essential information to describe your data collection and or analytic approach.

In terms of results or findings, one need not attempt to present all or even most of a study's findings but should provide the major or most important discovery. This would be the finding contributing to the major takeaway point. You may be able to work in more than one, but keep an eye on the word limit for the abstract.

Similarly, writing under the abstract heading of "Discussion" could include implications, conclusions, and/or applications but need not involve all of these alternative slightly different foci. Somewhere in the abstract, highlight the uniqueness and contribution of the study. Do not lose sight of the study's major strength.

TABLE 11.1 Abstract Structured Formats

Format	Reference
Introduction Methods Results Discussion (the IMRAD format)	Pearce, P. F., & Ferguson, L. A. (2017). How to write abstracts for manuscripts, presentations, and grants: Maximizing information in a 30-s sound bite world. *Journal of the American Association of Nurse Practitioners, 29*(8), 452–460. https://doi.org/10.1002/2327-6924.12486
Introduction Purpose Method Results Implications and Conclusions	Freysteinson, W. M., & Stankus, J. A. (2019). The language of scholarship: How to write an abstract that tells a compelling story. *Journal of Continuing Education in Nursing, 50*(3), 107–108. https://doi.org/10.3928/00220124-20190218-04
Background/Purpose Methods/Interventions Analysis/Results Conclusions/Implications	Pierson, C. A. (2016). Structured abstracts improve clarity and reach your intended audience. *Journal of the American Association of Nurse Practitioners, 28*(7), 346. https://doi.org/10.1002/2327-6924.12392
Problem Investigated Participants or Data Sources Method—Essential Features Findings Conclusions, Implications, or Applications	American Psychological Association. (2020). *Publication manual of the American Psychological Association* (7th ed.). https://doi.org/10.1037/0000165-000
Objectives Methods Results Conclusions	*Journal of Research in Crime & Delinquency* https://journals.sagepub.com/author-instructions/JRC
Background Aim Method Results Conclusions	Hartley, J., & Guillaume, G. (2017). Thirteen ways to write an abstract. *Publications, 5*(11), 1–7. https://doi.org/10.3390/publications5020011

Note that some journals (e.g., *Journal of the American Association of Nurse Practitioners*) require structured abstracts for qualitative and quantitative research articles but unstructured abstracts for clinical case studies, education, and health policy manuscripts (*Journal of the American Association of Nurses*, n.d.).

Also, the maximum length of the abstract may vary by the type of article written. Understand what is required of the abstract before you start writing.

What Are Examples of Structured Abstracts?

In this section, excerpts from a wide variety of professional journal articles have been extracted to provide examples of the different styles and approaches used by authors to summarize their studies.

Calloway and colleagues (2022) used 12 sentences in their abstract of an article entitled "Stakeholder Perceptions of the Efficacy, Barriers, and Facilitators of Telemental Health Clinical Experiences During COVID for Nurse Practitioner Students."

ABSTRACT

Background: Telemental health services grew during the COVID pandemic, resulting in psychiatric–mental health nurse practitioner students obtaining clinical hours through this modality. Although patient outcome data demonstrate the efficacy of telemental health services, data on the efficacy of learning through telehealth clinical experiences are lacking.

Purpose: To explore perceptions of learning through telehealth clinical experiences by students, preceptors, and faculty and to identify perceived barriers and facilitators to facilitating telehealth clinical experiences.

Methodology: Mixed-methods exploratory study using web-based, researcher-designed, cross-sectional surveys eliciting perceptions of learning and perceived barriers and facilitators to telemental health clinical experiences sent to current and former PMHNP students and their preceptors of a state university in the southwest along with PMHNP faculty in the National Organization of Nurse Practitioner Faculties. Students and preceptors were offered the option to participate in a semi-structured interview.

Results: Twenty students (35.7%), 22 preceptors (24.7%), and 19 faculty (25.3%) participated in the surveys. Three preceptors and three students volunteered for interviews. Telemental health clinicals were perceived by students as equivalent to or superior to in-person learning. Preceptors rated the teaching/learning environment through telemental health as equivalent or better as compared with in-person clinicals with two exceptions. Faculty-rated greatest barrier to telemental health clinicals was telephone visits because of technology issues.

Conclusions: Telemental health clinicals can provide a high-quality learning experience for students.

Implications: Preceptors should be provided with resources for facilitating telemental health clinicals. Ongoing discussions regarding the number of clinical hours recommended through telehealth are needed.

Keywords: Clinical; education; nurse practitioner; telehealth. (p. 1216)

Note that this journal helpfully includes key words as a part of the abstract. Key words are useful when searching for other, similar articles. Key words may be taken from the title or from the body of the abstract. Not all journals require key words with the manuscript, and those that do often ask for three to five. Submitting key words to the journal helps editors know which pool of peer-reviewers might be interested in reading the manuscript.

In deciding upon key words, you may find it helpful to look at electronic databases that index the journal you are considering for submission. To take an example, *PsycInfo* contains a search box for the APA's Thesaurus of Psychological Index Terms. Using it, you could learn that "left-handedness" is not indexed. When your keywords are found in the indexes of electronic databases, it makes it easier for those conducting specific subject searches to find your published article. Similarly, *Medline (ProQuest)* contains a thesaurus search box for Medical Subject Headings (MeSH). Search the *Medline* thesaurus and you can find that "left-handed DNA" *is* an indexed term there.

In the next example, Armes and colleagues (2020) in the article "Secondary Trauma and Impairment in Clinical Social Workers" describe their mailed survey sent to a national sample of clinical social workers. They accomplish this in seven sentences.

ABSTRACT

Background: Secondary traumatic stress (STS), symptomatology resulting from indirect exposure to trauma, is one potential negative effect from engaging in clinical social work. Yet, little is known about the relationship between STS and workers' distress and impairment due to their work.

Objective: The purpose of this paper was to explore STS in a national sample of clinical social workers (N = 539).

Method and results: A structural equation model demonstrating good model fit indicated that STS mediated the association between trauma exposure at work and reports of significant distress and impairment (β = .08, p < .01; 95 % CI = .03, .12). Likewise, STS mediated the association between working with children aged 13 and under and reports of significant distress and impairment (β = .05, p < .05; 95 % CI = .02, .09). Results indicated that the model accounted for 25% of the variance in significant distress and impairment ($R2$ = .25, p < .001) and 5% of the variance in STS ($R2$ = .05, p < .05).

Conclusions: Implications for agencies working with child welfare are provided, including a discussion addressing STS and significant distress and impairment at the individual and larger agency levels. (p. 1)

Mongilio (2022) in an article entitled "Childhood Head Injury as an Acquired Neuropsychological Risk Factor for Adolescent Delinquency" uses four headings and seven sentences in her abstract.

ABSTRACT

Objectives: This study aims to parse out the effects of childhood head injury (HI) as an acquired neuropsychological deficit that impacts adolescent delinquent behavior, while accounting for other early-life risk factors and potential temporal ordering.

Methods: Nationally representative prospective data from the UK Millennium Cohort Study (MCS; N = 13,287) and a series of logistic and binomial regressions are used to examine the relationship between early-life risk factors, HI, and adolescent delinquent behavior. Methodological considerations from clinical HI research, such as the use of an orthopedic injury comparison group, are incorporated.

Results: Findings are consistent with the conceptualization of HI as an acquired neuropsychological deficit, in that childhood HI increases the risk of early- and adolescent-onset delinquency, sustained delinquent behavior from childhood to early adolescence, and participation in a greater variety of delinquent behavior.

Conclusions: Childhood HI is relatively common, as over 27% of the sample reported at least one HI. The importance of HI as an acquired neuropsychological deficit and its relevance as a risk factor for later criminal behavior is reiterated. Future research should examine the importance of developmental period effects and mechanisms underlying this relationship. (p. 756)

Macgowan and colleagues (2022) developed an abstract of their meta-analytic study entitled "Eye Movement Desensitization and Reprocessing Therapy to Reduce PTSD and Related Symptoms Among Forcibly Displaced People: A Systematic Review and Meta-Analysis." This abstract involves eight sentences.

ABSTRACT

Purpose: This study is a meta-analysis on the efficacy of eye movement desensitization and reprocessing (EMDR) in reducing Post-Traumatic Stress Disorder (PTSD) and co-occurring depression, and anxiety symptoms among forcibly displaced people.

Methods: A search was followed by data extraction and assessment of risk of bias. Within- and between-conditions effect sizes of posttest and follow-up outcomes using a random effects model were examined, with heterogeneity and subgroup analyses.

Results: Twenty-two studies (N = 1964) were included and seventeen (N = 1652) had complete data for the meta-analysis. There were medium to large effect size reductions on PTSD, depression, and anxiety within-conditions. EMDR was more effective than other conditions at posttest for PTSD symptoms but outcomes for the posttests and follow-ups for depression and anxiety were inconclusive.

Discussion: EMDR effectively reduced PTSD symptoms, depression, and anxiety among forcibly displaced people. More studies with larger samples and better designs are needed. (p. 863)

In the last example, Wilson and colleagues (2022) in an article entitled, "Tiny Homes Are Huge for People Living With Serious Mental Illness" were able to create an abstract in six sentences.

ABSTRACT

Purpose: A formative evaluation examined the acceptability and feasibility of tiny homes for people living with serious mental illness (SMI).

Methods: The evaluation included four focus groups with people with SMI and service providers (n = 28) and eight overnight stays with people with SMI.

Results: The analysis identified six recommendations for tailoring the design of the tiny homes and the community where the homes will be located to meet the needs of people living with SMI. The recommendations for the design of the tiny homes included maximize natural light and outdoor spaces, design flexible living spaces, and ensure accessibility. The recommendations for the design of the surrounding community included ensure privacy, build a community, and maximize residents' connectivity.

Conclusions: This research serves as a starting point for interventions that aim to develop housing that is both affordable and tailored to the needs of people with SMI. (p. 816)

These examples, chosen from a variety of journals, show how truly brief abstracts can be. Four of the five examples were under 200 words, and four of the five involved eight or fewer sentences. While this small sample is not representative of the larger universe of all journals, it at least provides some notion that abstracts don't have to be all that difficult to construct. Did this quick review shatter your illusions about how detailed or difficult they must be to develop? Were you worried about pointing out the limitations of your study? (Of course, you may still aspire to publish in a journal requiring longer and more detailed abstracts.) As you have been reminded before, be familiar with the journal to which you are planning to submit your manuscript.

Also, in case you didn't make the association, abstracts required for presenting at national conferences are usually developed in the same way as those for professional journals, but there could be some slight changes depending on the conference. Learning to write abstracts for journals easily translates into skills for developing abstracts for conferences.

> *I have only made this letter longer because I had not the time to make it shorter.*
>
> Blaise Pascal, philosopher, mathematician, scientist, inventor, theologian

From my perspective, the takeaway point about abstracts is that they don't have to be too complicated or perfect. In fact, they can't be because there may be word count restrictions mentioned in the journal's author guidelines. The best you can do is to try and capture the essence of what needs to be reported under each heading so that your abstract is informative while also (hopefully) alluring the reader to go further into the manuscript.

How Do I Compose an Eye-Catching Title?

Unlike the abstract, which is absolutely the last piece of the manuscript I write, I sometimes have an inspiration for the title in the early stages of drafting a manuscript. Other times, the title seems to suggest itself after I have finished a portion of the manuscript—for instance, the literature review or the discussion where I have had to think about the implications for the study.

Because it is the first thing a person will read of your manuscript, and perhaps the last, the importance of a good title should be obvious. The more your title invites readers, the more likely your published paper will be read, and possibly cited by others.

There are few hard and fast rules about creating a title, but here is what the last edition of the *APA Publication Manual* has to say about the topic: "The title should summarize the main idea of the paper simply and, if possible, in a way that is engaging for readers. … Although there is no prescribed limit for title length in APA Style, authors are encouraged to keep their titles focused and succinct" (p. 31). The *Publication Manual* also advises authors to avoid using implicit words in their titles such as "a study of," "an empirical investigation of," and to otherwise "avoid words that serve no purpose" and only increase the title length (p. 32). Shorter titles are associated with "higher numbers of article downloads and citations" (APA, 2020, p. 31).

The previous edition of the *Publication Manual* recommended that titles be restricted to 10 to 12 words, but that suggestion doesn't appear in the new edition. Particularly when scientific names of species are inserted into titles (as recommended in the seventh edition) one can understand why titles might be longer than 10 or 12 words. Personally, the only time I've been concerned about the title length is when I've been preparing an abstract for a conference submission and the guidelines specify a given limit. No point in having one's entry kicked out on a technicality! However, some journals do have specific requirements. This is what the *Journal of the American Medical Association* has to say as to title length:

> Please limit the length of titles to 150 characters for reports of research and other major articles and 100 characters for Editorials, Viewpoints, Commentaries, and Letters. For scientific manuscripts, do not use overly general titles, declarative titles, titles that include the direction of study results, or questions as titles. For reports of clinical trials, meta-analyses, and systematic reviews, include the type of study as a subtitle (e.g., A Randomized Clinical Trial, A Meta-analysis, A Systematic Review). For reports of other types of research, do not include study type or design in the title or subtitle. (Jama Network, 2023)

Authors can introduce their papers with a variety of different types of titles. For instance, Hartley (2017) catalogues 13 different ways, and others have provided even more subtypes for medical journals (Kerans et al., 2020).

Truthfully, it is not necessary to overthink this, as most titles would seem to fit in one of the selected categories of titles illustrated with my whimsical illustrations. Authors may choose to:

- **Announce a general topic** ("What Statistical Significance Testing Is, and What It Is Not")
- **Report findings** ("Consequences of Relying Upon Statistical Significance Alone: Some Medical Illustrations")
- **Mention a controversy:** ("Six Enduring Controversies in Measurement and Statistics")
- **Pose a question** ("When Is Statistical Significance Not Important?"). Note, however, a study by Hudson (2016) of over 150,000 articles from 36 disciplines contained in a United Kingdom database revealed that fewer than 10% of titles were worded with a question in such fields as public and allied health, psychology, biological sciences, chemistry, physics, mathematical sciences, computer science, and engineering. Articles in business, law, politics, social work, and educational journals were the exception with percentages ranging from 12% (business) to 19% (law and politics)
- **Provide options:** ("Options for Publishing Research Without Any P-Values," Also, ("Robust Regression Analysis: Some Popular Statistical Package Options")
- **Give a description or a primer:** ("Effect Size, Confidence Interval and Statistical Significance: A Practical Guide for Biologists")
- **Hook with a puzzle:** ("Some Puzzling Genetic Disorder Statistics"). Also: ("A Panorama of Statistics: Perspectives, Puzzles, and Paradoxes in Statistics")

As you may have noted, authors may use colons in their titles. Doing so is a way to "convey more information about a study" (Hallock & Bennett, 2021, p. 27) and gives the author another shot at capturing a reader's attention by presenting slightly different information about the paper. Looking back at my own publications, I have used colons in the majority of my titles. Hudson's (2016) study found that colon use varied widely by profession. They were used most often by the authors in the fields of geography, business, law, politics, social work, sociology, and anthropology—with about 50% or more of all the articles in these disciplines using a colon in the title. Sixty-one percent of the papers in education used colons. Along this line, Hartley (2017) has reported looking at 260 titles in higher education reporting research and also found that 60% used a colon. Thirty percent of the titles were expressed as a single sentence. Only about 10% were posed questions.

Advice from other sources provides the following suggestions about titles:

> - Avoid abbreviations (APA, 2020).
> - Avoid jargon, numerals (e.g., Part I), and placing locations in titles (Krausman & Cox, 2020, p. 1030).
> - Avoid irony and humor (Hyland & Zou, 2022).
> - In a study of undergraduates, Hallock and Bennett (2021) found that titles with colons were preferred over those without, long titles were preferred over short titles, and titles worded as a question were preferred. However, Hyland and Zou (2022) interpreted Hudson's (2016) study as stating, "Citations to papers were higher when the titles were shorter and contained colons" (p. 3), but Hudson did observe that results varied considerably among disciplines.

While it may feel like there is much to consider when thinking about what title to give your manuscript, I have found it helpful to write down four or five possible titles. Then I order them in terms of my favorites. I let them sit for several hours or overnight and then come back to them. Sometimes, my coauthors and I discuss our favorites and eventually reach an agreement. If you feel a draft title doesn't capture the essence of your paper, then try substituting words, striking out some, and penciling in others.

I don't believe most journal editors reject manuscripts based solely on reading just the title (unless you have submitted to a completely inappropriate journal). If a title can be improved, sometimes peer-reviewers will notice that and provide suggestions. Or, if they suggest major revisions to the manuscript, you may choose to modify the title to better reflect a new thrust. In other words, don't worry too much about the title.

> *Worrying is like a rocking chair. It gives you something to do, but it doesn't get you anywhere.*
>
> Van Wilder, fictional film character

Your Turn 11.1

Using one of the structured abstract formats (e.g., Introduction, Methods, Results, Discussion) found in Table 10.1, draft three or so sentences for each of the subheadings. Let it sit a while. When you go back to read it, what words are unnecessary that can be removed? Can you collapse your verbiage into two sentences for each heading without leaving anything important out?

(continued)

_____

_____

_____

_____

Once you are happy with that draft, check with one or two of the journals you are considering sending your manuscript to. Does it fit within their guidelines? If not, what do you still need to do?

_____

_____

_____

_____

When you have a final draft of the abstract, share it with your coauthor, mentor, or trusted friend. What feedback do they have?

_____

_____

_____

_____

Your Turn 11.2

After you have completed your abstract and possibly thought about key words that would help define and categorize your paper, try your hand at writing a draft title. While you are at it, write three or four titles—variations on a theme. Let them sit a while, and then go back to see which one you like best. If you don't like any of them, you might try using a thesaurus to see if any word substitutions provide more clarity. Could you remove any unnecessary words?

_____

_____

_____

_____

When you are finished with your title, show it to your mentor, coauthor, or trusted friend. What do they say about your title? (Note, when I am at this stage and really happy with the title, I might show it to others for approval; however, I tend to be protective of my titles when I like them. Might I tweak a title to incorporate feedback? Yes, of course.)

_____

_____

_____

_____

References

American Psychological Association. (APA). (2020). *Publication manual of the American Psychological Association* (7th ed.). https://doi.org/10.1037/0000165-000

Armes, S. E., Lee, J. J., Bride, B. E., & Seponski, D. M. (2020). Secondary trauma and impairment in clinical social workers. *Child Abuse & Neglect, 110*(Pt 3), 104540. https://doi.org/10.1016/j.chiabu.2020.104540

Calloway, S., Hilliard, W., & Jimenez, R. (2022). Stakeholder perceptions of the efficacy, barriers, and facilitators of telemental health clinical experiences during COVID for nurse practitioner students. *Journal of the American Association of Nurse Practitioners, 34*, 1216–1224. https://doi.org/10.1097/JXX.0000000000000776

Freysteinson, W. M., & Stankus, J. A. (2019). The language of scholarship: How to write an abstract that tells a compelling story. *Journal of Continuing Education in Nursing, 50*(3), 107–108. https://doi.org/10.3928/00220124-20190218-04

Grech, V. (2022). WASP (write a scientific paper): Preparing an abstract. *Early Human Development, 125*, 51–52. https://doi.org/10.1016/j.earlhumdev.2018.06.005

Hallock, R. M., & Bennett, T. N. (2021). I'll read that! What title elements attract readers to an article? *Teaching of Psychology, 48*, 26–31. https://doi.org/10.1177/0098628320959948

Hartley, J. (2017). What works for you? The choice of titles for academic articles in higher education. *SHRE News Blog.* https://shreblog.com/2017/05/26what-works-for-you-the-choice-of-titles-for academic-articles-in-higher-education/

Hudson, J. (2016). An analysis of the titles of papers submitted to the UK REF in 2014: Authors, disciplines, and stylistic details. *Scientometrics, 109*(2), 871–889. https://doi.org/10.1007/s11192-016-2081-4

Hyland, K., & Zou, H. (2022). Titles in research articles. *Journal of English for Academic Purposes, 56*, 101094. https://doi.org/10.1016/j.jeap.2022.101094

Jama Network. (2023). *Instructions for authors.* https://jamanetwork.com/journals/jama/pages/instructions-for-authors#SecTitle

Journal of the American Association of Nurse Practitioners. (n.d.). *Abstract.* https://journals.lww.com/jaanp/Pages/informationforauthors.aspx#Abstract

Kerans, M. E., Marshall, J., Murray, A., & Sabate, S. (2020). Research article title content and form in high-ranked international clinical medicine journals. *English for Specific Purposes, 60*, 127–139. https://doi.org/10.1016/j.esp.2020.06.001

Krausman, P. R., & Cox, A. S. (2020). Writing an effective title. *The Journal of Wildlife Management, 84*, 1029–1031. https://doi.org/10.1002/jwmg.21881

Macgowan, M., Naseh, M., & Rafieifar, M. (2022). Eye movement desensitization and reprocessing therapy to reduce PTSD and related symptoms among forcibly displaced people: A systematic review and meta-analysis. *Research on Social Work Practice, 32*, 863–877. https://doi.org/10.1177/10497315221082223

Mongilio, J. (2022). Childhood head injury as an acquired neuropsychological risk factor for adolescent delinquency. *Journal of Research in Crime and Delinquency, 59*(6), 756–790. https://doi.org/10.1177/00224278221081140

Pearce, P. F., & Ferguson, L. A. (2017). How to write abstracts for manuscripts, presentations, and grants: Maximizing information in a 30-s sound bite world. *Journal of the American Association of Nurse Practitioners, 29*(8), 452–460. https://doi.org/10.1002/2327-6924.12486

Piedra, L. M. (2022). The mighty abstract: An overlooked element of peer review. *Qualitative Social Work, 21*(3), 475–482. https://doi.org/10.1177/14733250221095125

Pierson C. A. (2016). Structured abstracts improve clarity and reach your intended audience. *Journal of the American Association of Nurse Practitioners, 28*(7), 346. https://doi.org/10.1002/2327-6924.12392

CHAPTER 12

What Do I Need to Check Before Submitting My Final Draft?

Having invested a great deal of time to complete a final draft, you do not want to get into such a big hurry to submit it that you rush your manuscript barefoot, shirtless, and possibly in need of a shave out the door. Recently, I was reading a published article that I was pleased to find and planned to incorporate a portion of its results in a project that would soon be published. As I went to double-check the passage that I wished to cite, I realized something was wrong. The text of the article didn't agree with the findings presented in its table. I emailed a colleague of mine to see if I had missed something important. He confirmed what I had discovered—that either the table was in error, or the authors had drawn upon the wrong data from the table when writing the findings narrative. Although I'm sure the authors were embarrassed by my email, I recommended that they inform the journal of the problem so that an erratum could inform future readers. What this brief story demonstrates is the importance of proofreading to identify microstructural problems.

How Do I Proofread for Microstructural Issues in the Manuscript?

Microstructural problems, like the previous example, include a lack of agreement between numerical values reported in the narrative and in tables—that is, inaccurate data—but also grammatical and spelling issues that running the editor functions of grammar and spell-check on your computer do not always catch. This is why proofreading is so important.

Writer and blogger, Derek Haines (2022) has on his website, *Just Publishing Advice*, recommendations about proofreading:

> "To use online editing tools and a grammar and spelling checker … is not proofreading. It will not result in an error-free text. … It is impossible to

proofread on a screen. ... Electronic tools are very poor at understanding words in context."

"Go to the beginning of the text and start reading out loud. ... Using your eyes and ears together will find more errors than your eyes alone."

"Never rush the task of proofreading. ... You can never do it in a hurry. ... Make sure you have plenty of time and no distractions. You need to concentrate, so turn off the music and television."

"To proofread your writing, always leave it for a day or even longer before you start. You need to disconnect from the writing process before you can begin to be analytical."

> Microstructural issues your online editing tools may not catch can include these things:
>
> - Inappropriate punctuation. For example, the first word inside a quotation begins with a capital letter; periods and question marks go inside quotation marks, not outside; and check for missing quotation marks.
> - The wrong verb tenses.
> - Acronyms and abbreviations that are used before they are explained. Example: "OOHC was on the increase. Administrators appointed a task force to examine numbers of children in out of home care."
> - Autocorrections that aren't correct. Online editing tools sometimes don't recognize typos even though the terms don't fit the sentence or its context. Here is an example of the intended sentence: "The authors were dismayed by their lack of significant findings." Notice now the version with the wrong term in the sentence: "The authors were dismayed by their lack of significant fins." Since "fins" is a legitimate noun, the grammar checker on my computer does not catch this typo. What about yours? Typos or incorrect "autocorrections" may not be identified by software editors when the terms are found in a dictionary.
> - Quotations without a page or reference source.
> - Tables and figures without captions or headings.
> - Overly long sentences. I had an instructor once advise, "Don't let your sentences grow to over 30 words." One website recommends that average sentences should not exceed 20–25 words in length (Enago Academy, 2021). If you are a brilliant writer, you can ignore this suggestion. For most of us, however, excessively long sentences make for a more laborious reading experience. Fun it is not.
> - Words that you commonly get wrong. For example, complement and compliment.

- Spell out numbers that begin sentences. Don't start sentences with numeric values like this: "55 students participated in the survey. 114 declined participation."
- Check for capitalization issues. Look at these three examples: (a) *Tourists at Pennsylvania's capitol saw the governor in shorts that day.* (b) *Attendees from three zoom meetings were contacted.* (c) *Blacks and whites were proportionately represented in the survey.* Note that "capitol" should be capitalized when it is a proper noun as it is in (a). "Zoom" would be capitalized because it is a specific type of electronic meeting, and "whites" would be capitalized as well as "blacks."
- Unnecessary words. Shorten sentences (particularly in abstracts!) by removing words when you can:

    "What kind of mature tree has vicious thorns on it?" (Original sentence)

    "What mature tree has vicious thorns?" (Cleaner, simpler sentence)
- Repetition in word usage. A two-sentence example:

    "As undergraduate students consider their ability to interact with and utilize research to inform their practice, practice doing these discussions can be essential. Learning how to utilize research to inform their practice take time and *practice*." Redundancy like the sentences above scream, "I didn't take enough time to think about these sentences!" If authors don't appear to value the sentences they write in their manuscript, then why should you as a reader, peer-reviewer, or journal editor? In the example, you can see how using fewer words or a thesaurus would greatly improve the writer's presentation of ideas.
- Ideas, concepts, and words of others, factual statements, and direct quotations are documented.

You know you should proofread, but you must also be deliberate and thoughtful. As Haines (2022) has suggested, do it without rushing and without distraction. Slow reading is difficult for Type A personalities to do. When we read or skim at a high rate of speed, our minds can fill in a missing word or not stumble when the wrong form of a word is used. However, we can slow our reading down by taking a blank index card and allowing our eyes to view only one line at a time on the printed page. Or we can read our manuscript out loud. Both of these methods work if you don't have access to a really top-notch assistant or coauthor who is skilled at proofreading. Although I have never tried it, Haines also suggests starting with the last sentence in the piece and reading each sentence from the end to the front of the manuscript to allow for a singular focus on the sentences.

How Do I Proofread for the Macrostructure in the Manuscript?

Once the microstructural proofing is finished and a relatively "clean" manuscript free of misspelling, grammatical issues, repetitive words, or information have been addressed, then the manuscript should be read for the intellectual argument it presents, its organization, and the integrity of the piece.

Allow me to explain why you might want to do a slow, reflective reading of your manuscript before you launch it. Let's start with a story about a manuscript I was asked to review by a journal's editor. Beginning with the first page, I was quite impressed with the authors' excellent writing. It seemed like it would be a slam dunk of an acceptance with a "well done!" coming. However, as I cruised into the *Results* section, I was struck by two things. First of all, I was completely baffled as to why their systematic literature view included articles that they earlier had indicated would be excluded. They had found a large number of articles and spent a good deal of time highlighting them, but then like sheep that had wandered away without a thought to their destination, they ended up far from their original aim.

Perhaps the authors recognized this late in the development of the manuscript and hoped the reviewer wouldn't notice. If they had simply asked themselves with each study added to their review, "Does it provide information about this type of intervention?" and then eliminated those not qualifying, I could have gladly recommended the manuscript be published. However, they didn't appear to have conducted even this minimal level of checking their data, and the manuscript was rejected.

I have no explanation as to how this could have happened. Maybe the senior author gave the second author the idea for the study and then trusted that it had been conducted properly, not giving it the attention needed. Maybe the author who did the majority of the database searching wasn't clear on what constituted the intervention of interest. Could the paper have been produced by two students still learning and not having a writing mentor? Since there were at least two authors, I wondered if each one had been in charge of their own section and didn't ask any hard questions of the other author.

At any rate, when there are multiple authors writing on the same manuscript, additional care must be taken to allow the work to speak with a consistent voice. Otherwise, there may be phrasing or style differences in the writing—which can be quite noticeable at times. When there are multiple authors, it is best if the most experienced or skilled writer reads the whole manuscript several times to smooth out any valleys or hills in the writing. Certainly, every coauthor should read the whole manuscript multiple times but be alert to stylistic differences that hint at or reveal an assembly of the paper by two or more individuals.

The editor of a nursing journal has written, "I often receive manuscripts that are written by more than one author and no one author edited the manuscript for a consistent style. For example, the writing changes from third to first person in the middle of the manuscript. Another problem is that information is repeated unnecessarily which is a distraction to the authors' main message ... one author must edit the manuscript to have one consistent writing style" (Morton, 2020, p. 2). It is important that each author feels comfortable discussing sections written by others. One should not be too shy to point out issues not caught by the author of another section. One author should not have to do all the thinking, editing, and revising for others. Without the necessary back-and-forth discussion about what works and what doesn't, a manuscript will never achieve its best chance at success with multiple authors.

Read for Organization

Sometimes when we look back over a long section, we can discover that a later paragraph does a better job of explaining or introducing things than the first paragraph. It may make sense to keep all of the paragraphs, to give them a slight reorder, or maybe the first paragraph is not really needed. Read for smoothness. Look for any spots where you have to slow down to understand a sentence or passage. (This works better when the material has gotten "cold" on you.)

In the same way, unnecessary sentences can reduce the clarity of a paragraph, and possibly put the reader to sleep. A slow, thoughtful reading of each stand-alone section of the manuscript (e.g., the Discussion or Conclusion) may reveal sentences that can be removed and maybe even a paragraph or two. Check your headings and subheadings to make sure they accurately communicate what is coming next in the manuscript.

> *Examine every word you put on paper. You'll find a surprising number that don't serve any purpose.*
>
> William Zinsser, *On Writing Well. The Classic Guide to Writing Nonfiction*

Kallestinova (2011)—you'll remember her from the first chapter—adds to the discussion with her "Rule 7: Revise your paper at the macrostructure and the microstructure using different strategies and techniques. Receive feedback and revise again" (p. 190). For her, reading macrostructure includes thinking about the logic of the presented ideas and the organization, content, and flow. The microstructure level includes items that we have already discussed (e.g., the individual words used, spelling, and grammar), as well as sentence structure.

One set of authors (Hirschey et al., 2019) have reported designing a writing program for students enrolled in a doctor of nursing practice degree. One component was a writing checklist for their students to use. A portion of their checklist addresses specific questions you might also want to consider as part of your slow reading for macrostructure:

> Does each paragraph have one clear main point?
> Are there logical bridges from one sentence to another?
> Are the foci of the first and last sentences of the paragraph consistent?

Beside these three bullets, I would add this question: Is there a smooth transition from one section of the paper to the next? Actually, your reader needs to see the logic in the ending of one paragraph and the starting of the next. Think conversationally. You wouldn't describe the last Cincinnati Reds game you attended in one paragraph and then start a new one about an event that happened at your Senior Prom without some sort of transition. We need the bridge or transition to know how these two events relate to each other.

Give thought to what macrostructural areas need to be policed in your manuscripts. For instance, if you know that you tend to write very long paragraphs, you might want to see if they can be broken up with a new heading or subheading. Trust me, your readers won't mind at all. In fact, they may think of you as a skilled writer because you don't lull them to sleep with your constant verbiage. Using an adequate number of headings and subheadings is a good discipline for you too. They keep you honest and from straying away from what you ought to be discussing. In my opinion, it is better to have more than too few. If you overdo it, they can always be removed at the final draft stage when you read for macrostructure and organization.

Be a Skeptical Reader

Have you ever given a presentation where you were feeling seriously underprepared or where you were caught napping in a sunny warm zone of naive thinking that you were well prepared but then verbally attacked by a skeptical person or persons in the audience? If so, then you will appreciate the value of reading your manuscript not as the aspiring author but in the role of a skeptical reviewer. Lord knows many reviewers are skeptical readers. They are not the protective parent of your manuscript but truly objective readers.

Skeptical readers may look at your *Introduction* section and ask, "Why is this important?" Or, "Why should I care about that problem?" Will your Introduction answer their questions?

In the *Literature Review* section, there are wonderful hiding places where the skeptical reader may spring up for a confrontation. Questions they may ask can include, "Why is the literature review so brief?" Or, "Why did you go into so much depth and include studies that aren't directly related?" Defend yourself by being clear on the purpose of your literature review and the relevance of each study discussed. Questions can also arise about the time period your review covered. Did you go back 5 years, 10 years, or 20? Is there a logic to the years you covered? Are there any classic or important studies you should acknowledge outside that window of time? Any salient studies that you possibly missed as you look back with a critical eye?

Skeptical readers will want to know why the theory or theories in that pretty basket with a nice ribbon on top were chosen. Are there others that aren't so dated or have greater empirical support? Any that you wish you had mentioned instead?

In the *Method* section, skeptical readers may wonder if you could have analyzed the data a different way, used a different instrument, or observed the intervention for a longer period of time. Can you defend the data collection method, the variables chosen? Did you leave out any vital details? If modifications to the original design had to be made, were these mentioned in the limitations?

In the *Results* section, are the findings reported objectively? Could there be any bias that you didn't recognize initially? Have you answered the research questions that you set out to explore?

Skeptical readers in the *Discussion* section will be looking particularly at your implications. The ol' "So what?" question will be set and ready to spring. So, do you have real, meaningful implications? If not, don't pretend or stretch the truth. Expand future research suggestions if needed. Have you discussed similar studies? What were their implications? Did you make too much of your implications or too little of your limitations? Are there any limitations you didn't mention that a skeptical reader may sniff out?

My intent in this segment of the chapter was not to make readers even more fearful of the peer-review process but only to help you to read your manuscript more objectively. Learning to read your own material soberly as if written by someone else allows you to see possible areas where it could be strengthened. It also helps to harmonize the sections and creates a strong macrostructure. When you are able to put on the objective lens and revise accordingly, you may find that the comments you receive from reviewers are only minor recommendations. As an educator, I tried to impress upon my students that it is the *details* that matter in their writing. It's the details that researchers love and care about—so don't overlook them.

How Many Times Should I Revise My Paper?

Early in my life, I learned the necessity of reading my drafts multiple times. Perhaps my first lesson came after I received a portable Smith-Corona typewriter for Christmas in high school and sometime in January proudly typed a 10th-grade composition out for my English teacher, Mary Bush—a perpetually frowning individual who secretly cared for her students but never showed it and didn't have a clue about how to relate to teenagers. I typed my homework assignment on my new olive-green typewriter, proud of its almost professional appearance, even though I had to "hunt and peck" to find the keys, a year before I had the benefit of a typing class or discovered Liquid Paper Correction Fluid.

I was darn proud of the typed paper I handed in but soon learned that Mrs. Bush didn't heap any praise on my fledgling effort or recognize that I was the only one in class who didn't make her plod through scrawly adolescent penmanship trying to decipher the meaning or intent of hastily scribbled thoughts. Instead, she pointed out each and every one of the typos I had made—including those I had recognized but thought they were close enough to correct that they would be overlooked as she read for content. She *did* read for content, but as an educator, she thought it imperative to identify every misplaced comma, every misspelled word, every incomplete thought, and so on. I got her drift. To do well with writing, one has to be careful about what appears on the page.

Possibly because I was a little insecure about my ability to write well, or wanting to wrestle an accolade or two out of Mary Bush, I began the habit of doing a rough draft before every final draft. Later, as a professional, after receiving a few rejections from journals, I realized that publishing was a highly competitive enterprise and that I needed to read each manuscript as a skeptical or critical person would, assaying and analyzing each sentence, paragraph, and page. (Thank you, Mary Bush.) Early on, I created a rule for myself—I had to produce another draft if I found at least one misspelled word. Then, slowly, I tried to read as a journal reviewer, a skeptical reader might. After checking for any format issues, I began trying to develop a mindset that would probe the areas where I thought my manuscripts might be weak. For instance, I looked to see if I overgeneralized the findings or made assumptions without any evidence.

> *No first draft fulfills all the requirement of being a good writer. One has to take pain in rewriting it often as to remove irrelevance from it. Like a sculpturist, one has to remove the unnecessary stuff from the first draft before giving a finishing touch to it ... the real craft of editing will make the piece a masterpiece.*
>
> Doshi (2019, p. 59)

In short, I acquired a habit of making five to six revisions of a manuscript before believing that I had done all that I could do to make the paper professional, presentable, and publishable. I know there are those who can publish with one or two drafts, but they may be just more skilled than me. Through trial and error, I've learned what works for me—as everyone serious about publishing should do for themselves.

CHAPTER 12 WHAT DO I NEED TO CHECK BEFORE SUBMITTING MY FINAL DRAFT?

Final Checklist for the Manuscript

- ☐ The Abstract. Does it fit the word limit and conform to the journal's format?
- ☐ The Abstract. Have you provided key words?
- ☐ Tables and Figures. Are they accurate with the descriptions in the narrative?
- ☐ Tables and Figures. Do they all have captions or titles?
- ☐ The Manuscript: Are the pages numbered?
- ☐ The Manuscript: Are the number of pages or word count in compliance with the journal's guidelines?
- ☐ The Manuscript: Have you provided headings to guide the reader?
- ☐ The Manuscript: Have you checked the microstructure by running the spelling, grammar, and editor functions in your Word document?
- ☐ The Manuscript: Are all direct quotations correctly attributed?
- ☐ The Manuscript: The macrostructure has been examined by a slow, thoughtful reading.
- ☐ References. Are they in the appropriate format for the journal?
- ☐ Overall Length of Manuscript. Does it conform to the journal's guidelines?
- ☐ Title Page. Is it properly formatted with your contact info?
- ☐ Comments. Delete all comments.
- ☐ Track Changes. If you have used this feature, accept all changes, and save with no markup.

Your Turn 12.1

Are you aware of any unnecessary words that you tend to overuse? Would it be worthwhile to search specific terms to see if you have used such words as any of these:

Actually, Very, Completely, Extremely, Totally, Fairly, Incredibly, Really.

_____

_____

Your Turn 12.2

When you have checked your manuscript for microstructure issues, what have you found? Is there any pattern that you recognize? That is, do you tend to do these things often? What can you do to ameliorate the problem?

_____

_____

_____

Your Turn 12.3

Do you have the patience to do a slow reading of your manuscript? If not, can you make a deal with yourself to read 3 full pages, and if you find three errors or things you want to change, then read 3 more pages?

_____

_____

_____

If you start reading for problems at the beginning of the paper with each new draft, then that portion probably has been polished enough. Start your reading with the section that has been read the fewest number of times.

_____

_____

What did you learn from your slow reading that you need to be more alert to next time?

Resource

Beard, R., Myhill, D., Riley, J., & Nystrand, M. (Eds.) (2009). *The Sage handbook of writing development*. SAGE Publications.

References

Doshi, H. M. (2019) What makes you a good writer? Tips from literary stalwarts. *IUP Journal of Soft Skills, 13*(2), 55–61.

Enago Academy. (2021). *Top 6 tips to optimize sentence length in your research paper.* https://www.enago.com/academy/how-to-optimize-sentence-length-in-academic-writing/

Haines, D. (2022). The slow art of proofreading a text the right way. *Just Publishing Advice.* https://justpublishingadvice.com/the-slow-method-of-proofreading-the-right-way/

Hirschey, R., Rodgers, C., & Hockenberry, M. (2019). A program to enhance writing skills for advanced practice nurses. *Journal of Continuing Education in Nursing, 50*(3), 109–114. https://doi.org/10.3928/00220124-20190218-05

Kallestinova E. D. (2011). How to write your first research paper. *Yale Journal of Biology and Medicine, 84*(3), 181–190.

King, S. (2000). *On writing: A memoir of the craft.* Scribner.

Morton, P. G. (2020). Why was my manuscript rejected? *Journal of Professional Nursing: Official Journal of the American Association of Colleges of Nursing, 36*(2), 1–4. https://doi.org/10.1016/j.profnurs.2020.02.006

CHAPTER 13

What Is the Process for Submitting My Manuscript?

Before submitting your manuscript, it is assumed you have:

> **Final Checklist Before Submitting Your Manuscript**
>
> ☐ 1. Reviewed and revised my manuscript at least three times.
> ☐ 2. Completed the Final Draft Checklist in Chapter 12.
> ☐ 3. Identified a journal where I intend to send my manuscript.
> ☐ 4. Are familiar with the articles the journal typically publishes.
> ☐ 5. Read the journal's "Instructions for Authors."
> ☐ 6. Feel that my manuscript is properly formatted and a capable candidate for the journal.
>
> If you can check all six boxes, then you are *almost* ready to proceed with submitting your manuscript.

How Do I Submit My Manuscript?

The submission process is actually quite simple but almost always involves going to the journal's website and following the directions to upload files of an electronic copy online. While there are thousands of journals, many of them use the same online electronic software (editorial submission and manuscript processing systems) to facilitate their work. The software systems used by numerous journals are known as Editorial Manager, Manuscript Central, and ScholarOne. Given the abundance of journals, the information in this section of the book provides general information; it is beyond the scope of this chapter to describe the specific system each journal may use.

Almost all journals except for the smaller ones will require you to submit your paper electronically through an automated submission system. The software is quite powerful, creating meta-data that allows the journal editor to do such things as conduct duplicate submission checks by similarity of title, author, and abstract, to search for potential reviewers using keywords both within the journal and outside. Further, editors can track and manage the number of manuscripts that have received the required number of reviews, and the number of submissions still needing additional reviewers. Automatic reminders can also be sent out to reviewers who have not completed a review. These systems can do even more tricks that we don't need to go into (see, for instance, Elsevier, 2020).

A benefit to authors, besides the timely processing of manuscripts, is that once the submission process has been completed, authors can often follow the status of their submission in a general way. You might, for instance, learn that it has been sent out to all reviewers.

As a first step to submitting, you normally will be required to register with a username and password. You may be able to use your ORCID ID if you have one. ORCID stands for Open Researcher and Contributor ID and addresses the problem of finding articles by an author sharing the same name with many others (e.g., John Williams). ORCID creates a unique fixed or constant digital identifier for researchers that journals can use to keep records of author publications, the reviews conducted by peer-reviewers, and lots more. There is no fee for individual researchers to obtain an ORCID ID. Membership fees are paid by organizations. The nonprofit organization states that the ORCID (a 16-digit number) provides an "unambiguous record of research." Benefits to funders include "trustworthy award attribution" and better transparency to avoid conflicts of interest and so forth. Registration is simple at their website (https://orcid.org/register), but it may also be provided to you by the journal where you are submitting.

Before discussing the actual process of submitting your work, let's explore the questions a journal's website may ask you.

What Issues Might Journals Be Concerned About That Might Escape Me?

You may be thinking, prior to submitting your manuscript, that the main thing the journal will be interested in is the originality of your research or whether it is "good" enough to meet their expectations. However, journals have more concerns than that. These concerns amount to a prescreening that could divert your manuscript from ever reaching a peer-reviewer. Typically, the online submission process contains a series of "Yes/No" questions that will smooth the way for your paper to proceed forward, stop it cold, or perhaps result in the editor launching an email to obtain additional information. The questions journals ask will naturally vary by discipline and journal and will not necessarily follow in the order in which they are discussed in this chapter.

In addition to the "Yes/No" questions, you may find others that ask you to complete a form such as what each coauthor contributed to the article.

Publishing Rights

You may find that the journal provides a checklist, and the first item may be, "Have you read our author's guidelines?" Although I've never tried, I think it is at least possible that the journal's electronic submission system might not allow you to go further with your submission if you check "No." Editors don't want to waste their or their peer-reviewers' time and effort with those who could potentially be submitting a paper that is inappropriate for their journal.

A second question might ask you to confirm that you have not submitted your manuscript (simultaneously) to another journal and that it has not been published elsewhere. This makes sense. The rule you must follow is to never submit to more than one journal at a time. Each journal you submit to wants the first right of acceptance or rejection. If your manuscript is rejected, then fine, submit it to a new journal. Remember that peer-reviewers are unpaid volunteers; no one associated with a journal wants to be the backup bride or groom at the altar—a situation that could arise if an author "shotguns" the manuscript to multiple journals at the same time.

Once a journal has accepted your manuscript and published it, the journal owns the publishing rights. You surrender your copyright to it. As an author, you do not have any legal ability to take the paper and publish it elsewhere unless the publishing rights are returned to you. A question on the website might ask if you own the copyright. Saying "No" means that another publisher holds the copyright and will likely prevent a review with the current journal.

Once you have a published article, you might be approached by a professor or editor who wants to use your published article as part of a collection in an edited book. In order for the article to be printed again, the journal that published your paper will have to be contacted and return their rights to you as an author or to the publishing company planning the new book.

But back to submitting your work—you may be asked if you acknowledge and agree on behalf of yourself and your coauthors to the publishing terms and the extent to which you can share the published article or its content. Because you have authored the published paper does not necessarily mean that you can share it across personal media platforms, post it on your personal website, give it to friends or colleagues, or hand copies away at the supermarket. Journals may give you permission to share copies with your students if you are teaching or may allow a specific number of copies to be made from their protected website.

The website may specifically ask if you have assigned or already licensed the content or rights to the manuscript to any other third party that would be in conflict with the journal's publishing terms. Because journals want you to realize the implications of assigning your rights to the journal, another question might ask if you are one of the named authors of the paper. They don't want an office assistant, graduate assistant, or a feckless, uninformed individual to submit on your behalf.

Another question may ask if you are using any material (figures, diagrams, tables, photos, or a large amount of text) that has been previously published. Typically, figures, artwork, and so forth are contained in separate files, not placed in the main document file. Use of these items in your manuscript could involve securing permission from the previous journal or publisher and could complicate the publishing of your manuscript. Usually, it is the corresponding author's responsibility to obtain written permission from the original source when an author wishes to reproduce any material from a third party.

Once you've been screened and informed regarding the legal issues associated with publishing rights, the journal may lighten things up a bit and give you a chance to enter your manuscript title and abstract. It may ask if this paper is being submitted in response to a call for papers for a specially edited issue. At this point, the journal may allow you to upload your completed manuscript. However, the journal may have another series of questions with other concerns.

Protecting the Peer-Review Process

You may be asked to upload two copies of your manuscript. One copy will be a complete manuscript file with a title page containing the names of all authors and their affiliations and email addresses, as well as the contact information for the corresponding author, abstract with key words, and references. The journal may ask you to list all funding sources on the title page and may ask for even greater detail about the grant information. Psychology journals expect a running head (an abbreviated title shown in the header) to be shown on the title page and throughout the manuscript. Do not create a running head containing your name (e.g., Royse. Healing from trauma). Some journals may ask for a word count on the title page, too.

The other manuscript copy will *not* contain any identifying information about you or the other authors; you will be anonymous. This is the copy that will be sent out to peer-reviewers. Remove personal references by disguising any citations to previous work you and your coauthors have written using this in-text format: [Authors, 2019]. When the manuscript is accepted, you can complete the citation(s) and restore the correct information in your reference list with a final manuscript sent to the editor.

Journals may also just request one copy of the main body of the manuscript with the title page and cover letter uploaded as separate files to allow for blind peer-review. In this instance, the only identifying information about the authors should be contained in the cover letter and title page—nowhere else in the body of the manuscript. Cover letters are not necessarily needed. Go with what the author guidelines instruct you to do. Journals will sometimes provide text boxes so that you can type or paste in content like abstracts, running heads, and keywords so that you don't have to upload files. If you have something out of the norm to explain to the editor about the manuscript (not that it is your mother's favorite), you may be able to convey that information in a special textbox or find a way to attach a cover letter. Note that the editor will *not* be favorably swayed by the fact it took you 18 months to polish the manuscript to a high gloss. However, it is okay to give the editor a "heads-up" in a cover letter for something truly relevant they may need to pass along to the peer-reviewers. Just remember to keep it short, and if you include a cover letter, use your organization's letterhead, and address the editor by their name.

Note that the *APA Publication Manual* (APA, 2020) recommends three to five key words listed one line below the last line of the abstract. Choose your keywords carefully, as they are what will help editors find reviewers and potential readers to discover your paper in the databases when they are conducting literature searches. As suggested earlier, you may want to do a little research to make sure you are using the same keywords associated with articles in the same vein as yours. You may want to consult the Thesaurus Psychological Terms found in the database *PsycInfo* or the thesaurus found in *Medline* to align your key words with subject terms used in their indexing.

Editors appreciate good labels on your uploaded files. If the title of your manuscript is: "Healing From Trauma: New Lessons From the COVID Epidemic," your files might be labeled this way:

> Healing from trauma.complete ms
> Healing from trauma.de-identified.ms
> Healing from trauma.cover letter
> Healing from trauma.title page
> Healing from trauma.abstract

Their Other Informational Needs

The journal may ask if you are using a database that you will be sharing. (If so, you may need to include a Data Availability Statement explaining the allowed use of the data, the conditions under which it can be accessed, and where it is located.)

Expect a question regarding whether your study included human participants and another asking for confirmation that you have obtained formal approval for your research from an Institutional Review Board or Human Subjects Review Committee. If the reviewing committee waived approval, this should be explained in the manuscript. A third question might appear asking for confirmation that any participants identified in the manuscript have provided written consent and reviewed the manuscript. (This situation will not occur often but might exist in a case study.) Similarly, another question may ask if individuals who are identified in the acknowledgments of the manuscript are aware of their inclusion and give their approval. You may be asked to confirm that the paper being submitted meets all ethical guidelines and legal requirements. You could be asked if there is any possible conflict of interest in your reporting of the research or findings. A conflict of interest could arise if you received remuneration associated with the research being reported.

You may encounter a journal that allows you to recommend reviewers. If so, you'll have to add their affiliations and contact information also. Any you recommend should be an "arm's length" away from the conduct or writing-up of your research. That is, they should not be close friends, associates, coworkers, persons you are related to, or anyone who contributed to the manuscript. They should be an expert or knowledgeable about the subject you are writing about, but not someone who participated in the data collection and so forth. Some editors may not feel that one's dissertation advisor would be objective and independent enough. Don't recommend reviewers unless the journal asks for suggestions.

Lastly, you may be asked to review the electronic proof associated with the files and information you have submitted. Then, you could be asked to confirm that everything is ready to be submitted.

Most journals provide FAQ and Support/Help links in case the author has difficulty uploading files or getting something to work correctly on their website. You should receive an email confirming your submission was received. And of course, you will receive another email weeks later after a decision has been made on your manuscript.

The warrior knows that peace does not come from control but from relinquishing control. Everything in life that you try to control that is outside your control will steal from you your peace. You must choose to take hold of what you can control and let go of what you cannot. You cannot control the outcome, but you can control the process.

Erwin McManus, megachurch pastor, California

How Long After Submission Before I Will Hear From the Journal?

The length of time taken to review a manuscript and respond to authors will vary greatly depending on the journal. Since reviewers are often university faculty and unpaid for their reviews, it is difficult for editors to speed up reviews. At certain times of the year (e.g., summer and spring breaks, the beginning and end of semesters), faculty may be even less available. Also, even dependable reviewers can become ill, need surgery, or become burdened with projects of their own. They can also slow up when they have become burned out as a result of too many manuscripts being sent to them to review. And to be honest, reading a couple of awful ones makes a reviewer less eager to read the next one. Manuscripts can get put aside and sometimes forgotten about. Editors can do little about this. They can send reminders that a review is due or overdue, and if nothing is forthcoming from a reviewer, then they must reassign the manuscript to someone else—which adds to the length of time it takes to decide on the paper. Another problem that could impact the review time is that editors may have difficulty finding reviewers for certain manuscripts—especially if the journal does not have a strong bench of reviewers with the particular expertise needed to evaluate it.

All that said, authors should be prepared for it to take 10 to 12 weeks or a little longer, in most cases, before they hear from a journal that is not open access. Although it is good to remember that electronic links are not permanent and often change, here is additional information found on the internet that may be helpful:

> Reviewers for the American Psychological Association's journals are asked to complete reviews within 30 days (https://www.apa.org/pubs/journals/vio/guidelines-for-reviewers).
>
> For Springer's journals, the goal from submission to first decision, "in most cases the decision is made in less than three months" (https://www.springer.com/journal/11280/submission-guidelines#:~:text=Time%20to%20First%20Decision%3A%20From,in%20less%20than%20three%20months).
>
> Wiley's *Journal of Management Studies* attempts to respond "within approximately three months" https://onlinelibrary.wiley.com/pb-assets/assets/14676486/JMS_Submit_an_Article-1509475375000.pdf. However, its *Journal of Bone and Mineral Research* states, "A decision is generally rendered within 20–30 days of submission" (https://asbmr.onlinelibrary.wiley.com/hub/journal/15234681/homepage/review_process).
>
> The website for Taylor & Francis journals says, "Journals usually ask reviewers to complete their reviews within 3–4 weeks" (https://editorresources.taylorandfrancis.com/managing-peer-review-process/#:~:text=Journals%

20usually%20ask%20reviewers%20to,reviews%20within%203%2D4%20weeks).

Open-access journals tend to respond to authors quicker. For instance, PLOS ONE in 2021 reported the time to the first decision was between 48 and 53 days—but then again, you are paying a premium for getting your work in print (https://journals.plos.org/plosone/s/journal-information).

Don't sit around and wait to hear from the journal. Start your next project. It will go faster given all you have learned from this one!

> **Your Turn 13.1**
>
> Have you conducted a Google search to learn if there is any information about the response time for the journal to which you are considering sending your manuscript?
>
> _____
>
> _____
>
> _____
>
> If not, could learning about a slow response time make you rethink submitting to that journal? Is there another journal that might be equally appropriate for your paper that reports a speedier response time?
>
> _____
>
> _____
>
> _____
>
> Do these two journals have similar impact factors? Which one has the highest impact factor?
>
> _____
>
> _____
>
> _____

> **Your Turn 13.2**
>
> Do you have a second writing project in mind? If yes, is it one that will take a long time to develop, or have you already begun the groundwork? What can you begin within a week after submitting your manuscript?
>
> _____
>
> _____
>
> _____
>
> If you don't have another idea or a project with data ready to analyze, where might you look or who could you talk with? Don't take more than a week to begin investigating a topic for your next project. You know how to do this. Time is precious. Make a plan. At least, list some steps that must be made.
>
> _____
>
> _____
>
> _____

Resources

Enago Academy. (2021). *How do online manuscript submission systems work?* https://www.enago.com/academy/how-do-online-manuscript-submission-systems-work/

Engineering Our Way. (2021, September 20). *How to submit your manuscript in a journal???* [Video]. YouTube. https://www.youtube.com/watch?v=3-o8i3o8YEk

Learn With SciTech. (2022, February 14). *Manuscript submission process ✩ How to submit research articles to Elsevier Publisher* [Video]. YouTube. https://www.youtube.com/watch?v=XDBr48uVI7s

Learn With SciTech. (2022, February 28). *Manuscript submission process ✩ How to submit manuscript in Springer Publisher* [Video]. YouTube. https://www.youtube.com/watch?v=5Zo5s6miUx0

References

American Psychological Association. (APA). (2020). *Publication manual of the American Psychological Association* (7th ed.). https://doi.org/10.1037/0000165-000

Elsevier. (2020). *Brief introduction to Editorial Manager (EM)*. https://supportcontent.elsevier.com/Support%20Hub/Journals/30146_EM_Highlights_for_Editors_Jan_2021.pdf

CHAPTER 14

My Manuscript Was Rejected. What Do I Do Now?

How Do I Step Away From the Ledge? Understanding My Emotions

Imagine you have submitted your manuscript and later it is rejected. What are your options? What do you do now? Should you send it to your laptop's recycle bin? Start all over again? Write an appeal letter to the journal editor? Or perhaps find a good bottle of bourbon and a friend to consume it with?

If your manuscript has been rejected, two possible emotions can result, and you may feel them both at once. Your first emotion may be a sense of loss or sadness, a feeling that you weren't meant to be published. Although you really labored over the piece, you may feel that the doors to journal publishing will never be open to you—a severe implication for your career if you are an academic. You may hear a tiny voice in your head whispering that you aren't smart enough to have an aspiration to be an academic or writer. It may accuse you of being stupid. (These scripts are a lot easier to ignore, however, if you *never* heard them as a child or if you have already had success with publishing.)

With regard to feeling down in the dumps, it is an honest and quite human emotion after you have invested weeks in developing a manuscript, reading it again and again to eliminate any imperfection but somehow not creating the right manuscript for the journal. However, don't let any negative insinuations in your head prevent you from objectively evaluating reviewers' comments and your prospects after another revision and resubmission to a new journal.

Anger is the other emotion that likely will arise. Again, this is a legitimate emotion, and while I don't advise punching the wall or throwing your laptop against it, you hopefully will have a way of managing your anger—possibly by putting on your workout clothes and running a mile or two, meditating, or distracting yourself by going to a movie or binge-watching streaming videos.

How appropriate is it to feel anger? It is an authentic response when you read petty criticisms of your manuscript, comments that don't make any sense at all, where the reviewer misinterpreted something or was such a micro-manager that few paragraphs have escaped a withering rewrite comment or critique.

Even in writing this chapter, my blood pressure spiked as I looked over and read a reviewer's remarks about an old manuscript. Take this comment, for instance: "The last paragraph in the literature review is 'intrusive' without a heading." My coauthor and I had no idea what the reviewer was talking about—why was it intrusive? When we revised the manuscript, we addressed other comments, and when we came to that one, we wrote, "We don't agree" to the editor. The same reviewer followed the intrusive comment with another one accusing us of dishonesty: "The numbers in the subjects section seem too exact, and make me suspicious." Our crime? We rounded our data (using one third and two thirds) in describing the number of credit hours college students in the sample had completed. Lastly, in our survey, we did not capture any data about race/ethnicity, but we estimated that 10% of the sample might have been African American. Yet the reviewer commented, "The wording about ethnicity needs to be cleaned up. Either note the percents or don't reference them." Despite that reviewer's irritating comments, the paper was published.

Being prepared for possible bad news and realizing that the journal's acceptance rate is not likely to be 100% might help with not becoming consumed with anger. However, even Cindy Peternelj-Taylor (2018), editor of the *Journal of Forensic Nursing*, refers to writing being "unnerving," as we are "haunted by the ghosts of our past high school English composition classes" (p. 1). She has written, "I still cringe when I read reviewers' feedback and even now turn to my mentors for sage counseling" (p. 2).

Give some thought to how you might handle the bad news of a rejection—it just might soften the blow if such news comes your way. Even in the face of possible rejection of our efforts, writers write because they must. This is how Bonnie Miller-McLemore, professor of religion, psychology, and culture, emerita, has described her feelings about writing (2016):

> The compulsion to write—and for me, it is a kind of compulsion, even preoccupation as much as occupation—is about more than cash flow, which is fortunate since the dollar per hour for academic publication is ridiculously minuscule. Beyond job security and recognition, many of us write because some part of ourselves comes alive, and, for many in pastoral theology, our very lives and those of others depend on it. There is something in the sheer pleasure and power of it—those moments when words appear that seem so right, something not yet known or thought, words that capture a truth that evaded us until it appeared, hidden in what psychoanalysis would call the subconscious (personal and collective) or, for those convicted about life's deeper meaning, received from a power beyond ourselves.

That moment—and it flits by and away, returns on occasion, cannot be commanded—is when I love to write (in addition to the moment when I am finished). We hope when others read that sentence they will gasp "yes" and maybe even "thank God, someone put *that* into words," as we have done as we have read. (p. 814)

Can There Be a Bad Apple in One's Set of Reviewers?

Yes, of course. You may get a bad, belligerent reviewer your first time out—just the luck of the draw—or later after you have been lulled into thinking they are nothing more than fallacious myths circulating among those who write for professional journals. Reviewers may differ with authors at just about any point in the manuscript. For instance, they can take a different view of how your data should have been analyzed, interpreted, or reported, and the findings or conclusions drawn. In an article that examined traumatic events happening during participants' childhood, the Survey Research Center of our university surveyed a state-wide random sample of adults. After a blistering four paragraphs of one negative reviewer's comments, here's a final one we received:

> This poorly conceived and injudicious "study" is, in my opinion, essentially an opinion-piece thinly disguised as research. The authors give little evidence of competence in designing research, analyzing findings properly, interpreting data correctly and with appropriate caution, and discussing implications of research responsibly. If (journal name deleted) published it, I believe it would bring the reputation of the journal into question.

I immediately fired off a letter to the editor complaining about the venomous review in a 3-page single-spaced letter refuting the reviewer's remarks. Among the points I made was that in our cross-sectional telephone survey (with a known level of confidence and 4% sampling error), a committee of social science faculty reviewed every question. Further, the director of our Survey Research Center was a sociologist, a product of the University of Chicago, and obtained experience at the National Opinion Research Center. Among the other facts I provided was that at that point in my career, I had already had

> *Whenever you have a good idea, it's inevitable some people will criticize it and deny it. Some people will try to prove it wrong.*
>
> Eugene Parker, astrophysicist, predicted the existence of solar wind

40 peer-reviewed journal publications and two published textbooks, with a third one due out in 4–5 months. I am not saying that the manuscript couldn't have been improved, but I am suggesting that something touched the nerve of this one reviewer. (Quite frankly, I suspect the reviewer was a survivor of childhood trauma who had never adequately dealt with it.) There was no justification for our being so fiercely attacked. The manuscript was an early one looking at how traumatic events in childhood could affect adults in a nonclinical adult sample.

Should I File a Protest With the Editor If I Get a Terrible Review?

Does it make sense to protest an editor's decision not to accept a manuscript? I don't think so. The letter we wrote to the editor didn't seem to matter to the editor—she did not even give us the courtesy of replying to our letter. Needless to say, I never submitted anything else to that journal. We revised the paper, sent it to another journal, and it was published under a different title.

Another well-known expert also agrees with my position:

> The plain truth is that writing such letters would not change anything. Recently, an interviewer asked a well-published faculty member if he ever protested journal decisions. The author answered with one word, "Yes." The interviewer then asked if protesting ever worked. The author again answered with one word, "No." (Belcher, 2009, p. 391)

The good news is that truly bad apples are rare—you shouldn't discover many of them over a career of writing. However, there is no protection against bad luck—which can strike the first time or the seventh time. If your other reviewers are fair and objective, try not to let the offensive one get under your skin (but of course they will). Just don't attack the reviewer personally, in a "revise and resubmit," make the revisions suggested by the other reviewers, and do what you can to address any of those stemming from the deviant one. It may turn out that the editor will realize that the one reviewer was "off their game" and not expect you to jump through hoops that were too small or too high. If the journal sent a flat-out rejection, then cool off, read all the reviewers' comments a day or two later, revise, and resubmit to another journal.

Success consists of going from failure to failure without loss of enthusiasm.

Winston Churchill

How Do I Deal With Reviewers' Comments That Seem "Off"?

Perhaps most journal reviewers are faculty members who may slip into a "teaching mode" at times, which can feel like an affront to your knowledge of the problem, population, or methodology. Keep in mind that reviewers don't know you personally or your prior accomplishments. The majority of journals use double-blind review procedures where the manuscript is de-identified. Journals can be even triple-blind where even your identity is not known to the editor. Reviewers may be reacting to one sloppy paragraph or something in your rush to finish that you forgot to add. Sometimes after reflection, you can see why that suggestion was made or how it might be useful.

In another vein, writers sometimes get comments from reviewers that seem as if they are trying to clandestinely promote their own publications. Here's one example my coauthors and I once received:

> The author's revisions strengthen the manuscript. The author has done a good job of responding to the reviewers' suggestions, with one exception. We had asked the author to draw on an article recently published in this journal (journal name and author deleted), but for some reason the author did not do this. The article is directly related to the author's paper. The author should cite this article and note consistencies and inconsistencies in the two studies' results. We would be remiss if we did not note the connections between these two papers.

Since reviewers are often experts in the field or topic in which your manuscript is situated, they may feel slighted if somehow your literature search didn't identify one or more of their works. You do the best you can, but sometimes you miss things when reviewing literature for inclusion in a manuscript. Once my coauthor and I got a kind letter from a faculty member at another university who had read our article and noted that we missed his article published 31 years earlier (our review had only gone back 28 years). He further added, somewhat sweetly, that we also had missed finding his dissertation. He was right. We didn't find either of those two resources, but I didn't mind hearing from him—it was collegial and informative, not mean.

An editor of a nursing journal has said this about responding to reviewers: "The most effective response to reviewer comments is to make the suggested changes. Authors who argue with many reviewer comments will have difficulty with publication" (Conn, 2022). If you get a comment that is definitely not relevant because the reviewer misunderstood something or missed material already there, simply note that in correspondence back to the editor. Martin (2008) also suggests that sometimes it is possible to make "a small change—modified wording, or an extra sentence—so that you can say you've responded" (p. 310).

The comments I've shared here from reviewers don't mean that *you* will get wacky or mean, offensive comments. Over a career of publishing, I've received relatively few comments that were insulting or hurtful. Most of the requests for revisions I could understand, and the great majority of them resulted in my adding details to the manuscript that improved it. You may not like or agree with every recommendation you will receive from reviewers, but if the revisions don't take a great deal of time, it is better to give the reviewers what they want and get the paper published than it is to feel insulted and a need to pull your manuscript and send it to another journal.

After the Initial Shock of Rejection, What Do I Do?

First thing. *Don't take the rejection personally.* The reviewers don't know your identity, and you don't know them. Yes, it may feel like the reviewers insulted you or slapped you across the face, but they don't know who you are. Even if you have published previously and cited yourself in the references, the journal would have asked you to manage it this way in your manuscript: (Author, 2021). Once the paper is accepted, then the author's name is inserted back into the manuscript. While it may be possible for a reviewer to track down an unidentified reference, my hunch is that few reviewers would take the time to do it. Just to be clear, the point here is that the odds are against the reviewer knowing who you are, so don't take any criticism personally or catastrophize the review. It is not the end of your career. A rejection doesn't mean that you will be on some kind of a "blacklist" or have trouble publishing future papers.

Second thing. If your manuscript is not accepted for publication, read completely through it, and then put it away for 2–3 days—particularly if you feel your emotions rising. Give yourself time to cool off and then consider the editor's letter and the reviewers' comments when you are less emotional. *Do not write the editor an angry letter* complaining and boasting of your prior publications, your Ivy League degree, your membership in Phi Beta Kappa. It won't matter. You are not in the driver's seat on the submission.

Third thing. When you must revise, try to view see why you got the comment from the reviewers—take their perspective. Is it possible that the reviewer is correct—that your literature review is not organized tightly enough? Do you have any findings that don't relate to your stated purpose? If the reviewer's remarks strike you as overly harsh, Martin (2008) advises that you show them to an "experienced colleague and ask for a judgment: Are they really as bad as they seem?" (p. 309). They may not be asking you to pole-vault 16 feet after all. Martin further recommends that you look especially at the editor's suggestions and focus on one at a time. He says that "looking at a list of criticism can be demoralizing: the task seems too big" (p. 309).

Reviewers' comments can be viewed as an "obstacle course," and if you love challenges, that's a fine way to engage in the process of creating a revised version of your work. However, if you feel defeated by the battalion of acrid criticisms all bristly and armed with sharp instruments hiding behind the defensive wall of the editor, take on the comments one at a time. Look back at the manuscript to see how you can make repairs. Start with the comments that will be quick and easy to make. Can you insert another sentence or two to address a specific reviewer's comments? Is a new paragraph needed?

You may find other comments that will take more time to address. For instance, you might be asked to analyze the data with a different procedure. You should get consultation if the statistical procedure is an unfamiliar one. It could turn out to be impossible to do with your data. You could find a comment or two that you don't understand at all. In that situation, it is usually helpful to have a conversation with your writing mentor or someone with recent publications about how to handle the comment. Once in a great while, you might need to ask the editor for clarification.

Journal editor Conn (2022) has "unpacked" the review process by noting reviewers may suggest the following:

> New replacement citations for older ones
> Hypotheses or research questions where none exist
> Requests for data not possessed by the author ought to be acknowledged as a limitation
> Alternative interpretations of the findings that could be added to the *Discussion* section

Journal editors typically evaluate manuscripts in terms of three categories. Based on comments from the reviewers, they may *accept, accept with revisions*, or *not accept*. Even if a manuscript is accepted, they may ask for one or two things to be added or modified—usually no big deal. If a submission is accepted with revisions, this indicates there were several aspects of the manuscript that must be addressed. Journals may have slightly different names for their categories. For instance, the "accepted but revise" might be labeled "provisional acceptance." Usually, reviewers' comments are fairly clear and are more likely to be requests for more details or suggestions that the author revise the implications—either adding to or deleting a few of those. They may question why a sociodemographic variable was not explored—or note that cited literature wasn't included in the reference list. Reviewers sometimes ask for information that was not collected or available from the secondary data set used. Just remember, they haven't seen your data.

Occasionally, the journal editor may ask for a major revision that requires quite a bit more work. This may come about because your exploration was quite novel and interesting to read, or the literature review was inadequate, not broad enough, or simply not pertinent. You could also be asked to cut pages from an overly long article.

One thing to know about journal editors (as opposed to a single reviewer) is that a suggestion may not really be a suggestion but an actual directive—if you don't make the adjustment in the way "suggested," the editor may send it back to you a second time to fix.

Occasionally, after you have made a recommended revision, the editor could decide to reject the manuscript after all. This has happened rarely to me. Each time it left me wondering whether my revisions weren't close enough to what the editor wanted, or perhaps the editor received a stronger paper—or one that met a need such as being shorter or having a sexier title able to attract more readers to the journal. You'll never know for sure, so it is best to let it go.

Odd things happen. I had an editor give a "revise and resubmit" to one of my manuscripts. The chief request for revision involved data that I didn't have (county-level data). I explained that nicely but still got the rejection. The editor then wrote me back and asked me to be a reviewer for his journal. I didn't respond.

Fourth thing. Create and keep a list of the revisions you make. Better yet, keep a folder of your original draft, the revised draft, and any correspondence from the journal. I've never had the wrong version of a manuscript published by accident, but I have found typos and tables that didn't get produced exactly as they should have been. Don't worry about editors comparing your original manuscript against the revised one to look for every possible change. Most editors, I believe, are mostly concerned with how you have responded to their and the reviewers' comments. For that reason, you shouldn't ignore any suggestion but find a way to accommodate it, if you possibly can. Explain when you can't make tweaks or incorporate a reviewer's recommendation.

Does a Revise-and-Resubmit Email Mean That My Manuscript Was Accepted?

Depending on how you look at it, the revise-and-resubmit email is exactly like the "glass is either half full or half empty." If you are optimistic, full of determination, and plan to see the manuscript through to publication, then yes, the email can be viewed as a tentative acceptance. If it had been a complete rejection, they would not have asked for revisions. So, take the advice offered in this chapter and carefully shore up all of the paper's weaknesses, proofread, and double-check and then cheerfully send it off again.

If you are a pessimistic person, you might believe that your manuscript is not good enough to be published, and if that attitude carries forward in your revision effort, then, sadly, your effort will be only half-hearted because the reviewers only wanted to cruelly torture and have another opportunity to slice your manuscript into hundreds of pieces.

Personally, I usually believe that a revise-and-resubmit communication shows a definite interest in my paper, and while I rarely am excited about spending more time making it in the image held by another academic reviewer, I begin revising optimistically and hope that it will see publication. In decades of writing, I've only had maybe two or three manuscripts where my polishing and responding to a *revise and resubmit* was not successful. It is helpful to believe that a revise and resubmit from an editor means that someone, somewhere, believes there is merit in the manuscript and wants to see you successful with it. After they have read the original manuscript, sent it to reviewers, read their comments, and read your revisions and revised manuscript, they have an investment in you. One editor reviewing a paper that a doctoral student and I wrote together had us go through about five revisions (but it might have been six!) before she was satisfied that our revise-and-resubmit paper was acceptable to her. How's that for an investment of her time?

What Are the Reasons Journals Reject Manuscripts?

Once a manuscript is sent to a journal, it is received by the journal editor who examines it to determine if it is within the scope of the journal and consistent with the guidelines that authors are supposed to follow. Is it a good fit for the journal? A quick assessment may be made of the quality of the piece regarding its appearance (e.g., unprofessional?), written communication skills (poor?), methodology, references (well-formatted, inadequate number?), unsupported claims, ethical issues, and so forth.

One journal editor summarized the reasons for rejection as "fatal flaws in research design or execution, inadequate development, unresolved concerns with interpretation or overstatement, an absence of relevant or meaningful insight, or poor journal fit" (Pollock, 2019). The first review by an editor includes basic issues of the manuscript's quality and writing structure as well as fit. Perhaps the majority of manuscripts "submitted to high impact journals in the medical field are rejected in this first stage (Smith, 2006)" as cited in Mendiola-Pastrana et al. (2020, p. 183).

Here is a table (Table 14.1) I've prepared of reasons provided by editors from three different journals explaining why manuscripts to their journals are

TABLE 14.1 Reasons Journal Editors Reject Manuscripts

Journal of Professional Nursing	Journal for Continuing Education in the Health Professions	Journal of Bodywork & Movement Therapies
Not a match for the journal or its scope	Outside of journal's scope, format	Outside of journal's scope
Topic not interesting; no new information	No new contributions to knowledge**	Lack of relevance or contribution to literature
Author guidelines not followed	Disregard for author guidelines	Lack of adherence to "Guide for Authors"
Confusion between fact and opinion	Writings not substantiated with literature	Claims of fact not supported with citations
Student papers not formatted for journal	Informal or subjective writing	Inappropriate writing style
Miscellaneous: No consistent style, multiple voices, topic too broad, too many purposes, no defined audiences, multiple audiences	Miscellaneous: plagiarism, poorly referenced work, excessive jargon	Miscellaneous: poor quality of English, too much overlap with other papers, lack of adherence to standard scientific reporting guidelines
No review of the literature*	Inadequate introduction	
Wrong method used to answer question*	Serious methodological problems	Leaps of logic and fatal flaws
No IRB approval*	Lacking informed consent	
Sample size is too small*	Sample size too small	
Author created instrument with no reliability or validity*	Instruments not validated for study group, obsolete instruments**	
Conclusions not supported by data*	Conclusions not related to results**	
Morton, P. G. (2020). Why was my manuscript rejected? *Journal of Professional Nursing, 36,* 1–4.	Mendiola-Pastrana, I. R. et al. (2020). Peer-review and rejection causes in submitting original medical manuscripts. *Journal for Continuing Education in the Health Professions, 40*(3), 182–186.	Chaitow, S. (2019). The life cycle of your manuscript: From submission to publication. *Journal of Bodywork & Movement Therapies, 23,* 683–689.

*Reasons for rejecting research manuscripts
**Expert reviewer comments

rejected. Note the similarity in the first five categories across all the journals. Clearly, it pays to know—actually, to study—the journal to which you are submitting, to follow their guidelines for topics, length, referencing format, and much more. You increase your chances of getting your manuscript accepted when you are compliant with a journal's scope and guidelines.

How Do I Go About Revising a Manuscript for Resubmission?

As identified by one journal editor (Pierson, 2016), there should be four steps in this revising process. Her first step is to *Read* the peer-reviewers' comments and your manuscript with an "objective eye." This should not be hasty, get-it-done-as-fast-as-possible reading, but slow, line-by-line reading. If you aren't the best proofreader, you may want to read it out loud or in a different way. For instance, print it out and use a straight edge to focus your attention on each sentence. When you feel a sentence or paragraph can be improved, make a note to yourself, or rewrite the section before continuing.

The second step is to *Reflect*, to consider what you are reading. Try to view the manuscript from another perspective. Could anything be misinterpreted? Does it flow logically? Is there anything left out?

The third step is to *Revise/Rewrite*. Pierson (2016) advises that you pay attention again to the prior reviewers' comments as you revise. Your organization, use of headings, and proper format should guide and lead readers. See if you've created any detours or distractions. If you receive several comments where reviewers had trouble understanding your writing, you might want to consult with someone who can help with editing your revision.

The fourth step for Pierson (2016) is to *Respond* and by that she means that you have a reply for every issue raised in the peer-reviewers' comments. A journal may require that you highlight new text in yellow, prepare a table showing reviewers' comments and your response to them, or have other requirements such as a narrative about the changes made. If you do not agree with a comment, then you need to explain why you are not revising to address that concern. You do not get to pick and choose which comments to respond to but need to at least explain why you won't be addressing any specific comment with a revision.

If peer-reviewers made so many suggestions that you are exhausted just thinking about the effort required to address them all, or if they have suggested that there are problems too large to overcome, then you should possibly consider abandoning the manuscript. This is your decision where you have to weigh the odds of success against the investment of additional time. However, Pierson (2016) wisely advises,

> If you have received a request for revisions, you have already passed a big hurdle. The editors and reviewers have concluded that your manuscript is appropriate for the journal, but it just needs some additional work to make it the best it can be. You throw away that advantage when you decide not to resubmit and look for another journal. If your original submission had been completely inappropriate, it would have been rejected by the editor. (p. 408)

What Happens to a Revise-and-Resubmit Manuscript After It Is Submitted Again?

Typically, the revisions to a manuscript come weeks or maybe even months after it was first received by the journal. This will require the editor to examine the peer-review comments and/or instructions sent back to the author. The newly revised manuscript will then be read to see if the suggestions made by reviewers were made or if any were missed or unattended, which might require that the manuscript be sent back to the author. (Editors may finally reject at this point any manuscript where the author did not fully comply with instructions. Others may simply return the manuscript and ask again for the suggested revisions to be made.)

If the suggested revisions were considered minor and successfully addressed, the editor likely will not forward the paper back to one of the original reviewers, but accept the manuscript for publication. If, however, there were several major issues where revisions were needed, then the manuscript will be sent to at least one and maybe all of the original reviewers to determine if the revised manuscript meets with their approval.

Can I Submit a Rejected Manuscript to Another Journal?

Yes, and you should. Here are encouraging words from a journal editor:

> The rejection of a manuscript can make some leery of further participation in research activity. A more productive approach, however, is to make the rejection a learning opportunity to strengthen future efforts. It is possible that rejection can ultimately improve scholarship more than having an inadequate manuscript accepted. This comes back to objectivity. Those who choose to stay engaged and grow from any experience may well become productive contributors and effective educators of the next generation. (Pollock, 2019, p. 1).

Yes, resubmit. However, first, you must do the hard work of understanding why your manuscript was not accepted on the first attempt. Study and reflect upon the editor's and/or peer-reviewers' comments. Consult with another established author or your mentor to see if there is anything they would have done differently or if there is any additional issue you haven't addressed. These two efforts should not be rushed. Yes, sometimes a manuscript was simply fine in its original state but not a good fit for the journal, so a lot of additional work may not be needed. Don't rush to resubmit to a different journal because you are thinking all of their peer-reviewers were idiots, that the journal didn't like you, or that this version of the manuscript will probably be rejected anyway. Believing any of those three versions of the truth will surely be the "kiss of death" to the manuscript you submit to the second journal. Proofread, let it rest, then go back and read it closely, slowly, one more time before you send a revision off. Your efforts will then have a much better chance of success!

If you are excessively compulsive (a little bit does no harm, usually), you might enjoy checking out the article "How to Alienate Your Editor: A Practical Guide for Established Authors" by Stephen Donovan (2005). Donovan lists 25 or more mostly humorous bullet points that serve as things no author should ever do—whether "established" or not.

What Is the Rule of Three?

If after reading this chapter you are still a little discouraged about the rejection you received or fear receiving, this last piece is for you. It is how I decided to handle my disappointment years ago.

Early in my career, I experienced rejection just like everyone else writing for professional journals. I learned that even a manuscript soundly thrashed by one set of reviewers could be welcomed by another journal and its reviewers. I developed what I call "the rule of three." It goes like this: when a manuscript has been rejected, it is revised each time by incorporating the best of the last reviewers' comments and sent to another journal. If rejected a second time, it gets revised once more and sent to a third journal. I decided not to give up on a manuscript until it had been rejected three times. (At least once, however, I sent out a manuscript four or maybe five times, finding success with the last journal. I spent that much effort because I believed in the worth of that manuscript.)

I tell graduate and doctoral students that the rule of three can also be applied to their plans for writing. That is, there should be: (a) the article that you are currently writing or finishing up; (b) the "bones" of an article that you have already given thought to by choosing a good research question, begun searching to confirm a gap in the literature, started or developed a protocol for the IRB, or perhaps previously collected data waiting to be analyzed; (c) you have a very rough idea "on the drawing board" for a third manuscript. Such a plan requires that once you complete your current article (a), then you immediately begin with the project or data "on the back burner" or (b). In other words, when (a) is launched, (b) moves into the (a) slot, (c) moves into the (b) slot, and then as you commute to work or school, you think about a new project to move into the (c) slot. That way if one project gets rejected three times, you have other projects at the ready and needing your attention.

Hang in there. Be tenacious. Do not give up easily. Sometimes when I've had a rejection or feel a little depressed, I like to think of myself as a boxer. In that role, I have prepared my body to take blows. Life will always give us blows, but what matters most is whether I'm still standing at the end of the bout.

Boxing is a violent sport, and for those of you who might find that imagery offensive, there's also the parable of the sower who cast his seed and some fell on the path where birds ate it, some fell upon rocky soil, or where the thorns grew, but seed also fell on good soil where it thrived (Matthew 13: 3–9). If one manuscript falls on rocky or thorny soil, cast it again!

> *I'm a great believer in luck, and the harder I work the more I have of it.*
>
> Thomas Jefferson, prime author of the Declaration of Independence, third U.S. president, author

Your Turn 14.1

While none of us have crystal balls to foretell the fate of our submitted manuscript, it perhaps could be useful to give thought to how we could positively respond if our first submission to our first-choice journal receives a rejection.

_____

_____

_____

How do you think you might respond after receiving an email rejecting your manuscript from an editor?

_____

_____

(continued)

Drawing upon this chapter, what do you think might be a healthy, positive way that you could respond?

Your Turn 14.2

On a happier note than the Your Turn 14.1, suppose your first submission to your favorite journal results in a revise-and-resubmit email from the editor. As you read the comments, you find several from one reviewer that get under your skin like a slender splinter.

How will you respond? What will be your strategy?

Who could you talk to about your plan for responding?

Resources

Chauvin, N. C. (2021). The banality of law journal rejections. *Minnesota Law Review, 106*(1), 18–25. https://ssrn.com/abstract=3872992

Garand, J. C. & Harman, M. (2021). Journal desk-rejection practices in political science: Bringing data to bear on what Journals do. *Ps-Political Science & Politics, 54*(4), 676–681. https://doi.org/10.1017/S1049096521000573

Muir-Cochrane, E. (2013). What do journal editors want? ... and everything you wanted to know about the peer review process for journal publication. *Nursing and Health Sciences, 15*, 263–264. https://doi.org/10.1111/nhs.12092.

References

Belcher, W. (2009). Responding to a journal's decision to reject. *IETE Technical Review, 26*, 391–393.

Conn, V. S. (2022). Revising manuscripts to address reviewer requests for additional content. *Western Journal of Nursing Research, 44*, 355. https://doi.org/10.1177%2F0193945920956597

Donovan, S. K. (2005). How to alienate your editor: A practical guide for established authors. *Journal of Scholarly Publishing, 36*(4), 238–242.

Martin, B. (2008). Surviving referees' reports. *Journal of Scholarly Publishing, 39*(3), 307–311.

Mendiola-Pastrana, I. R., Hernández, A. V., Pérez Manjarrez, F. E., López, E. O., Romero-Henríquez, L. F., & López-Ortiz, G. (2020). Peer-review and rejection causes in submitting original medical manuscripts. *The Journal of Continuing Education in the Health Professions, 40*(3), 182–186. https://doi.org/10.1097/CEH.0000000000000295

Miller-McLemore, B. (2016). Getting it write: On the craft of academic writing. *Pastoral Psychology, 65*, 803–820. https://doi.org/10.1007/s11089-016-0707-3

Peternelj-Taylor C. (2018). Do you have a writing mentor? *Journal of Forensic Nursing*, *14*(1), 1–2. https://doi.org/10.1097/JFN.0000000000000188

Pierson, C. A. (2016). The four R's of revising and resubmitting a manuscript. *Journal of the American Association of Nurse Practitioners*, *28*, 409–409.

Pollock, N. W. (2019). Rejection under peer review. *Wilderness & Environmental Medicine*, *30*, 1.

Smith, R. (2006). Peer review: A flawed process at the heart of science and journals. *Journal of the Royal Society of Medicine*, *99*, 178–182.

CHAPTER 15

What's Needed to Write a Book Proposal?

What's Needed for a Book Proposal?

1) Having an Original Idea for the Book

We all have ideas, sometimes they are good and productive; at other times, they are nothing but quickly conceived and poorly assessed notions that are as ephemeral as a dream, evaporating in the hard light of reality. What is an original idea? The kind of idea that if someone told it to you first, you'd slap your knee and say something like, "Damn, that's a fine idea!" or at least, you'd think it silently to yourself. It *has* to be an idea that others will agree is a good one, and the idea has to be sellable too. That is, it must have a certain appeal, and you as a salesperson must be able to interest others in buying the idea. You must be able to sell it. Someone (e.g., a publisher) must be willing to get behind and support it.

The world loves innovation, new ideas, new presentations, and unique or unorthodox examinations of the every day, off the well-worn path of previous interpretations. Thus, your idea should have some ability to promise an exciting experience, something like taking a bite of a fresh, crisp apple or taking a ride in a convertible on a summer morning. Your originality might come from a new style, or perspective, recently uncovered information, or bundling existing information differently in a more relatable and tidier package.

If you've just finished months of writing a thesis or dissertation, it may seem more mundane than exhilarating right now. However, if you turn the spotlight to the discovery, the unique findings or contributions it makes, that is where the originality may be waiting for an introduction to the larger public.

How Do Authors Find Ideas That Become Published Books?

Controversies

Some authors make a name for themselves by becoming iconoclasts—attempting to topple some enshrined theory, theorist, or classic work. Take the case of anthropologist Margaret Mead, author of *Coming of Age in Samoa: A Psychological Study of Primitive Youth for Western Civilization* in 1928. In that early book, she suggested, "The struggles of female adolescence might substantially lessen were girls able—as she claimed they generally were in Samoa—to dally with sex" (Dreger, 2011, p. 1341).

This is what a current anthropologist has written about Mead:

> At the time of her death in 1978, Margaret Mead was one of the three best-known women in the United States and America's first woman of science. A prolific author, sought-after public speaker, icon, and oracle, Mead was the public face of anthropology and its ambassador to the world for much of the twentieth century. She spoke to the great issues of her time and was widely recognized for her many contributions. After her death, she was awarded the Presidential Medal of Freedom by President Jimmy Carter. (Shankman, 2009, p. 1)

However, another anthropologist (Derek Freeman) claimed in a 1983 book after Mead's death (*Margaret Mead and Samoa: The Making and Unmaking of an Anthropological Myth*) that two of her young female Samoan informants had "lied to Mead" (Sullivan, 2012, p. 2) and misrepresented their society as sexually permissive. In short, he challenged her portrayal of Samoan adolescence. Although Freeman published three books (1983, 1996, and 1999) on his hoaxing hypothesis, another anthropologist, Paul Shankman published his own book reviewing Freeman's work. He was able to conclusively show that "Freeman was able to advance his argument only by selective use of information, including the creative use of partial quotations, and the strategic omission of relevant data at crucial junctures in his argument" (Shankman, 2009, p. 12).

For better or worse, books get written about controversies. As for Mead's 1928 book, after all of this time, it is still in print—almost a hundred years later! However, taking the role of critic or heretic involves a certain amount of risk-taking, which may not be a path that many would want to take.

Ideas are around us everywhere, sometimes they are whispering softly, and if we are not so busy or bored, we may hear suggestions. Like footprints in a snowy field, we should allow our curiosity to follow these for a while, to see where they lead, what they may reveal to a sleuth able to see the subtle indentations.

Value-Added Information to a Common Human Experience

Sometimes we need fresh ideas to jumpstart our thinking. One resource available would be to consult a listing such as one that *Smithsonian Magazine* publishes periodically called the "Ten Best Science Books" (Spring et al., 2022). Recently, three books from their list jumped out at me as good creative ideas. In the first two examples, almost all of us have had some experience with COVID, and in the second example, most of us at some point have experienced a broken heart from a lost relationship. How do these become fresh ideas?

Example 1
Inspired by the recent COVID-19 epidemic, which affected us either directly or certainly indirectly, author David Quammen interviewed 95 scientists to understand the virus, its origin, mutations, and what we learned that enabled our responses. The book he wrote was called, *Breathless: The Scientific Race to Defeat a Deadly Virus*. Of course, this was not the first or only book written about the COVID experience, I could have highlighted many others as well. See, for instance, Michael Lewis's 2021 book, *The Premonition: A Pandemic Story*.

Example 2
In *Heartbreak: A Personal and Scientific Journey* (2022) Florence Williams details a midlife divorce and interviews psychologists and neuroscientists for her own healing and to learn what science knows about heartbreak. While many of us have experienced the misery of lost relationships and grieved them, few of us have poked into the science of our feelings in the way that Williams has done. As I read more about her, I also learned that her experience as a nursing mother gave her the inspiration for another book, *Breasts: A Natural and Unnatural History* (which was a Notable Book of 2012, the *New York Times*, and also received the *Los Angeles Times* Book Prize in 2013).

Example 3
Sometimes authors can take the mundane and provide a new horizon. Sarah Everts introduced readers to a world of new information in her 2021 book, *The Joy of Sweat*. Like the other two, this book brings knowledge that forces readers to think differently about perspiration, in a sense, to put on new lenses to see the landscape better.

Passion for a Subject
Science writer Riley Black takes the reader back in time 66 million years ago before a giant asteroid hit the earth and obliterated 75% of the species at that time. She uses artistic license to imagine what life was like before the collision based on current science and paleontology. See *The Last Days of Dinosaurs: An Asteroid, Extinction, and the Beginning of Our World* (2022; one of *Smithsonian Magazine's* Best Science Books of 2022).

Here's a footnote on Riley Black. Although when we are unpublished, we may think that others have it easier, maybe because they have more resources and can afford things like professional proofreaders and editors, or perhaps because they have had more education or are products of Ivy League Schools. But what does it take to become an author? Riley failed out of Rutgers University twice and on the third attempt decided to leave two courses short of her bachelor's degree. What she had was a fascination with dinosaurs since childhood and began writing about paleontology "out of enthusiasm." Here's a short piece from an interview with her:

> I actually wanted to write a book before I started blogging. I was tired of seeing books about evolution gloss over paleontology as an unimportant discipline. So I got the unreasonable idea of trying to write one myself despite having never written anything more substantial than a high school newspaper op-ed in my life.
>
> I had no idea how to write a book, and it took at least three years before *Written in Stone* came together in a coherent way. My blogs were my training grounds. They offered me a space to practice any time I wanted to, and also to collect and store ideas that might be useful for the manuscript. (Shipman, 2013)

What Riley Black has is a passion for paleontology that has led to writing at least 10 books in English and others under her former name, Brian Switek. She has also written an incredible number of articles and blogs for *Smithsonian*, and numerous other pieces for *National Geographic*, *Scientific American*, *Nature*, and other well-known magazines and journals.

What Is Needed Besides Great Ideas?

2) Great Writing Skills

The sad truth is that just having a good idea may not be enough for you to get your foot in the door with book publishers. They are in the business to make money. If you don't have a strong track record as a productive scholar, journalist, or blogger, you are going to have something of an uphill task to get publishers to pay attention to you. If you send editors an idea by email or letter, you may not get a response. Forget attempting to reach them by phone. (See the talk from the Harvard Club at the end of the chapter under "Resources.")

The basic PhD dissertation, although it may have taken many months of planning, collecting, and analyzing data, is not going to be a PASS GO! card that will impress most editors. Dissertations are often highly specialized on a narrow topic. They are not written for the average reader but for the academic. The doctoral candidate's job in that piece of research is to show a knowledge of the literature, topic, and methodology. Dissertations can be full of jargon, statistics, tables, appendices, and even notes. Most of these features don't help publishers sell books, and they would want them severely minimized or removed from any book you might think about preparing. Sales, for them, means generally reaching a general audience of the public (trade books), although some do target specific university courses and niche audiences. A finished thesis or dissertation viewed by itself is not evidence that you can reach and engage the larger public; it only means that you have completed your degree requirements. Although your thesis or dissertation may be superb, your major professor or committee may have had a large role in editing the dissertation—thus obscuring the doctoral student's contribution to the writing. All that said, yes, sometimes dissertations do become scholarly books. Don't ask me how often this occurs, but my best guess is that it is somewhat rare. If your spouse or loved one couldn't make it through reading your dissertation, well—you can see the point about having an idea that will interest the general public.

The news you may not want to hear is that you likely will have to demonstrate great writing skills outside of and apart from your thesis/dissertation. You can do this by having to your credit multiple publications, not necessarily all in the same two or three journals. However, pieces in popular magazines might count favorably, as they could highlight your ability to write for the general public. Although publishers seem to be predisposed to favor book proposals (more about developing one of these later) from authors who have already published a book (as opposed to numerous articles), the dedication, self-discipline, and creativity required to publish multiple articles is often good and perhaps satisfactory evidence for many book acquisition editors. Take your dissertation (if you have one) and pull out one, two, or three publications from it. Build your CV first; establish you can write and then set your sights on developing a book. This is a strategy also recommended on the Taylor & Francis (n.d.) website "Turning Your PhD Into a Successful Book," which states, "In the majority of cases, PhD research is published in the form of journal articles. In some cases, the research is published in a book."

In my own case, I was teaching a research methods course when one day I was struck by the fact that the textbook we were using had been written by a sociologist. I thought to myself, "Why aren't we using one by an author in my field (social work)?" By that time, I had published a number of articles, and it occurred to me that writing a chapter seemed to be about the same amount of work as drafting an article for publication. All I needed to do was to think of the project as developing 12 to 15 professional journal articles. So, after doing a little investigation, I created a list of 14 publishers and sent each a book proposal. (More about developing proposals a bit later.) On the negative side, I got positive interest from only two of the 14 publishers. A short time later, I did receive a contract although most of the publishers never bothered to respond. The second publisher expressed interest about 6 months or longer after I had already committed to the first one. That book, my first one, has gone through eight different editions and has been continuously in print since 1991. It only takes one interested publisher. A little more than a year after publishing the first book, I published a second book as well.

What If You Don't Have an Amazing Writing Ability?

There is a short, pithy response to this question; however, it is one I believe to be true. If you don't have good writing skills, then you must develop them. There are many ways to polish your writing, such as working with a more experienced author and reading books and magazines on how to self-edit and write well. You might even consider hiring an editor on your own for a special project. If you are able to work as a paid blogger for a magazine, besides the pay, you can get helpful advice from your magazine editor. Even if you create your own website and shoulder all the costs yourself, there is probably a payoff as you respond to readers and learn to respond to their interests, questions, and feedback. You'll be communicating with people who have the same interests as you.

As we have discussed earlier in Chapter 4, if you know your writing skills need improvement, you can also sign up for journalism at your local university, look for workshops or opportunities to work with faculty or coauthors, and search for learning opportunities. If you are still a student, you might want to negotiate something like an independent study with a faculty member where the focus of your experience will be on developing a manuscript for possible publication.

Writer's Digest and other organizations hold conferences every year and offer a great deal of practical wisdom to aspiring authors. Also, you can Google "writer's conferences," and you'll find sites such as these three loaded with conferences for the whole year all across the country:

> (https://book-publicist.com/the-top-writers-conferences-for-2023-by-book-publicist-scott-lorenz/);

> (https://www.awpwriter.org/wcc/directory_conferences_centers)

> (https://publishedtodeath.blogspot.com/p/writers-conferences.html).

It is safe to say that the wide variety of conferences offers something for everyone, although many of them seem to be more for writers of fiction than nonfiction. Selected conferences can have a narrow focus (e.g., legal writing, specific genres of fiction), but most combine several types of writing (e.g., biographical, poetry, playwriting, and children's literature). An advantage of attending a conference targeting your interest is that there are often special sessions on self-publishing and marketing, as well as opportunities to hear from and meet literary agents. You can find conferences that provide writing consultations, "critique boot camps," and active writing workshops. If your preference is to author a novel, there likely are creative writing courses at your closest university, and a number of instructional courses for writing fiction and poetry can be found online.

What Else Is Needed Besides Originality and Great Writing Ability?

3) A Book Proposal!

Having read the book this far, you might be nurturing an idea or planning to author a book. It may be an idea very much in its infancy, but one you can envision growing to full scale. Good for you! This segment of the chapter will outline what you must prepare to sell your idea to the book publisher of your choice. (Skip this section if you are going the self-publishing route.)

While most publishers will ask for the same basic information to be provided to them about your planned book (see the following), individual publishers may ask for slightly more or less information, depending on their particular areas of focus and interest. Tailor your description to the informational requirements specified by the publisher. To save yourself time and energy, Google "Publisher Name" and "book proposal." For instance, Harvard University Press (n.d.) states, "We do not publish original fiction, original poetry, religious inspiration or revelation, cookbooks, guidebooks, children's books, art and photography books, *Festschriften*, conference volumes, unrevised dissertations, or autobiographies."

What they *do* publish is also outlined:

> Harvard University Press publishes thoughtful books for both scholars and educated general readers in history, philosophy, literature, classics, religion, law, economics, public policy, physical and life sciences, technology, history of science, behavioral sciences, and education, along with reference works in a wide range of fields. (n.d.)

The book proposal contains a cover letter to the acquisition editor, the document (prospectus) describing and pitching your proposed project, and information about you (e.g., your CV), your projected audience, and the niche the book will fit in. Start by describing your planned work and answer such questions as those in the textbox below.

Information to Provide in a Book Proposal

Project Overview

- What is the working title?
- Who will be the target audience to buy the book (general public, students, professionals)? What special field/discipline/or specialty would be interested? Is there a secondary audience?

- If a book for students, at what level? Will it be a primary text or a supplement?
- Has the project been completed? If not, when is it expected to be finished?

Book Description
- What is the book's approach? What is the rationale for the book? How will it be similar to and different from other books on the topic?
- What does a detailed table of contents look like? (Include a brief description of each chapter.)
- Will it have any outstanding features? (List three key features.)
- What is the expected length (number of words)?
- Will it be a single or coauthored text or an edited volume/case study/reader?

Competition
- What are the top competing books? What are their strengths and weaknesses? (Mention them by author and title, year, and possibly price.)

Marketing
- What is an estimate of the potential market audience?

Writing Sample
- A sample of your writing showing your style/pedagogy. Typically, publishers will ask for one to three chapters. Some publishers, however, may prefer that you not send chapters initially but wait for an invitation. That is, they don't want unsolicited manuscripts.

Qualifications
- A current CV or resume showing education, previous publications, and relevant professional experience or qualifications for the project is needed. If you have a very lengthy vitae, you might consider cutting it down to 3 to 5 pages. While a 25-page CV is impressive, most acquisition editors don't care about the committees you have served on, the number of dissertations you've directed, and so forth. A shorter CV is more memorable.

Your cover letter should succinctly introduce the idea for your proposed book and the need for it, as well as something about yourself in about a page. Editors will be especially interested in your publications or special expertise related to the book's subject. Any files you send should be in Microsoft Word, double-spaced. Large publishers will have more than one acquisition editor.

Find the appropriate editor responsible for reviewing projects in the area in which you are writing. Send your materials by email. Don't send paper copy chapters, as these may not be mailed back. Make sure your name and contact information are on the prospectus, as well as in the cover letter. Your total proposal could range from about 15 to 20 pages excluding any sample chapters.

In terms of how long you may have to wait to hear something, probably the shortest amount of time will be 3 to 4 weeks, although a flat-out desk rejection could come sooner if the proposal is sent to the wrong editor or publisher, or is inappropriate for some major reason. Be prepared to wait longer than a month to hear something. Editors may not consult outside reviewers at this stage but rely upon internal staff (e.g., in marketing and production and other editors). However, other publishers may send your proposal out to reviewers for comments if they like your proposal.

> *Putting a book together is interesting and exhilarating. It is sufficiently difficult and complex that it engages all your intelligence ... it is life at its most free, if you are fortunate enough to be able to try it, because you select your materials, invent your task, and pace yourself.*
>
> Annie Dillard, *The Writing Life*

Do I Need a Literary Agent?

The short answer to the question is, "It depends." If you are interested in selling a book in the trade market to the general public, then yes, you will need an agent. If your aspiration is to reach the *New York Times* Best Sellers' List, you will need an agent. However, if your goal is to publish a college textbook or a monograph with a small publishing company, then you don't need a literary agent and can contact companies directly yourself. If you are a writer of fiction, yes, you will need an agent unless you go the route of publishing short stories to literary magazines to build up your resume and then are lucky enough to get discovered by an agent who loves your work and wants to sign you.

I don't claim any special expertise or knowledge about agents or publishing creative works of fiction. However, I did author a novel once and had an agent for about a year. She never disclosed to me who she was sending my novel to, where it had been rejected. If memory serves correctly, I heard from only one editor who read several chapters. While the editor was associated with a well-known publishing house, her letter thanked me but kindly suggested the manuscript was not of the literary quality she was seeking. Although the agent charged no fees, and indeed, made no money on me, it was a frustrating experience. I wanted to know where she had sent the manuscript, what she heard informally about the book, but this information was never shared with me. At some point, she seemed to just give up on the project—though I never heard that officially from her. From a strictly quantitative stance, it was hard to know if that manuscript was turned down four times or 20 or more. To a writer, there's a world of difference. It is easy to suspect the worst when you don't know.

Perhaps ten or more years later, I tried it again and developed a second novel. At a writing conference, I had a brief conversation with an agent who expressed interest in the new manuscript and told me to send it to her. I did. Months went by, and I never heard anything. After about 7 months, I spent several thousand dollars and self-published it. Almost a year to the day after I sent the manuscript, she called me one Sunday morning and was interested in representing me. I told her I had self-published the book but was happy to pull it off the market and sign with a publisher. She told me to see how the sales are going, and if the book sold well, to contact her again. The book never came within 10 miles of making back what it cost me to publish it. Part of the explanation, I would argue, is that a book has to be marketed for the world to know about. Amazon, the world's largest bookseller, uses an algorithm, so the best-selling books on any topic or those with similar titles are those that pop up first. A book that has barely sold any copies may not show at all or is so far down the list as to be in book purgatory for the rest of its life. When writing this I googled, "How many books are there on Amazon" and found a post that said Amazon had 33 million books in 2017. A 2022 post said there were 12 million books on Kindle. Marketing, making the book visible to the public, is a must! A book will not necessarily be sold just because it is listed on Amazon. Aspiring authors, beware!

What About Self-Publishing?

See the last three sentences in the previous paragraph. Self-publishing is incredibly easy, whether you do it alone with Amazon Publishing or contract with a "vanity" press that will do whatever you need for a price: proofreading, supplying a front and/or back cover, artistic layout, and so forth. In fact, a 97-year-old former college professor of mine recently added to his list of 11 self-published books on Amazon with his autobiography that runs to four volumes. Unless you know him personally and spell his name correctly, I'm not sure as a casual reader you would ever come across one of his books. An email from him indicated that his prime motivation was not to make money but wanting his grandchildren to have the books to remember him. Nothing wrong with that.

Before you succumb to the intoxicating siren call of the self-publishing presses, please realize that authors who go this route often have boxes of their books gathering dust in their basements or garages. This is after appealing to a local bookstore or two, perhaps purchasing a booth at a book fair, and sending emails to all of one's friends and family members. Unless you are just lucky or highly skilled with social media, you may never break even on a self-published book.

Publishing with established publishers with marketing departments gives you "reach" into places where you can't go with email blasts and communications, booths at various conferences where your prospective audience will attend, and sometimes (e.g., college textbooks) with regional representatives who may contact faculty about your book and forward copies. The self-publishing companies you find on the internet do not attempt to market your book. In fact, even some established publishing companies that have names you might recognize do very little to promote a book. Even if you have a book that is well-written, some books just never take off and become popular.

Book reviewer extraordinaire, Steve E. Gump, with close to 100 book reviews at the *Journal of Scholarly Publishing*, has written this:

> I have self-consciously avoided reviewing self-published books in part because I see publishers as arbiters of standards and, therefore, as a means of quality control. For advice on writing, I respect the gatekeeping function of serious publishing houses, since it suggests I won't be led completely astray. (Plus, given the importance of peer review, scholarly publishing functions in a world of checks and balances. Shouldn't scholarly readers, at least, want to focus on writing that has been checked and balanced?) Besides, isn't self-publishing essentially a form of vanity publishing? (2020, p. 314–315)

I don't think Gump's position is very different from most editors who commission or receive book reviews. Self-published books are not seen as being of the same quality as books coming from large publishers. However, later in his 2020 review, Gump begins talking about a book that is "remarkable both for being self-published and for being a necessary, useful book" (p. 315). He concludes his review by saying that the author's work "opened my eyes to the possibilities of self-publishing" (p. 319).

Certainly, there are many (don't ask me how many) authors who have made fortunes with self-publishing—usually writing fiction. This doesn't mean that you should or shouldn't try self-publishing—only that you look before you leap. Beware of the companies that expect you to do all the marketing yourself and want you to buy a large quantity ahead of time that might be difficult to peddle at your local bookstore.

On the plus side, you can purchase from the majority of the self-publishing companies all of the services you might need associated with producing a book: line-by-line editing, formatting, indexing, book design, cover page artwork, and so forth.

Barbara Sarnecka (2020) has described her reasons for self-publishing her academic book and also the cost she experienced ($10,000). Obviously, the cost might not be something everyone can afford—particularly at the start of a career. I believe it is possible to self-publish for less than she experienced.

A recent development has been the arrival of open-access books. A company based in Croatia and London, IntechOpen, has produced a large number of books containing chapters written by various authors. I know this because I have been contacted and invited numerous times by email to contribute to books they were assembling. For approximately $1,880 dollars, I could write a chapter having these characteristics:

> Be 10 to 20 pages long
> Provide a context-setting introduction
> Have at least one section and subsection
> Show original research from my field
> Include references

One portion of their website (https://www.intechopen.com/series) says that "Early online publication after acceptance assures research is made available to the scientific community without delay." Publishing ahead of the book's completion, I guess, could be important in rapidly changing or developing fields. The best advantage, however, seems to be the immortality one would achieve, "Your work will be permanently available online, free to download, share and read." Doesn't permanently mean forever?

One last story, if you are a faculty member and hoping to use (and require) your self-published book in your college courses, you might want to check with your dean or someone in the administration to see if that poses an ethical conflict of interest. One faculty member at my university got into trouble because of profiting off a book he was requiring in his courses. I'm not sure of all the issues involved, but it could be that the decision to use that specific book was not made by a faculty committee in his college. One would be well advised to go through all of the appropriate approval processes to prevent the same difficulty with a self-published book of your own. (No need to worry about profiting from an open-access book.)

Let's now turn our attention again to the possibility of trying to sell a good idea to an academic or trade publication.

Can I Send My Book Proposal to More Than One Publisher at a Time?

Unlike submitting a manuscript to a professional journal that relies on the good graces and volunteerism of unpaid reviewers, book publishing companies are a business, and all of their staff and even their reviewers are paid. I see nothing unethical about submitting a book proposal to more than one publisher at a time.

If my doctor told me I had only six minutes to live, I wouldn't brood. I'd type a little faster.

Isaac Asimov, author, and editor of approximately 500 books

Resources

From Dissertation to Book. A talk at the Harvard Club with Elizabeth Knoll, formerly executive editor at large for Harvard University Press; Philip Laughlin, senior acquisitions editor, cognitive science, philosophy, linguistics, and bioethics, MIT Press; and two professors from Harvard share their insights and experiences. https://hwpi.harvard.edu/files/faculty-diversity/files/from_dissertation_to_book.pdf

Germano, W. (2016). *Getting it published: A guide for scholars and anyone else serious about serious books.* University of Chicago Press.

Hayden, T., & Nijhuis, M. (2013). *The science writer's handbook: Everything you need to pitch, publish, and prosper in the digital age.* De Capo Lifelong Books.

Luey, B. (2008). *Revising your dissertation.* University of California Press.

Nijhuis, M. (2016). *The science writer's essay handbook: How to craft compelling true stories in any medium.*

Penn, J. (2018). *How to write nonfiction: Turn your knowledge into words.* Curl Up Press.

Portwood-Stacer, L. (2021). *The book proposal book: A guide for scholarly authors.* Princeton University Press.

Rabiner, S., & Fortunato, A. (2003). *Thinking like your editor: How to write great serious nonfiction—and get it published!* Norton.

References

Dreger, A. (2011). The trashing of Margaret Mead: Anatomy of an anthropological controversy. *Archives of Sexual Behavior, 40,* 1341–1343. https://doi.org/10.1007/s10508-011-9843-0

Freeman, D. (1983). *Margaret Mead and Samoa: The making and unmaking of an anthropological myth.* Harvard University Press.

Freeman, D. (1996). *Margaret Mead and the heretic.* Penguin Books.

Freeman, D. (1999). *The fateful hoaxing of Margaret Mead: A historical analysis of her Samoan research.* Westview Press.

Gump, S. E. (2020). Barbara W. Sarnecka. The writing workshop: Write more, write better, be happier in academia. *Journal of Scholarly Publishing, 51*(4), 314–320.

Harvard University Press. (n.d.). *Proposal guidelines.* https://www.hup.harvard.edu/resources/authors/proposal.html

Mead, M. (1928). *Coming of age in Samoa: A psychological study of primitive youth for western civilization.* William Morrow.

Sarnecka, B. W. (2020). Why would a professor self-publish a book? *Journal of Scholarly Publishing, 51*(4), 309–313. https://www.muse.jhu.edu/article/760735

Shankman, P. (2009). *The trashing of Margaret Mead: Anatomy of an anthropological controversy.* University of Wisconsin Press.

Shipman, M. (2013, August 16). How dinosaurs actually lived: An interview with Riely Black. *Science Communication Breakdown*. https://sciencecommunicationbreakdown.wordpress.com/2013/04/16/riley-black/

Spring, J., Kranking, C., Black, R., Falk, D., Alex, B., & Kim, S. E. (2022, December 7). The ten best science books of 2022. *Smithsonian Magazine*. https://www.smithsonianmag.com/science-nature/the-ten-best-science-books-of-2022-180981235/

Taylor & Francis. (n.d.). *Turning your PhD into a successful book*. https://authorservices.taylorandfrancis.com/blog/get-published/turning-your-phd-into-a-successful-book/#:~:text=In%20the%20majority%20of%20cases,is%20published%20in%20a%20book

Index

A

abstract
  examples, 180–184
  purpose of, 176–177
  structured, 178–180
  writing good, 177
academic writing style, 99–101
acquired immunodeficiency syndrome (AIDS), 23–24
addictive behaviors, 83
American Psychological Association (APA), 81
American Psychological Association's Thesaurus of Psychological Index Terms, 31
APA Publication Manual, 112, 143, 153, 185
Association of Writers and Writing Programs, 69
authorship, 53–55
  sharing with students, 55–56

B

Beall's List of Potential Predatory Journals and Publishers, 76
Belcher, Wendy, 7, 47–48
Black, Riley, 231–232
blog writing, 18
book proposal
  cover letter, 235
  information to provide in, 235–236
  original idea, 229–232
  writing skills, 232–234
book reviews, 16–17
Breasts: A Natural and Unnatural History, 231
Breathless: The Scientific Race to Defeat a Deadly Virus, 231

C

CESNET, 139
child abuse, 27–28
coauthorship, 52–53
commitment to schedule, 9
confidence building, 13
Contributor Roles Taxonomy (CRediT), 53
controversies, 229–230
critical feedback, 12, 16
Critical Incident History Questionnaire (CIHQ), 141
Cumulative Index to Nursing and Allied Health Literature (CINAHL), 76, 121
curriculum vitae (CV), 3

D

data analysis, 143–145
design of method section, 133–136
desk rejections, 82
Directory of Open Access Journals, 84–86
Discussion section, 23, 55, 63–64, 114, 150–152, 176
  comparison with previous studies, 164–165
  conclusions, 169–171
  issues or flaws in study, 165–167
  purpose of, 162
  questions, 171–172
  starting, 162–164
  suggestions for future research, 167–169

E

editors, 93–94
Educational Testing Services, 69
engaging readers, 115–120
equipments for writing, 9–10
Everts, Sarah, 231
experiences with publishing, 1–3

F

fear of failure, 11–12
first-person narratives, 13–16
foster parenting, 24
Freeman, Derek, 230
Frontiers in Psychology, 85

G

Google Scholar, 85
Graduate Writing Center, 5
grammar self-assessment, 106–107

H

Haines, Derek, 191
Heartbreak: A Personal and Scientific Journey, 231
HIV-prevention communications, 46
hypotheses, 39

I

idea development
  life experiences, 23–26
  literature search, 26–29
  people resources, 29–31
  reading and, 21–23
  research discussions, 23
impact factors, 78–81, 85
International Committee of Medical Journal Editors (ICMJE), 55
Introduction, Methods, Results, and Discussion (IMRAD) template, 112
introduction section, 113–115
  literature review, 121–126
  unneeded content in, 120–121
  with controversy, 117–120
  with question or problem, 115–117

243

J

JAMA, 87
Journal of Forensic Nursing, 10, 12, 213
Journal of Pediatric Psychology, 113
Journal of the American Association, 87
Journal of the American Medical Association, 185
Journal of Trauma Nursing (JTN), 82
Journal of Youth and Adolescence, 45–46
journal publishing business, 16–17
journals
   acceptance rates, 80–81
   audience of, 82
   author guidelines, 82–84
   impact factors, 78–81
   legitimate, 78–80
   predatory, 75–78
   selection of, 86–88
The Joy of Sweat, 231
Just Publishing Advice, 191

K

Kubrick, Stanley, 29

L

language used in TED talks, study, 44–46
The Last Days of Dinosaurs: An Asteroid, Extinction, and the Beginning of Our World, 231
legitimate journals, 78–80
   American Journals, 79
   impact factors, 78–81, 85
Lewis, Michaelc, 231
life experiences, 23–26
literary agent, 237–238
literature review, 121–126
literature search, 26–29

M

magazines, 17–18
Mead, Margaret, 229–230
measures, 141–143
MEDLINE, 76
mentorship, 68, 172–173
method section
   basic information, 132–133
   data analysis, 143–145
   design, 133–136
   measures, 141–143
   participants, 136–138
   procedures, 138–140
   subheadings of, 145–146
microstructural issues on online editing tools, 192–193
Miller-McLemore, Bonnie, 213
Mindful Self-Care Scale (MSCS), 142
Minnesota Satisfaction Questionnaire (MSQ), 143
Multifactor Leadership Questionnaire 5x-Short (MLQ-5x) instrument, 143

N

Nelson Memo, 86
Niles, John Jacob, 30

O

occupational therapy (OT), 43
organizing principle, 39–40
out-of-scope submissions, 82

P

participants, 136–138
passion for subject, 231–232
peer-review, 2, 92–93
   author's role, 96–98
   editor's role, 93–94
   peer-reviewer's role, 94–95
   protection of, 205–206
   role of, 92–93
   tactics to impress reviewers, 101–102
Perceived Stress Scale (PSS), 142
Peternelj-Taylor, 10, 12
physical therapy (PT), 43
plagiarism, 46–49
PLOS Global Public Health, 85
PLOS Medicine, 85
PLOS One, 85
poems, 18
poetry journal, 3
predatory journals, 75–78
   checklist of characteristics, 77
The Premonition: A Pandemic Story, 231
Prince of Tides (Pat Conroy), 23
problems in research projects, 35–36
procedures, 138–140
proofreading, 191–193
   checklist, 199
   headings and subheadings, 195
   microstructural proofing, 194–195
   read for macrostructure and organization, 195–196
   rules, 195
   skeptical reading, 196–197
   slow reading for macrostructure, 196
prostitutes, interviewing, 33
publishable manuscript, developing, 21
publishing rights, 204–205
PubMed, 85

Q

quality time, 6

R

reading, 21–23
recaptured time, 4
rejection of manuscript
   dealing with reviewer comments, 216–217
   emotions related to, 212–214
   filing of protest with editor, 215
   initial shock of, 217–219
   negative reviewer's comments, 214–215
   reasons for, 220–222
   submission to another journal, 223–224
remuneration, 18
research discussions, 23
Research on Social Work Practice, 83–84
research questions, 39
   approaches to developing, 42–43
   clarity of, 41
   criteria, 42
   examples, 43
   focus of, 41
   importance of, 39–40
   in journal articles, 43–46
   issue of plagiarism, 46–49
   originality, 41
   parts, 42
   PICO framework, 42–43

relevance, 41
researchable, 42
research questions, sources for, 25
research/writing group (RWG), 67
results section
 information, 151–152
 length, 150–151
 number of tables, 155–158
 starting, 152–153
 structure, 153–155
revision-and-resubmission of manuscript, 219–220, 222–223
revision of paper, 197–198
rule of three, 224–225

S
Satisfaction with Life Scale (SWLS), 141
scientific scholarly work, 54–55
Seinfeld, 14
self-publishing, 238–240
Shankman, Paul, 230
skeptical readers, 196–197
Smithsonian Magazine, 230
social work magazines, 17
space (physical and emotional) for writing, 8–9
 minimizing background noise, 8
subheadings, 145–146
submission of manuscript, 202–203, 240
 Data Availability Statement, 206–207
 length of time taken to review a manuscript, 208–209

originality of research, 203
publishing rights, 204–205
recommend reviewers, 207
research approval, 207
"Yes/No" questions, 204
survivor's guilt, 28
swampy writing, 103–108
 self-assessment, 107–108
 writing tips, 105–106
Switek, Brian, 232
Symmes, John Cleves, 123

T
titles, 184–187
 length, 185
 suggestions about, 187
 types of, 185–186

V
value-added information, 230–231
viability of idea, assessment of
 checklists, 34–35
 evaluation by closest friends or support systems, 31–32
 feasibility/practicality, 32–33
 gap in literature, 31
 interesting basis, 31
 sponsored or financial support, 32

W
Web of Science, 85
White House Office of Science and Technology Policy, 86
Williams, Florence, 231
workshops, 65–66

writer's conferences, 234
Writer's Digest, 234
writing boot camps, 66–67, 69
"writing buddy" approach, 67, 69
writing coaches, 69
The Writing Life (Annie Dillard), 8–9
writing mentors, 60–62
writing partner
 advantages, 56–57
 disadvantages, 57–59
 giving feedback to, 62–64
 receiving feedback from, 64–65
 rules for choosing, 59–60
writing project, viability of, 33–35
writing skills, ways to improve
 Association of Writers and Writing Programs, 69
 Educational Testing Services, 69
 mentorship, 68
 self-improvement strategy, 69
 workshops, 65–66
 writing boot camps, 66–67, 69
 "writing buddy" approach, 67, 69
 writing coaches, 69
 writing support groups, 67–68
writing support groups, 67–68, 70–71
writing time, 3–7
 extended or binge-writing episodes, 6
 protecting, 5

www.ingramcontent.com/pod-product-compliance
Lightning Source LLC
Chambersburg PA
CBHW080409300426
44113CB00015B/2449